The Arminian Confession of 1621

The Arminian Confession of 1621

Translated and Edited by
Mark A. Ellis

Pickwick Publications
A division of Wipf and Stock Publishers
Eugene, Oregon

THE ARMINIAN CONFESSION OF 1621

Copyright © 2005 by Mark A. Ellis. All rights reserved. Except for brief quotations in critical publications or reviews, no part of this book may be reproduced in any manner without prior written permission from the publisher. Write: Permissions, Wipf & Stock, 199 W. 8th Ave., Suite 3, Eugene, OR 97401.

Paperback ISBN: 9781597523370

Hardcover ISBN: 9781498247511

Table of Contents

INTRODUCTION	vii
ORIGINAL PREFACE	1
THE CONFESSION OR DECLARATION OF THE REMONSTRANT PASTORS	
Chapter 1: On the Sacred Scriptures	35
Chapter 2: On the Knowledge of the Essence of God	44
Chapter 3: On the Holy and Sacred Trinity	51
Chapter 4: On the Knowledge of the Works of God	53
Chapter 5: On the Creation of the World, Angels and Man	54
Chapter 6: On the Providence of God	58
Chapter 7: On the Sin and Misery of Man	63
Chapter 8: On the Work of Redemption, and the Person and Offices of Christ	69
Chapter 9: On the Knowledge of God's Will, Revealed in the New Covenant	74
Chapter 10: On the Commandments of Christ in General: Faith and Repentance, or Turning to God	76
Chapter 11: On Faith in Jesus Christ	78
Chapter 12: On Types of Good Works, and and Exposition of the Decalogue	83
Chapter 13: On Governing and Denying Ourselves, and Bearing the Cross of Christ	90
Chapter 14: On Prayer and Thanksgiving, and the Lord's Prayer	96
Chapter 15: On Special Callings and the Commandements and Traditions of Men	102
Chapter 16: On the Worship and Veneration of Jesus Christ, the Only Mediator, and the Invocation of the Saints	103
Chapter 17: On the Benefits and Promises of God, Principally of Election to Grace, or Calling to Faith	105

Chapter 18: On the Promises of God that are Performed in this Life to Those Who Are Converted and are Believers, that is, Election to Glory, Adoption, Justification, Sanctification and Sealing............................. 110

Chapter 19: On the Promises of God Pertaining to the Life to Come, or the Resurrection of the Dead, and Eternal Life.. 114

Chapter 20: On Divine Threats and Punishments of the Wicked Pertaining both to this Life, and the Life to Come: Reprobation, Hardening, Blinding and Eternal Death and Damnation... 115

Chapter 21: On the Ministry of the Word of God, and the Orders of Ministers... 117

Chapter 22: On the Church of Jesus Christ, and Its Marks................................... 121

Chapter 23: On the Sacraments and Other Sacred Rites 124

Chapter 24: On Church Discipline... 129

Chapter 25: On Synods or Councils, and their Manner and Use........................... 132

CONCLUSION.. **137**

• INTRODUCTION •

Some will think it strange that one not from the Arminian tradition would undertake the translation of this first and very important Remonstrant confession.[1] My initial exposure to Arminian theology came when, as a Calvinist pastor of a Reformed baptistic church, a friend challenged me to read Jacobus Arminius' (1560-1609) works.[2] Having been taught he was both Socinian and Pelagian, I was surprised how Calvinist his affirmations sounded about trinitarianism, Scripture, original sin and the necessity of grace. This led to a broader study of those who shared Arminius' theology, with special emphasis on his protégé, Simon Episcopius (1583-1643), the primary author of this confession.[3] The Remonstrants published the *Confession or Declaration of the Remonstrant Pastors* shortly after the Synod of Dort.[4] They intended it as a concise, easily understandable statement of their faith and a corrective to what they viewed as the misrepresentations published in the *Acts of the Synod of Dort*.[5]

The impetus for a new translation of the *Confession* is its value as a primary source of early Remonstrant doctrine. In the desire to help English readers maintain the "feel" of the original and assist in finding the corresponding passages in Latin, the translation largely maintains the flow of the text, although it divides longer sentences and moves verbs to the beginning of sentences, often substitutes participles for nouns and infinitives and sometimes uses synonyms even when cognates were available in English.[6] Nevertheless, the style remains complicated and some sentences are long. Whitaker's Words[7] and Lewis and Short's Latin Dictionary[8] guided word selection. Italics in the Latin are from the original and brackets in the English indicate the addition of words for comprehension.

Different theological traditions will find this book useful for different reasons. Those from an Arminian tradition may want to compare their theology with that of the early Remonstrants. Certainly it is much easier to consult the *Confession* than wade through Arminius' private and public disputations, orations and treatises. One must keep in mind, however, that the *Confession* does not reflect Arminius' theology alone. It also represents those who were "Arminian" before Arminius (such as Wtenbogaert and older pastors), together with Episcopius' own creative impulses.

The *Confession* also offers benefits to those from Calvinist/Reformed backgrounds. It dispels common misrepresentations, such as the Arminians were Socinians, an accusation the Arminians' opponents brought against them from the beginning of the conflict.[9] In chapter three of the confession, the Remonstrants gave a clear repudiation of Socinianism's denials of the divinity of Christ and the trinity and provided an orthodox declaration of trinitarianism, the eternal generation of the Son and procession of the Holy Spirit and the sharing of the divine nature by both.

More common are accusations of Pelagianism. The *Confession* gives ample evidence that the Remonstrants did not hold to Pelagius' theology.[10] Whereas Pelagius taught Adam's sin affected himself alone and only served as a bad example for his descendents, the Remonstrants affirmed that all men except Jesus Christ were "involved and implicated"

v

in Adam's sin and so were subject to "death and misery" and "destitute of true righteousness necessary for achieving eternal life, and consequently are now born subject to that eternal death...and manifold miseries" (7.4). Whereas Pelagius defined grace as the native ability conferred through creation, together with a mind illuminated by the preaching of the law, the Remonstrants affirmed grace is a "special work" which only functioned in those who believe (7.1), and that under the Law, grace was "revealed it only from afar, obscurely and almost as if through a lattice." While Pelagius thought there were those even in the Old Testament who attained sinless perfection through the Law, the Remonstrants affirmed that even in the Old Testament "they were not entirely lacking those who believed in God by the assistance of that divine grace and by faith walked blamelessly and sincerely before him" (7.8). In contrast to Pelagius' belief in human ability, the Remonstrants wrote that "(we) could neither shake off the miserable yoke of sin, nor do anything truly good in all religion, nor finally ever escape eternal death, or any true punishment of sin. Much less could we at any time obtain eternal salvation without it or through ourselves" (7.10). They reaffirmed human inability and the necessity of grace in (8.1, 8.2.2) and that salvation is the work of God (9.2). It is only by grace that people "may really believe in their Christ the Savior, obey his gospel and be freed from the dominion and guilt of sin, indeed also through which they may really believe, obey and be freed"(9.2) The Remonstrants clearly were not Pelagians.

If not Pelagians, were they semi-Pelagian? Domingo Bañez (1528-1604) coined the term in the sixteenth century to refer to the doctrines of the Jesuit thinker Luis de Molina (1535–1600) in the controversy between Dominicans and Jesuits over grace and free will, which paralleled discussions among Protestants. The term entered Protestant theology through inclusion in the Lutheran Formula of Concord (1580). It defined "…the error of the Semi-Pelagians, who teach that man by virtue of his own powers could make a beginning of his conversion but could not complete it without the grace of the Holy Spirit." Semi-Pelagianism began as a reaction by monks who agreed with Augustine on the doctrines of original sin, the inability of man to perform any act of saving worth and the necessity of illumination, but defended the freedom of the will by attributing to it the initial act of faith. Fallen sinners initiate and God responds. They also taught that people could, of themselves, freely accept and persevere in grace.[11] Again, if one allows history to define labels, neither Arminius nor the Remonstrants were semi-Pelagian. They made this plain in the original Remonstrance of 1610,[12] and repeated the same in the *Confession* (17.6). They stressed "that the grace of God is the beginning, progress and completion of all good, so that not even a regenerate man himself can, without this preceding, or preventing, exciting, following and cooperating grace, think, will, or finish any good thing to be saved, much less resist any attractions and temptations to evil." They differed with their opponents not over the necessity of grace, but in their belief that a person can "despise and reject the grace of God and resist its operation, so that when he is divinely called to faith and obedience, he is able to render himself unfit to believe" (17.7).

In the end, one wonders why those who look to Geneva would need to resort to fabricating or extrapolating their differences with the Remonstrants. The Remonstrant rejections of unconditional election, limited atonement, irresistible grace and perseverance, together with the unique doctrines they affirmed in the *Confession* (such as multiple definitions of election) are *per se* reasons enough to declare that they represented an alien theological development.

On the other hand, those from non-Arminian theologies may also find ideas they appreciate. Many from the "lordship" perspective will value the Remonstrant emphasis on repentance, that it is a requirement for salvation, that it precedes faith and that the biblical authors understood that when Scripture mentions "faith" alone it included the idea of repentance. We within the Baptist tradition will resonate with Remonstrant efforts to write a confession which was an accurate expression of their faith, yet did not violate liberty of conscience and avoided the chains of creedalism. We affirm with them the perspicuity of the Scriptures, soul competence and the priesthood of the believer.

We also see in the *Confession* that the Remonstrant challenge was not merely doctrinal. From its inception, the Remonstrants considered their movement as a rejection of Reformed scholasticism as a theological method.[13] Certainly Arminius viewed himself this same way. On October 8, 1603, shortly after his installation as professor at Leiden, Arminius observed his first student-led disputation on original sin. He was critical of the presenter for depending too much on logic and too little on Scripture. He then used this occasion to challenge his colleagues to abandon what he called "the cumbrous mass of scholastic assertions" for what he termed an "earlier and more masculine method of study" of the Scriptures.[14] If someone were to discount this protest as merely "typical" of the time, this seems strange in light of his criticizing men who were in a position to point out his own inconsistencies. This criticism becomes even more interesting if the source of this "earlier and more masculine method of study" was none other than John Calvin. We find an indication of this a letter Arminius wrote two years before his death:

> But after the reading of Scripture, which I vehemently inculcate more than anything else, which the entire academy can testify and of which my colleagues are conscious, I encourage the reading of the commentaries of Calvin, which I extol with the greatest praise…. For I say that he is incomparable in the interpretation of Scripture, and his comments are better than anything which the Fathers give us.[15]

These examples evidence that Arminius perceived differences between his theological method and that of other Reformed scholastics and was attempting both to sway his students away from theological speculation toward the more biblical theological method of Calvin.

Episcopius adopted Arminius' perspective on Reformed rationalism and speculation and removed himself even further. For example, Episcopius began his private disputations by repeating his emphasis on biblical, practical theology, limited by the constraints of the text.[16] He pointedly refused to comment on some subjects, such as details about angels, which he viewed as "scholastic innovations." He repeated his rejection of Reformed scholasticism in his farewell address to his students,[17] and incorporated it into the *Confession*.[18] That 17th century Calvinist Reformed theologians were sensitive to these attacks can be seen in the writings of Gisbert Voetius, who tried to counter Remonstrant accusations of excessive speculation, innovation and "bogging down" on small points and *minutiae*.[19]

We find in the *Confession* a corollary to the rejection of Reformed scholasticism, the Remonstrant insistence that all true theology was entirely practical and not speculative or theoretical.[20] Whatever the modern equivocations over the meaning of "speculative theology," for Episcopius it signified theology which was derived from reason rather than from Scripture and served to satisfy theological curiosity rather than promote the worship of God. As Episcopius wrote in the introductory section of his *Theological Institutes*,

"Theology is not a speculative knowledge, but practical. Nor is it, as some desire, partly speculative and partly practical. Still less, is it as others desire, the greatest part being speculative. It is purely practically."[21] This emphasis on theology as a practical science became one of the hallmarks of Remonstrant theology.

Having mentioned Simon Episcopius numerous times in the introduction and given his general obscurity among modern scholars, it would be helpful to include some information about his life and work. Episcopius was singularly responsible for the survival of the Remonstrant movement after the Synod of Dort.[22] We may rightly regard him as the theological founder of Arminianism, since he both developed and systematized ideas which Arminius was tentatively exploring before his death and then perpetuated that theology through founding the Remonstrant seminary and teaching the next generation of pastors and teachers.[23]

His given name was Simon Bisschop, which he later Latinized according to the academic practices of his day. He was born to Reformed parents in Leiden and from early childhood showed keen intellect and great promise in Greek and Latin. In spite of his family's humble financial circumstances, private and public benefactors provided him with the best education available in the Netherlands. He entered the University at Leiden in 1600, where he formed his close relationship with Arminius. That Arminius was an orphan and Episcopius lost both parents to plague during this time may have fostered their friendship.

After receiving his master's degree on February 27 1606,[24] he continued in academic life at the university through participation in daily disputations and attendance at the lectures of the three professors of theology, Franciscus Gomarus (1563-1641), Lucas Trelcatius (1573-1607) and Arminius. During this time open conflict broke out between Arminius and Gomarus.[25] We know little about how much Episcopius entered the debate, but nearly every letter he wrote during this time to his brother, Rem Bisschop, contained references to Arminius.[26] His association with Arminius created problems for him in Amsterdam[27] and later at Franeker, where he had gone to study Hebrew under Ioannes Drusius.[28] Arminius' death in October 1609 compounded frustration with grief.[29]

Episcopius' recognition among those who shared Arminius' theology grew quickly. In May 1610 he was appointed pastor in the small town of Bleyswick. In 1611, he was chosen as one of six to represent the Remonstrants at a conference called by the government to try to resolve the growing conflict. In 1612, the curators of the University of Leiden formally recognized his theological leadership among the Remonstrants by inviting him to succeed Gomarus as professor of theology, an appointment which aroused bitter enmity among Calvinists. It is likely that, on account of the influence his appointment gave to the spread of Remonstrant opinions, this was a significant factor leading up to the Synod of Dort in 1618.

Theological and political turmoil brought the Netherlands to the brink of civil war in the years leading up the synod and troubled both Episcopius and his family.[30] Persecution progressed to the point that on August 30, 1618, Johannes Wtenbogaert, the political leader of the Remonstrants, heeded the advice of his colleagues and fled the country.[31] In his absence the leadership of the Remonstrants fell to Episcopius. On September 20, Episcopius received a letter from the States of Holland and West-Friesland inviting him to represent the University at the national synod. The synod began on November 17 and one of the first acts was to change Episcopius' status from a representative to a subpoenaed person.[32] The Remonstrants knew this ended their hope for open debate and turned to other

means in order to gain a hearing. Episcopius asked for permission to address the Synod and then launched into an hour and a half oration detailing the Remonstrant position and their oppression at the hands of the Calvinist Reformed.[33] The speech was powerful and soon circulated throughout the Netherlands and beyond.[34] The Remonstrant protest, however, was short-lived. The president of the synod expelled them for refusing to cooperate,[35] and the synod decided to judge them from their writings.[36] It condemned their beliefs on April 24, 1619, civil sentences were pronounced on May 6 and on July 5 the leaders of the Remonstrants were loaded into wagons and driven into exile.

The exiled Remonstrants eventually settled in Antwerp, where in they formed the Remonstrant Brotherhood and selected Episcopius, Wtenbogaert and Nicholas Grevinchoven to form the "foreign directorship."[37] It was during these meetings that the Remonstrants discussed their need for a confession. Many were hesitant, fearful of establishing the same type of creedalism which had resulted in their persecution and banishment. The *Preface* to the *Confession*, which the Remonstrants considered an integral part of the document, emphasized its non-binding character. The society eventually judged it more important to prove their orthodoxy to those who wanted to assist them, to silence the misrepresentations of their opposition, and most of all, to encourage and unite the now distressed and scattered Remonstrants. They selected Episcopius and two others to write it, but in the end, he did the work alone. He completed the *Confession* on February 6, 1620 and the directory called a general meeting in Antwerp for the purpose of discussing it.[38] After some revisions, it was approved on February 8 and the gathering charged Wtenbogaert and Episcopius with making a Dutch translation which the Remonstrants approved and accepted on February 9. The Dutch edition was published in 1621,[39] the Latin in 1622.[40] The response from those friendly to the Remonstrants was immediate and gratifying to the Brotherhood.[41]

Episcopius lived in exile from 1619 until 1626, first in Antwerp and then alternating between Rouen and Paris. During this period he encouraged the Remonstrants who remained in the Netherlands and defended the movement from its opponents. By 1626 the persecutions in the Netherlands were beginning to abate. Prince Maurice was dead and his half-brother Henry, a Remonstrant sympathizer, was now leading the country. Episcopius arrived in Rotterdam in July. Wtenbogaert returned in September and resolved any potential leadership crisis by declaring Episcopius the director of the Brotherhood.[42]

Episcopius lived 16 years after his return from exile. He ministered at the church in Rotterdam, revitalized the church in Amsterdam (1629), founded the Remonstrant seminary (1632) and wrote and traveled much in support of the Remonstrant cause. During such a trip to Rotterdam a torrential rainstorm overtook him and having arrived too late to enter the city, he spent the night in the cold. The resulting fever left him permanently weakened. He fell ill again in similar circumstances in February 1643 and died peacefully on April 4. Four days later, his friends buried him in the Western Church by the side of his wife. His funeral was large, but the most poignant presence was that of Wtenbogaert. Van Limborch wrote that when he came into the room where Episcopius was laid, he approached the body and placing his hands upon the head cried out "O Head! O Head! How much wisdom there was within you!"[43] He had buried Arminius, and now he would bury Episcopius as well.

In sum, the *Confession or Declaration of the Remonstrant Pastors* treats the major areas of Christian doctrine as held by Arminius' colleagues and successors after the Synod of Dort. They published it to inform both lay and professional Christians about what they

believed and defend themselves against the attacks of their opponents. Their dominant concern was to expound what they believed were the central teachings of Sacred Scripture. This translation will not only allow the reader to directly interact with those theology was the object of the Synod of Dort, but also brings us into the thought and vocabulary of Simon Episcopius, the primary developer and defender of Arminius' theology.

I completed this translation while my wife Diane and I were on furlough from missionary service in Brazil. I am grateful to Dr. David Dockery and Union University for their kind hospitality during this time, with special mention to Todd Bradey and Suzanne Mosley of Student Ministries.

Mark A. Ellis, Ph.D.
Jackson, TN
June, 2005

Notes

[1] Although those who agreed with Arminius are often called Arminians, Arminius was merely a rallying point for many who represented the pre-Calvinist reformation movement in the Netherlands which looked more to Melanchthon, Bullinger and Hemmingius than to Calvin and Beza. Rather than calling themselves "Arminians," they took the name "Remonstrants" from the remonstrance (legal protest) they lodged with the government requesting protection from persecution. The church continues today as the Remonstrant Brotherhood. For a fuller presentation of Arminianism as a pre-Calvinist branch of the Dutch Reformation, see my dissertation, "Simon Episcopius and the Doctrine of Original Sin" (Ph.D. diss, Dallas Theological Seminary, 2002).

[2] Although many of Arminius' theological works were published individually, the Remonstrants published them collectively for the first time in *Opera Theologica* (Leiden: Goderfridum Basson, 1629). They are available in English in two versions, *The Works of James Arminius* (Reprint of the London edition [London: vols. 1-2, Longman, Hurst, Rees, Orme, Brown and Green; vol. 3, Thomas Baker, 1825-75]; Grand Rapids: Baker Book House, 1986, henceforth cited as *WA*), and *The Writings of James Arminius* (Reprint of 1853 ed. [Auburn and Buffalo: Derby, Miller and Orton]; Grand Rapids, MI: Baker Book House, 1956, henceforth cited as *WrA*).

[3] Episcopius' essential theological works, including orations and shorter treatises, were published in *Opera Theologica* (ed. Stephanus Curcellaeus, Amsterdam: Ioannis Blaev, 1650, henceforth *OTE*) and *Operum Theologicorum, Pars Altera* (ed. Philip van Limborch, Rotterdam: Arnoldum Leers, 1665, henceforth *OTPA*). His sermons were collected and published in *Predicatien van M. S. Episcopius* (ed. Philip van Limborch. Amsterdam: Isaak Pieterz., 1693).

[4] The Latin text used in this translation is from *OTPA* 1:69-94.

[5] Published in Latin as *Acta Synodi Nationalis* (Dort: Isaaci Ioannidis Canini Et Sociorum, 1620), and in Dutch as *Acta ofte Handelinghen des Nationalen Synodi* (Dort: Isaack Jans. Canin, 1621). Numerous translations are available in English.

[6] For example, I used "thoughts" to translate "cogitationes" even though "cogitations" exists in English, and "seeking" rather than "procuring" when translating "procurandum."

[7] http://users.erols.com/whitaker/wordsdoc.htm.

[8] http://perseus.uchicago.edu/cgi-bin/morphindex?lang=la.

9   See the anonymous *Een Kort en Waerachtich Verhael / wat voor een grouwelijck ghevoelen dat de Arminianen / Vortianen / ofte nieuwe Arrianen / Pelagianen / Socinianen / Samosatinianen ghesocht hebben in de Gehereformeerde kercke in te voeren / en in kort heir teghen gestelt het ghevoelen der Ghereformeerde kerche* (N.p.: "Ghedruckt buyten Romen," n.d.), published during the time of the conflict leading up to the Synod of Dort. Simon Episcopius was accused of Socinianism by Lubbertus Sibrandus while a student in Franeker, by Daniel Hensius while teaching at the University of Leiden and by the Leiden professors after returning to the Netherlands, but always proved himself orthodox when given an opportunity to answer his accusers. Regarding the absence of Pelagian or Socinian theology among the Remonstrants, see W. Robert Godfrey, "Calvin and Calvinism in the Netherlands," in *John Calvin, His Influence in the Western world*, ed. W. Stanford Reid and Paul Woolley (Grand Rapids, Zondervan, 1982), 104–05.

10 The Remonstrant rejection of Pelagianism had already been made plain in the Remonstrance of 1610, which stated in Article III, "That man has not saving grace of himself, nor of the energy of his free-will, inasmuch as he, in the state of apostasy and sin, can of and by himself neither think, will, nor do anything that is truly good (such as having faith eminently is); but that it is needful that he be born again of God in Christ, through his Holy Spirit, and renewed in understanding, inclination, or will, and all his powers, in order that he may rightly understand, think, will, and effect what is truly good, according to the word of Christ, John 15:5: "Without me ye can do nothing.""

11 Columbia Encyclopedia, 6th ed., s.v. "Pelagianism."

12 "Article IV: That this grace of God is the beginning, continuance, and accomplishment of all good, even to this extent, that the regenerate man himself, without prevenient or assisting, awakening, following and cooperative grace, can neither think, will, nor do good, nor withstand any temptations to evil; so that all good deeds or movements, that can be conceived, must be ascribed to the grace of God in Christ, but respects the mode of the operation of this grace, it is not irresistible; inasmuch as it is written concerning many, that they have resisted the Holy Ghost. Acts 7, and elsewhere in many places."

13 This perspective was defended by both James Nichols and W. R. Bagnall in their editions of Arminius' works. Bagnall wrote, "In view of his early training and the universal practice of the theological writers of that age, it might be expected that Arminius would adopt the phraseology and manner of the Schoolmen. This was, to some extent, true of him. Yet it will be found, we think, on the perusal of his writings, that he was less scholastic in his style and more practical and scriptural both in his views and in his mode of presenting them than most of his contemporaries." (W. R. Bagnall, "Preface," *WrA* [Baker: Grand Rapids, MI, 1977] 1: v).

14 Caspar Brandt, *The Life of James Arminius*, trans. John Guthrie [Nashville: E. Stevenson & F.A. Owen, Agents for the Methodist Episcopal Church South, 1857], 191-92).

15 "Sed post Scripturæ lectionem, quam vehementer inculco, & magis quam quisquam alius, quod tota Academia testabitur, etiam conscientia meorum collegarum, ad Calvini Commentarios legendos adhortor, quem laudibus majoribus extollo.... Dico enim incomparabilem esse in interpretatione Scripturarum, & majores faciendos ipsius commentarios quam quidquid Patrum Bibliotheca nobit tradit." Jacobus Arminius to Sebastian Egbert, 3 May, 1607, Christiaan Hartsoeker and Philippus van Limborch, eds., *Præstantium ac eruditorum virorum epistolæ ecclesiasticæ et theologicæ* (Amsterdam: Henricum Wetstenium, 1660), 236-37.

16 *Disputationes Theologiæ Tripartæ* (Amsterdam: Ioannem Blaev, 1644, henceforth *DTT*), 2.12, *De Creatione Mundi*. He repeated this sentiment in *DTT*, 3.8.1: "Sicut naturæ divinæ excellentia & supereminentia Deum cultu & honore dignum facit; ita opera quæ Scriptura ei tribuit, jus, auctoritatem, & potestatem postulandi à nobis cultum & obsequium eidem conciliant."

17 "ORATIUNCULA habita à M. SIMONE EPISCOPIO 13. Novemb. Anni 1618 in auditorio Theologico cum ad Synodum Dordracenam ab Illustr. Ordd. Hollandiæ evocatus discederet," in *OTPA*, pp. 170-172.

18 "As to thorny and excessively subtle questions, which are appropriate for universities and schools, and which neither help the knower nor hurt the ignorant, we have purposely abstained from them, leaving them to the idle and overly curious, and who have an incurable disease of disputing, to whom it is pleasurable to show their acumen, and from this laurel-cake they seek for fame in trifles" (*Preface*, p. 22).

19 Gisbert Voetius, "Selectæ Disputationes Theologicæ," in *Reformed Dogmatics*, ed. John W. Beardslee III (Grand Rapids: Eerdmans, 1977), 268, 278.

20 See the *Preface*, page 23. Note also the inclusion of sections which give specific applications for the content of each chapter.

21 "Theologiam non esse scientia speculativam, sed practicam: Nec esse, ut quidam volunt, partim speculativam, partim practicam, nedum, ut alii, maximam partem speculativam. Pure practica est" (*Institutiones Theologicae*, in *Opera Theologica* [Amsterdam: Ioannis Blæv, 1650], 1:4).

22 Important biographical sources for Episcopius are Stephanus Curcellæus' preface in Episcopius' *Opera Theologica* (Stephanus Curcellæus, "Præfatio Ad Lectorem Christianem," in *Opera Theologica* [Amsterdam: Ioannis Blæv, 1650]), and Philip van Limborch's more complete *Leven van Mr. Simon Episcopius* (In *Predicatien van M. S. Episcopius*, [Amsterdam: Isaak Pieterz., 1693]), which he augmented and republished as *Historia Vitæ Episcopii* (Amsterdam: Georgium Gallet, 1701). The only significant biography in English is Calder's *Memoirs of Simon Episcopius* (London: Simpkin and Marshall, 1835). Although Calder stated he relied heavily on van

Limborch for historical details (Calder, *Memoirs*, 71), much of his analysis is unique. These biographies do not discuss the content of Episcopius' theological works. Henrik Haentjens filled many such gaps with his 1899 doctoral dissertation, *Simon Episcopius als Apologeet van het Remonstrantisme in zijn leven en werken geschetst* (Anton Hendrik Haentjens, *Simon Episcopius als Apologeet van het Remonstrantisme in zijn leven en werken geschestst* [Leiden: A. H. Adriani, 1899]). In the 1960's, Gerrit J. Hoenderdaal provided important information concerning the relationship between Arminius and Episcopius in Gerrit J. Hoenderdaal, "Arminius en Episcopius," *Nederlands Archief voor Kerkgeschiedenis* 60 (1980): 203-35. See also extensive comparisons in my dissertation, "Simon Episcopius and the Doctrine of Original Sin" (Ph.D. diss, Dallas Theological Seminary, 2002)

23 One of the most important of his students was Stephanus Curcellus.

24 Van Limborch, *Vitae*, 4-5.

25 Van Limborch, *Vitae*, 5-7.

26 Haentjens, *Simon Episcopius als Apologeet*, 11.

27 He was blocked from entering the ministry there. See Calder, *Memoirs*, 53-54.

28 Calder, *Memoirs*, 56. Despite Arminius' warnings not to involve himself in debates, Episcopius disputed with Sibrandus Lubbertus over Romans 7 (Haentjens, *Simon Episcopius als Apologeet*, 14).

29 Episcopius travelled to be with Arminius as soon as he heard of his illness, and stayed with him at his bedside until he was assured Arminius would recover. Arminius died shortly after Episcopius returned to Franeker.

30 Rem Bisschop's home in Amsterdam was broken into and plundered under the watchful eye of at least one Calvinist Reformed pastor, Ursinus (Geeraert Brandt, *The History of the Reformation and other Ecclesiastical Transactions in and about the Low-countries: From the Beginning of the Eighth Century, Down to the Famous Synod of Dort, Inclusive: faithfully translated from the original Low-Dutch* [London: Printed by T. Wood for T. Childe, 1720], 2:95).

31 Van Limborch, *Vitae*, 5. Johannes Wtenbogaert (sometimes Uytenbogaert, Utenbogaart or Uitenbogaart) was a colleague of Arminius at Geneva, one of Arminius' staunchest defenders and primary leader of the Remonstrant movement. Regarding his relationship with Episcopius, Haentjens wrote, "There was also a growing attraction on the part of Episcopius for Wtenbogaert, and they developed such a strong relationship that they later spent their time in exile together. They complemented one another. Wtenbogaert took the lead in practical details, but in questions of scholarship he deferred to Episcopius, whose judgments he valued more than 'those of the greater and lesser gods'" (Haentjens, *Simon Episcopius als Apologeet*, 29-30). Wtenbogaert wrote the original Remonstrance of 1610 and outlived both Arminius and Episcopius. The standard work concerning his life is *Johannes Utenbogaerd en Zijne Tijde* by H. C. Rogge (Amsterdam, 1874).

32 The difference in status was significant. One could compare it to being moved from the panel of judges to being suppoened as a defendant.

33 The oration can be found in the Dutch version of the Acts of the Synod of Dort (*Acta ofte Handelingen*, 68-79), but was left out of the Latin (*Acta Synodi Nationalis*). The 23rd session appears on pages 64-66, complete with the accusations against Episcopius. Latin versions appear in van Limborch, *Vitae*, 145-167 and *OTPA* 2:1-4. One may find English translations in Calder, *Memoirs*, pages 284-315 and Brandt, *History*, 3:52-61.

34 Wtenbogaert heard about it even from exile, and wrote to thank Episcopius for it (Johannes Wtenbogaert to Simon Episcopius, April 25, 1619, in the Remonstrant Library in Rotterdam, and published in Rogge, *Brieven van Johannes Wtenbogaert*, #220. Quoted by Haentjens, *Simon Episcopius als Apologeet*, 50).

35 The president of the synod was Iohannes Bogerman, whose unique contribution to the persecution of the Remonstrants prior to the synod was translating Beza's tract defending the execution of heretics. His relationship with Episcopius was already strained because of Episcopius' speech, and Bogerman's attempts to prove Episcopius a liar. The conflict came to a head when he demanded the Remonstrant delegation sign yet another declaration of whether they still held to their opinions, and Episcopius responded with frustration, "Let it then be brought to us, and we will sign it." The president thought he was arrogant, and demanded each come before him to sign it. Bogerman became embarrassed by the dignity with which each came to his desk, lost control of himself and expelled them from the synod with accusations of "base artifices, cheats and lies" (Brandt, *History* 3:151-52).

36 Some of the strongest evidences of misrepresentation of Remonstrant beliefs by the Synod come from the letters of Walter Balcanqual. He served as a British delegate, was a committed Calvinist and held to particular redemption (Nicholas Tyacke, *English Arminianism*, 44-45, 92, 95-98). These letters were reports on the synod to the British ambassador Sir Dudley Carleton. He wrote that the British delegation had been criticized for attempting to define Remonstrant beliefs from those books in which "they spake best and soundest," while the tendency was to gather their sentiments "out of all places in their books, where they spake most absurdly, which we thought was very far besides the rule of charity." (George Balcanqual, Dort, to Dudley Carleton, February 9, 1619, in Hales, "Letters from Dort;" quoted by James Nichols, "A Brief Account of the Synod of Dort, Taken Out of the letters of Mr. Hales and Mr. Balcanqual, written from Dort, to the Rt. Hon. Sir D. Carleton, Lord Ambassador then at the Hague," in *The Works of Arminius*, London ed. [London: Longman, Hurst, Rees, Orme,

Brown and Green, 1825; reprint, Grand Rapids: Baker, 1986], 1:545). He noted that when Bogerman read from Episcopius, "the President picked out the worst part of it…which contained nothing but a bitter satire against Calvin, Beza, Pareus, Piscator, Whitaker, Perkins, Bogerman, Festus and twenty more. But in truth, through unhappily, yet it was finely penned" (George Balcanqual, Dort, to Dudley Carleton, February 15, 1619, in Hales, "Letters from Dort;" quoted in Nichols, "The Synod of Dort," 1:546). Finally, he criticized the delegates for distorting Remonstrant sentiments when he wrote, "They are so eager to kill the Remonstrants, that they would make their words have that sense which no grammar can find in them….They condemned the thing itself as a thing most curious, and yet would have it retained only to make the Remonstrant odious, though they find the very contrary of that they would father upon them in their writings" (George Balcanqual, Dort, to Dudley Carleton, February 19, 1619, in Hales, "Letters from Dort;" quoted in Nichols, "The Synod of Dort," 1:546). Blaising provides several examples of these misrepresentations (Craig A. Blaising, "John Wesley's Doctrine of Original Sin," [Ph.D. diss., Dallas Theological Seminary, 1979] 111-124).

[37] The meeting lasted from September 30 through October 4. Concerning this meeting, see Johannes Tideman, *De Stichting Der Remonstrantsche Bruderschap, 1619-1634* (Amsterdam, Y. Rogge, 1871), 1:118. Even though Wtenbogaert was present, Episcopius was chosen to chair the meetings. Ibid, 1:49.

[38] So wrote Haentjens, *Simon Episcopius als Apologeet*, 56. Although some have questioned the authorship of the *Confession*, its appearance without qualification in *Opera Theologica, Pars Altera* (Rotterdam: Arnoldum Leers, 1665, 2:69-94) supports that the first and second generation of Remonstrants attributed it to Episcopius. Nevertheless, comparisons with Episcopius' public and private disputations demonstrate that while the great majority of the *Confession* is clearly his work, there are those points at which Episcopius deviated from Arminius prior to the writing of the *Confession*, but Arminius' theology was reasserted in the *Confession*. I presume the other pastors in attendance were responsible for this reaffirmation of Arminius' thought.

[39] *Belijdnisse ofte Verklaringhe Van't ghevoelen der Leeraren die in de Gheunieerde Neder-landen Remonstranten worden ghenaemste, over de voornaemste Articulen der Christelijcke Religie* (N.p, 1621).

[40] *Confessio, sive, Declaratio, Sententiae Pastorum, qui in Foederato Belgio Remonstrantes Vocantur, Super Praecipuis Articulis Religionis Christianae* (Harderwijk: Theodorum Danielis, 1622). It was reprinted in *Opera Theologica, Pars Altera* (Rotterdam: Arnoldum Leers, 1665), 69-94, and later translated into English as *The Confession or Declaration of the Ministers or Pastors which in the United Provinces are called Remonstrants, Concerning The Chief Points of Christian Religion* (London: Francis Smith, 1676).

[41] Hugo Grotius' approval is especially interesting. See Hugo Grotius, Lutetiae (Paris) to Simon Episcopius, June 7, 1621, in *PEVE* (#198), 632-33. Grotius' words show his clear identification with the Remonstrants: "*Confessio* apud aequos homines, ut spero, nobis proderit." Episcopius' letter to Grotius immediately precedes this one in the 1660 edition (pp. 630-32).

[42] Haentjens, *Simon Episcopius als Apologeet*, 79.

[43] "O caput, quanta sapientia in te recondita fuit!" (quoted by van Limborch, *Vitae*, 320).

CONFESSIO, sive DECLARATIO,
Sententiæ Pastorum, qui in Fœderato Belgio
REMONSTRANTES vocantur,
Super præcipius articulis Religionis Christianæ.

The Confession or Declaration of the Pastors
which in the Belgian Federation
are called the Remonstrants,
on the principle articles of the Christian Religion.

PREFACE

PRÆFATIO,
AD LECTOREM CHRISTIANUM.

Non est dubitum, pie Lector, quin hæc, quæ à nobis editur Declaratio fidei variis ac diversis hominum judiciis obnoxia sit futura. Prout enim quisque apud animum suum de hujusmodi Declarationum tum necessitate, tum utilitate, tum forma ac modo statuit, ita etiam de hac nostra judicium facturus est.

Sunt, qui à Confessionibus aut Declarationibus omnibus prorsus abstinendum esse existimant, esque non modo non necessarias nec utiles Reipub. Christianæ, sed & illicitas, periculosas & noxias in Ecclesia esse consent. Sunt, qui Confessiones aut Declarationes in publicum edi, non quidem omnino inconsultum, nedum illicitum aut noxium arbitrantur, sed eas non nisi meris ac puris putis Scripturæ verbis concipiendas ac contexendas esse judicant. Sunt, qui Confessiones licet aliis quam nudis Scripturæ verbis conceptas non quidem omnino improbant, sed adeo generales ac breves esse volunt, ut nihil quod absolute ac precise necessarium scitu & creditu ad salutem est, contineant ac complectantur. Sunt denique alii ab his multum diversi, qui Confessiones ac Declarationes particulares de singulis etiam minutissimis controversiis, usque adeo non tantum utiles, sed & necessarias censent, ut sine iis Christianus ullus cœtus nec esse bene esse possit. Horum omnium tam varia, tamque diversa ac discrepantia judicia procul omni dubio expertura est nostra hæc Declaratio: & habent sane singuli hi speciosa & à verisimilitudine non prorsus aliena, quibus nituntur, opinionum suarum fundamenta.

A Preface to the Christian Reader

There is no doubt, godly reader, that the declaration of faith put forth by us will be subject to various and diverse judgments of men. For each will pass judgment upon our [declaration], just as he has determined in his own mind regarding either the necessity and usefulness, or the form and manner of such declarations.

There are those who think we should abstain from all confessions or declarations and judge that they are not only unnecessary and unprofitable for the Christian community, but also unlawful, dangerous and harmful to the church. There are some who think that it is not altogether unadvisable to set forth or publish confessions or declarations, much less unlawful or hurtful, but they judge that they ought to be conceived and woven from the pure and simple words of the Scriptures. There are others who do not entirely disapprove of confessions, even if they are not just conceived in the bare words of Scripture, but want them to be so general and brief, that they contain or include nothing which is not absolutely and precisely necessary to know and believe in order to be saved. There are also some, so very different from the others, who suppose that specific confessions and declarations concerning even the smallest and most minute controversies are not only useful and necessary, but also that no Christian church can exist well or even exist without them. Beyond all doubt, our declaration will be put to the test by all the diverse and discrepant judgments of all these, and they certainly have impressive and not entirely improbable foundations for their opinions.

Qui à Confessionibus aut Declarationibus prorsus abstinendum, aut eas non nisi meris nudis Scripturæ verbis concipiendas esse arbitrantur, (quales hoc sæculo non pauci alioquin pii & probi reperiuntur) ii, quantum nobis colligere licet, tria fere opinioni suæ prætexere solent. 1. Quod per eas Scripturarum majestati & authoritate non leve fiat præjudicium. 2. Quod Ecclesiarum seu conscientiæ ac prophetiæ libertati damnum ac detrimentum igens occasione earum adferatur. 3. Quod factionibus & schismatis in ecclesia lata fenestra per eadem aperiatur.

Ac primo quidem Scripturarum majestati non parum eo ipso derogari ac detrahi existimant, quod earum tum sufficientia, tum perspicutas in suspicionem aut dubium vocari videatur, quasi videlicet, eæ aut non contineant plene ac sufficienter omnia, quæ unicuique Christiano cœtu necessaria & utilia scitu, creditu, speratu ac factu sunt, aut saltem non eas usurpent loquendi formulas, quæ clare satis ac perspicue sensus divinos, imprimis ad salutem creditu necessaries & perutiles exprimant, sed phrasibus ac formulis humanis opus habeant, ut recte intelligi, & ad discrimen veritatis & falsitatis rite faciendum adhiberi atque usurpari possint. Unde deinde fieri dicunt, ut Scripturarum authoritas magis magisque labefactetur & tandem tota concidat, atque ad formulas illas humanas tanquam aut perfectiores, aut clariores recti falsique indices, paulatim transferatur. Et certe confirmare videtur horum hominum opinionem non leviter experientia multorum sæculorum, quibus id fere usu venisse inquiunt, ut, postquam Confessionum ac Declarationem formulæ in pretio esse cæperunt, iisque honor iste deferri, quasi abditos atque involutos Scripturarum sensus planissime exprimerent, eaque quæ ecclesiis Jesu Christi necessario tenenda sunt, clarissime atque evidentissime ob oculos ponerent, paulatim Scripturarum majestas atque authoritas inclinare, & sententiarum atque opinionum omnium ad Religionis negotium pertinentuim veritas simul ac necessitas ex

Those who judge that one ought to abstain from all confessions or declarations, or that they should not be formed except in the mere, unadorned words of Holy Scripture (of which there are presently found not a few otherwise godly and honest people), as far as we can gather, customarily give three pretexts to support their opinions. 1. Because by them the majesty and authority of the Scriptures suffer no light prejudice. 2. Because the liberty of churches or of conscience and prophecy are brought to great damage and detriment. 3. Because by them a wide door is opened for factions and schisms in the churches.

And indeed first they judge that by them the majesty and honor of the Scriptures is not a little diminished and withdrawn, for they appear both to call their sufficiency and clarity into suspicion and doubt, as if they either did not fully and sufficiently contain everything necessary and useful for every Christian congregation to know, believe, hope and do, or at least did not use those forms of speaking which express clearly and perspicuously enough the divine meanings which are savingly necessary and profitable to be believed. Instead, they needed human phases and forms in order to be correctly understood, and could be used for discerning between truth and falsity. They say that from this it follows, that the authority of the Scriptures is more and more shaken, and finally is completely destroyed, and little by little this authority is transferred to those human formulas as being more perfect or more clear indices of the right and the false. And it certainly appears that the experience of many ages more than a little confirms these men's opinions, when they say that for the most part it usually comes about that men began to hold formulas of confessions and declarations in esteem, and they were honored as if they most fully express the hidden and convoluted senses of the Scriptures, and most clearly and plainly put before one's eyes those things which are necessarily held by the churches of Jesus Christ. Little by little the majesty and authority of the Scriptures declined,

formulis illis pendere cæperit; adeo quidem, ut præterita & posthabita sacrosancta Scriptura; ad eas tanquam ad certissimas normas, ad regulas omni exceptione majores provocatum sit, & qui ad iis vel latum unguem discedere, licet sola Scripturarum reverentia motus citra ulteriorem ullam probationem, hæreseos postulatus & damnatus fuerit. Ac licet principio, inque ipsis, quod dicitur, formularum incunabulis id non acciderit, quin & cautionibus insuper, seu restrictionibus ac potestationibus, aliisque id genus modis obviam ac contraitum sit; tamen tractu temporis paulatim invaluit, & incrementa cæpit earum authoritas, arcanisque auctibus per intervalla & gradus sensim stabilita est & confirmata; donec tandem, radicibus profunde actis, tantum non supra ipsas Scripturas stare cæperit. Ita successu temporis Concilia quædam Oecumenica, quæque in iis conceptæ atque adsertæ sunt formulæ fidei seu generalia symbola tanti fieri cæperunt, ut iis par & æqualis cum ipsis Evangeliis authoritas à plerique attributa sit. Imo etiam quæ ab unico Augustino contra Pelagium disputata & determinata sunt, ætatis fluxu tandem eo dignitatis authoritatisque sunt provecta, (etiam apud eos qui alioquin Conciliorum & Patrum authoritatem permagni facere non solet) ut ad condemnationem cujusvis in ecclesia docentis sufficiat, si Pelagio tantum adsinis videatur ipsius sententia. Et ita facere in cæteris fidei quæstionibus accidere solere, atque ab omni retro ævo accidisse perquam specione ajunt. In summa, non temere isti conqueri videntur, formulas fere omnes cum ætate nimiæ authoritatis vires atque ancrementa capere; & ut sæpe non videantur palam atque aperte ad majestatem immodicam provehi aut proficere, reipsa tamen abire paulatim (non obstantibus etiam cautionibus ac potestationibus in contrarium) in immotos fidei canones & saltem secundarias regulas ac normas, & quidem tam secretis & imperceptibilibus motibus, ut ad culmen authoritatis plus quam humanæ & dignitatis supremæ fastigium non pervenire, sed pervenisse, neque adolescere, sed adolevisse comperiantur.

and it was held that the truth and necessity of all sentiments and opinions pertaining to the business of religion hung upon those formulas, to such a degree that, while neglecting and undervaluing the Sacred Scripture, they appealed to [confessions] as if they were most certain squares or indisputable rulers. He who departed even a fingernail from them, even if motivated by reverence of the Scriptures, was without any further proof condemned as a heretic. And although at the beginning, or as they say, in the infancy of these formulas, it happened that this [attitude] was blocked and resisted with warnings, restrictions and protestations and similar actions, nevertheless with the passage of time, their authority gradually prevailed and increased, and through unnoticed steps and degrees, it was imperceptibly established and confirmed. At last, having sunk deep roots, it finally established itself as superior to the Scriptures themselves. Thus with the passing of time, certain ecumenical councils, and the formulas of faith or the creeds which were formed and preserved by them, were held in such high esteem, that they were granted authority equal to that of the Gospels by the majority. Indeed, even more, those things that were disputed and determined by Augustine alone against Pelagius, finally, with the flow of time, were promoted to such dignity and authority (even among those who otherwise are not accustomed to make much of the authority of councils and fathers), that even if one's sentiments only seemed to approach Pelagius, this was sufficient to condemn anyone who so teaches in the church. And so it usually happens with other questions of faith, just as it has happened in every previous age, or so they very impressively affirm. In sum, they do not seem to complain rashly, that, with time, almost all formulas usually seize great authority and increasing strength. And even though they are not often seen openly and publicly to advance and achieve excessive greatness, yet by degrees they become (not withstanding cautions and protestations to the contrary) immutable canons

Libertati etiam ecclesiarum seu conscientiæ ac prophetiæ dammum ac detrimentum igens adserre formulas has arbitrantur, quod ubi eæ in ecclesiam admittuntur, fieri non possit, qion è vestigio posticam tyrannica etiam lex intromittatur, ut non nisi ad earum præscriptum sentire, loqui scribere, docere, conferre & Scripturas interpretari liceat; eas vero in dubium vocare, iisque, modeste licet, contradicere, nefas putetur. Nec deest prætextus: ut scilicet publica Ecclesiæ pax sarta tecta conservetur, confusion vitetur & libertas in licentiam non exeat: unde porro fieri dicunt, ut nemo, (imprimis si Reipub. etiam interesse credatur) vel inquirere audeat in formulas istas, & dogmata, quæ iis continentur, expendere ad veritatis trutinam, vel si quis ingenito & industria advocata in eas inquisierit, & in illis falsa quædam esse judicio suo deprehenderit, proferre illa in publicum, atque aperire ad aliorum emendationem sine manifesto periculo nequeat. Atque hac quidem ratione Confessionum & Declarationum hujusmodi formulas definere in ridissima vincula & compedes plusquam adamantinas, quibus libertas simul ac veritas arctissime adstringantur, qui semel receptus atque admissus est error, stabilis ac firmus, imo æternus reddatur.

Schismatis denique & secessionibus fenestram latam aperiri per hasce Confessiones & Declarationes, ajunt, quia illæ (ut quidem hactenus usurpatæ sunt) velut aperta & publica dissensionum signa sunt, quibus non aliter quam intergerinis quibusdam parietibus Christiani, quos conjunctissimos esse oportebat, quique in summa salutaris doctrinæ reipsa consentiunt, à se invicem disseparantur, dum hic quidem Pauli,[a] ille Cepha, iste Apollo, alius Christi se

of faith or at least secondary measuring rods and squares. Indeed, by such secret and imperceptible motions, they are found not to be arriving but to have arrived, nor to be growing but to have grown, to the height of superhuman authority and the peak of supreme dignity.

They also judge that these formulas greatly injure and damage the liberty of churches, or of conscience and prophecy, because where they are admitted into the church, it cannot otherwise be but that a tyrannical law is brought in by the back steps, so no one is permitted to speak, write, teach, discuss and interpret the Scriptures unless they agree with what [confessions] prescribe. And to call them into doubt, or to contradict them, even if in a restrained manner, is considered extremely wicked. Nor are they lacking an excuse, namely, that the public peace of the church must be preserved and protected, confusion avoided, and liberty not turn into licentiousness. From this they go on to say, that no one (especially if it is believed to be in the interest of the republic) may dare scrutinize these formulas or the teaching which they contain, or weigh them in the balance of truth, or if anyone by his genius and industry should examine them, and in his judgment discover some things to be false, he cannot make them public or disclose corrections to others without manifest danger. And certainly for this reason, such formulas of confessions and declarations ended up as most rigid chains and unbreakable shackles by which liberty and truth are most tightly restricted, and at the same time, error is both received and admitted, stable and firm, indeed, eternal.

Finally, they assert that a wide breach is opened by these confessions and declarations for schisms and secessions. For they have been open and public marks of dissensions, just as they are now, and Christians, who ought to be closely joined together and who really agree in the sum of saving doctrine, are divided from each another. One says he is of Paul,[a] this one of Cephas, that one of Apollos, and another of Christ, and every one believes that the purity of religion and

esse dicit: & intra suum quisque peculiarem cœtum, Religionis puritatem, vitæque immortalis spem consistere credit: adeo ut quisquis ad illum non pertinet, cælo & regno Jesu Christi tantum non exclusissimus censeatur. Unde odia deinde, & animorum studiorumque divortia æterna atque immortalia, non sine maximo Reipub. Christianæ dispendio oriri & quasi perenni forte fluere necesse sit.
a. 1 Cor. 3:12.

Hæc sunt fere præcipua firmamenta, quibus primi pariter & secundi nituntur, quibusque opinionem suam fulciunt: speciosa equidem, si prima fronte videantur, quippe quæ zelum non vulgarem pro divini verbi authoritate, pro conscientiarum libertate, pro ecclesiarum pace & concordia præ se ferunt: attamen quæ proprius introspecta, tanti nobis momenti visa non sunt, ut propter ipsa ab edendæ hujus declarationis instituto desistendum nobis esse putaverimus. Neque enim videntur nobis tam rem ipsam, quam vitium rei & abusum, qui optimis etiam ac per se saluberrimis rebus, veluti struma pulchro corpori, adnasci & adhærere non raro solet, non immerito reprehendere, & acriore vitii intuitu, & odio abusus alioquin justissimo, in rei etiam ipsius detestationem imprudenter ferri ac dilabi. Quod ut planum fiat, operæpretium erit nonnulla de Confessionum sive Declarationum natura, necessitate, utilitate, rectoque usu præmiterre: Inde enim & quantopere hallucinentur ii, qui eas omnino aversantur, ac sine delectu respuunt, & quis noster in hujus Declarationis editione finis ac scopus fuerit, clarissime apparebit atque elucescet.

Ad Confessiones igitur, sive Declarationis generatim quod attinet, eæ aliud nihil sunt, quam claræ ac dilucidæ certaque methodo propositæ fidei nostræ expositiones, quibus plures paucioresve sententiam suam super Religionis Christianæ articulis, seu ore seu scripto aperiunt, & Christiano orbi notam faciunt, ad divinæ veritatis illustrationem, calumniarum, quibus innoxii premuntur, averruncationem, & ecclesiarum in vera fide & pace ædificationem. Hæc

the hope of immortal life rests in his particular congregation, to such a degree that whoever does not belong to it is thought to be completely excluded from heaven and the kingdom of Jesus Christ. Finally, it is necessary that from this there arise and flow, as from a perennial, powerful spring, perpetual and undying hatreds and divisions of minds and affections, not without the greatest cost to the Christian republic.

These are generally the unique foundations on which both the first and second types depend, and by which they support their opinion. They are indeed impressive at first appearance, for they obviously set before them no common zeal for the authority of God's Word, for liberty of conscience and for the peace and unity of churches. Nevertheless, when properly examined, they do not appear so momentous that we should consider desisting from the intention of publishing our declaration because of them. For it appears to us that they most rightly reprove, not the thing itself, but its corruption and abuse, which, just as a tumor arises and clings to a most excellent body, is rightly removed. But one may imprudently be carried away and fall into detesting what is good, by focusing too sharply on the vice and hating the abuse. That this may be made clear, it is rewarding labor to set forth something about the nature, necessity, utility and right use of confessions or declarations. For from this it will more clearly appear, shine forth and become manifest how greatly they hallucinate who are wholly averse to them and indiscriminately reject them, and what is our purpose and scope in publishing this declaration.

Concerning confessions then, or what pertains to declarations in general, they are nothing but clear and distinct statements methodically put forth, by which many or few opinions concerning the articles of the Christian religion may be disclosed, whether by mouth or by writing, and made known to the Christian world for the illumination of divine truth, the turning away of slander by which the innocent are oppressed, and the edification of churches in true faith and

demun propria, vera & genuina Confessionum ac Declarationem natura atque indoles, ex qua de vera earum tum necessitate, tum utilitate, judicium faciendum est, neutiquam autem ex ingentio aut instituto eorum, qui Confessionibus & Declarationibus ad alios longe diversos fines abusi sæpe sunt. Etenim ea non Declarationum, sed declarantium vitia, & non Confessionum usus, sed abusus fuerunt, iique tales qui facile nisi per nos steterit ab ipsis Confessionum formulis separari possunt.

Formulas quidem hujusmodi præcipe atque absolute necessarias non esse haud illubenter admittimus: neque proinde nobis placet sententia eorum, quod quarto loco recensuimus, qui eas pro secundariis saltem fidei symbolis habent, quique si non ad esse, certe ad bene esse Christianæ Ecclesiæ præcise necessarias esse statuunt. Ubi enim recta & concors Scripturarum intelligentia locum habet, ibi aliis fidei formulis, aut phrasibus, quam quæ in Scripturis ipsis extant, simpliciter opus non est: & quæ in Scripturis extant formulæ, eæ ad fidem & salutem sufficiunt, sique ad earum dijudicationem adferatur animus, probus, docilis, ac divinæ veritatis studiosus, eaque insuper adhibeantur media, quæ adhiberi oportet, & tantarum rerum avidum lectorem decent, tam sunt claræ ac perspicuæ, ut cuilibet Christiano omni tempore abunde sufficere possint ac debeant ad perfectissimam divinorum sensuum Declarationem, tum pro se tum pro aliis inde depromendam. Nec enim dubitari jure potest, quin formulæ & phrases istæ quibus ipse Deus & Dominus noster Jesus Christus idiotis & plebeijs atque ineruditis hominibus olim sensa mentis suæ exprimere ac declarare voluit, nobis etiam hodie ad eadem illa sensa percipiendum & declarandum sufficiant; quum non minus nobis quam illis divinitus eo sine relicta & per Scripturam tradita sint, ut ex iis quæ rectum Dei cultum, æternamque salutem nostram & aliorum pertinent, hauriremus, & depromeremus. Ex quo efficitur, fieri omnino posse, ut sine formulis hujusmodi humanis non modo Ecclesia Jesu Christi sit, sed & eidem bene sit.

peace. In the end, this is the proper, true and genuine nature and character of confessions and declarations, from which their true necessity and usefulness must be judged, and not at all from the disposition and intentions of those who have often abused confessions and declarations for other far different ends. Because these were not the faults of the declarations, but of the declarers, and not the uses but abuses of confessions, and such that they might easily be separated from the formulas of the confessions themselves, unless we [would not].

We willingly admit that these formulas are not at all precisely and absolutely necessary, hence neither does the opinion please us which we mentioned in the fourth place, who hold them at least for secondary symbols of faith, and who establish them to be precisely necessary, if not for the being, at least for the well-being of a Christian church. For where a right and unified understanding of the Scriptures has place, there simply is no benefit for other formulas or statements of faith other than what exists in the Scriptures themselves. And those formulas which exist in the Scriptures are sufficient for faith and salvation. And if one brings with him a mind which is honest, teachable and eager for divine truth, in order to gain insights from it, and above all, use those means which must be used and which are fitting for an avid reader of such things, [the Scriptures] are so clear and easily understood that they can and should be abundantly sufficient at all times for every Christian to draw from them a most perfect declaration of the divine meaning, both for themselves and for others. For it is impossible justly to doubt, that those formulas and phrases by which God himself and our Lord Jesus Christ long ago wanted to express and declare their thoughts to ignorant, common and unlearned men, are no less sufficient today for us to understand and declare those same thoughts, when they were granted by divine inspiration and given through the Scripture for us as well as for them, that we might draw out and bring forth from them those things which pertain to the right

Interea quamvis præcise necessariæ non sint hujusmodi formulæ, non tamen idcirco etiam inutiles, adeoque illicitæ & noxiæ censendæ sunt. Etenim si inutiles non sunt, imo si certo respectu interdum necessariæ sunt prophetiæ, sive Scripturarum interpretationes, quas in Academis & Ecclesiis Doctores & Pastores singuli proponunt, aut quæ alioquin in cœtibus Christianorum fiunt, cum Scripturarum sensus ad ignorantes erudiendos, errantes in vitam rectam reducendos, hæsitantes sublevandos, contradicentes redarguendos, quantum fieri potest, familiaribus & clariis atque etiam extra S. Scripturæ usitatis formulis loquendi declarant & illustrant, utique non protest jure merito inutile videri, nedum illicitum aut noxium, si plures Ministri Jesu Christi consentientibus suffragiis, conjunctis studiis atque operis, ad majorem divinæ veritatis illustrationem, calumniarum depulsionem, plurimorum ædificationem, aliosve sanctos ad pios fines, sententiam suam super iisdem Scripturarum sensibus, idque certis ad conceptis formulis, publicitus pandant atque aperiant. Quinimo si rem procul omni affectu ac præjudicio recte putabimus, comperiemus ea posse incidere tempora, quibus non utiles tantum sed bene necessariæ Declarationes hujusmodi videri debeant. Etenim si foedi & crassi errores, Religioni Christianæ ad pietati noxii, sæculum nostrum occupent, si necessaria fidei capita negligantur, aut non nisi obiter curentur, non necessaria autem veluti necessaria sollicite inculcetur, utilia item à necessariis dogmatis non, prout oportet, discernantur, humanis denique commentis conscientiæ hominum adstringantur, & falsissima quæque placita Scripturarum verbis ac pharasibus pallientur, necessitas profecto imponitur Christianis omnibus ac singulis, maxime Ecclesiæ Pastoribus, ut qua ratione tot tantisque malis occurrere possint, serio intes se cogitent ac

worship of God, and the eternal salvation of ourselves and others. From this it follows that it is entirely possible that the church of Jesus Christ may not only be, but also be well without such human formulas.

Meanwhile, although such formulas are not precisely necessary, still they are not to be considered unuseful, and consequently illicit and harmful. For if prophesying or interpreting the Scriptures are not unprofitable, if indeed they are sometimes in certain respects necessary, as when presented by professors and pastors in universities and churches, or in Christian assemblies, when they declare and illustrate the meaning of the Scriptures, as far as possible, for teaching the ignorant, restoring the wandering into the right way, relieving the doubting, and refuting adversaries, by familiar, clear and common forms of speaking beyond the express words of the Scripture, then it cannot be considered useless, illicit nor harmful if the majority of ministers of Jesus Christ, by unanimous agreement and joint studies and labors, for the greater illustration of divine truth, the rebuttal of slanders and the edification of the greater part of men, or other holy and pious ends, publicly open and declare their opinions upon the same meanings of Scripture, or in certain composed formulas. On the contrary, if we consider the matter rightly without any emotion and prejudice, we will discover those times occur when declarations must be seen not only as useful, but very necessary. For if foul and crass errors, hurtful to Christian religion and piety, seize our age, if necessary points of faith be neglected or sought only in passing, if the unnecessary is pressed as if it were necessary, and likewise useful doctrines not distinguished from those that are necessary, as is right, and finally, if men's consciences are bound by human inventions, the falsest of which are cloaked with the words and phrases of the Scriptures, then certainly an obligation is laid upon all and every Christian, especially pastors of churches, to think and deliberate seriously among themselves by what means they may oppose such

deliberent; &, si cæcos ac miseros illos mortales divinorum sensuum clariore, quam quæ ante facta est, propositione atque elucidatione, veluti facula aliqua in tenebris accensa, utiliter ac prudenter juvari posse videant, in eo unanimiter & juncta quasi manu consentiant ac conspirent, ut sensus illos divinos formulis quibusdam jam olim utiliter receptis & familiaribus declarent & ob oculos iis ponant, si forte istarum auxilio errantes ex profundia ista caligine liberari, & in rectam æternæ salutis viam deduci possint.

Deinde, si contingat eos, qui utilem istam Reipub. Christianæ operam navant, nihilominus, uti fere sit, calumniis gravari, suspicionibus foedis ac turpibus maculari, & quasi diluvio quodam criminationum obrui, tanquam sublestarum omnium opinionum patronos, qui veteres vel omnes vel aliquas hæreses novo quasi paxillo suspendant, errores jampridem damnatos ex orco refodiant, qui in Religione nihil firmi, nihil solidi teneant, & tot tamque monstrosis opinionibus inter se divissi sint ac dissecti, ut portenta potius hominum, quam Christiani jure videantur; ecquis erit qui eos pretium operæ facturos, imo necessitate aliqua huc constringi non putabit, ut Declaratione publica & solemni calumnis tam atrocibus, & enormibus obviam eant, & sententiæ suæ ingenua Consessione testatum orbi Christiano faciant, qui & quales in caussa Religionis sint, quidque de præcipius fidei capitibus revera sentiant, istaque inculpata ratione, veluti obice ac repagulo, infamibus istis conviciis ac criminationibus solide opposito, famæ & existimationis suæ integritatem, vitaque innocentiam adserant bonisque omnibus probent? Imprimis si futurum videant, ut nisi id faciant, optimi quique ab ipsis alienentur, infirmi ab amore veritatis divertantur, aut alioquin animis ipsorum scrupuli non leves injiciantur, multis alioqui minime malis in erroribus suis manendi, aut ad pristinas sordes, quas deseruerant, veluti ad vomitum redeundi occasio detur, amici à benevolentiæ affectu retrahantur, atque à fraternitate divellantur, hostibus atque

great evils. And if they perceive that blind miserable mortals may profitably and prudently be helped by a more clear proposal and explanation of the divine meanings than which was earlier made, like some small torch lit in the darkness, they must unanimously and, as it were, with joined hands agree and plan how they may declare and set before their eyes those divine senses and meanings in certain formulas now long since profitably and familiarly received, if perhaps by their help the erring may be delivered from that profound darkness, and led into the right way of eternal salvation.

Then, if it turns out that those who perform this most useful service for the Christian republic (as it usually does) are weighed down with slander, stained with evil and disgraceful suspicions and almost covered with by a flood of accusations, as if they were the patrons of all wicked opinions who hang old heresies (either all or some) on a new peg, who dig up from hell heresies long since condemned, who in matters of religion hold nothing firm, nothing solid, and who themselves are so divided and even dismembered by so many and so monstrous opinions, that they justly appear more like human monstrosities than Christians, who is there who would think that they would not undertake, or even better, that they would not be bound by an obligation, to withstand such atrocious and enormous slanders by a solemn and public declaration [of faith], and to testify to the Christian world through a noble confession of their opinions concerning who and what kind [of people] they are in religion, and what reverence they feel concerning the principle points of faith? And by this unblamable means, like a bolt and bar firmly set against those infamous reproaches and accusations, demonstrate and defend to all good men the integrity of their reputation and honor, and the innocence of their lives? Especially if they see that, unless they do it, even the best men would be estranged from them, the weak will be turned aside from the love of the truth, or else no light scruples will be instilled in their minds, that an occasion

inimicis uberior calumniandi materia suppeditetur, atque per latus læsæ ipsorum existimationis divina veritas vulneretur, omnisque ipsorum labor, cura, industria atque opera, in illius promotione hactenus insumta, & porro insumenda, inutilis atque infrugifera reddatur? Certe qui ullo boni publici desiderio, ulla divinæ gloriæ cura, ullo veritatis pacisque Ecclesiasticæ studio tangitur, is non potest non credere, ac certo statuere, in tali casu necessitatem aliquam hominibus istis imponi, ut sese, si bona conscientia possint, & summi infimique id postulent, etiam conceptis formulis declarationum à criminationibus istis ac calumniis purgent, & universo orbi Christiano innocentiam suam testatam faciant. Neque vero ad calumnias istas diluendum satis videri potest, si intra meras & nudas Scripture phrases se contineant, & sententias suas totidem Scripturæ verbis ac phrasibus efferant. Etenim cum hoc ipsum crimini ipsis detur, quod sub verbis Scripturæ pessimos, & gloriæ Dei ac saluti hominum noxios sensus in sinu foveant, & vel ultro captata, vel ab aliis oblata occasione disseminent, ubi è re sua id futurum vident: utique velint nolint in eam rediguntur necessitatem, ut ad divinæ veritatis gloriam, infirmorum ædificationem, & calumniarum detectionem, ea ratione, quæ optima atque utilissima esse videtur, id est, publica aliqua sententiæ suæ declaratione, sese purgent, suæque fidei sinceritatem tueantur ac defendant. Quæ cum ita sint, tantum abest ut noxiæ aut inutiles per se videri debeant Confessiones, aut fidei declarationes, ut pro utilibus veritatis adsertionibus ac pæne necessariis maximorum malorum remediis, aliquando in Ecclesia Jesu Christi habendæ sint.

will be given to many who are less evil to continue in their errors, or to return to their former baseness which they had left just as to vomit, that the kind affections of friends will be withdrawn and brotherhood torn apart, that abundant material for slander will be supplied to their enemies and foes, and by their injured reputation the divine truth will be wounded, and all their labor, care, industry and work spent in promoting it will be rendered useless and fruitless? Certainly he who is influenced by any desire for the public good, any concern for the glory of God, any desire for the truth and peace of the church, cannot but believe, and certainly conclude that in such a case some necessity is laid upon those men, if they can [do it] with a good conscience and [if] men from the greatest to the least require it, [to] purge themselves from accusations and slander by the making of formulas of declarations and [of] testimony of their innocence to the whole Christian world. Nor indeed does it appear adequate to dilute such slander if they limit themselves merely to bare phrases of Scripture and publish their opinions in just the words and phrases of Scripture. For when they see that the accusation given against them is that, under the words of Scripture, they cherish in their hearts the worst things which are the most prejudicial to the glory of God and the salvation of men and disseminate them either when they can or when others permit, then whether or not they want, they are driven by necessity, for the glory of divine truth, the edification of the weak and the detection of slanders, by that means which appears best and most profitable, that is, that they purge themselves by some public declaration of their opinions, and uphold and defend the sincerity of their faith. When things are this way, instead of confessions or declarations of faith being seen as hurtful or useless in themselves, sometimes they must be held by the church of Jesus Christ as useful vindications of the truth, and almost necessary remedies of the greatest evils.

Veruntamen quia ea est plerorumque morta-

Nevertheless, the carelessness, sluggishness

lium sive inadvertentia, sive socordia, sive malitia, ut quæ per se utilia & pia officii nostri documenta, aut præsentissima magnorum malorum remedia esse possunt, ea accidente vitio atque abusu paulatim ain superstitiosa conscientiarum vincula, inque idola & venena noxia sensim abire ac degenerare sinant, imo non raro in damnum ac detrimentum optimarum rerum ipsi convertant, diligenter prospiciendum, & opera quam accuratissime danda est, ut ab abusibus & vitiis omnibus formulæ hujusmodi vindicentur, & rectus eaurum usus omni tempore sedulo inculcetur & asseratur, quod quidem commode fieri posse credimus, si tria hæc semper ante oculos versentur & sollicite observentur.

Primum, si authoritas nulla ἀνυπέυθενα id est, irrefragabilis & omni exceptione major in Ecclesia, quocunque titulo, prætextu aut specie, seu directe seu indirecte, in rebus ad Religionem pertinentibus, formulis hisce tribuatur, aut tribui concedatur, ita scilicet, ut conscientiæ ullorum hominum iisdem tanquam fidei regulis, sive primariis, sive secundaris adstringantur, aut obligentur: Quod quidem facile caveri posse dubio omni procul est, si eo tantum loco ac gradu habeantur, quo revera haberi debent, puta pro nudis fidei nostræ expositionibus, sive pro formulis ejusmodi, aut quæ definiant, aut statuant, quid pro vero, aut falso habendum, quid credendum, aut non credendum, qua ratione quid enuntiandum, aut proferendum sit: sed quæ dum tantummodo notum ac testatum faciant, quid pro vero ac falso habeant, quid credant, aut non credant, quomodo sensa mentis suæ enuntient ii, quorum formulæ & Declarationes propriæ sunt. Etenim si alio loco, aut majori in pretio non habeantur, periculum nullum est, earum authoritas non dicimus æquetur Scripturis, nedum præferatur, sed ne quidem ullum, quantumvis infimum, in Ecclesia locum inveniant. Nec enim, uti jam ante diximus, pro normis tum ac fidei regulis habenbuntur, ex quibus veritas, aut falsitas, hæresis, aut error cognosci possit ac debeat: quæque eo fine editæ sint, ut ex iis quid verum falsumve sit dignoscatur, aut deprehen-

or malice of most men is such that things which in themselves might be useful and pious documents of our duty, or most appropriate remedies of great evils, they permit them by reason of their additional vice and abuse to slowly degrade and deviate into superstitious chains of consciences and into idols and hurtful poisons. Not rarely they themselves change them to the damage and detriment of the best things. Therefore, it must be diligently watched and most carefully worked, that they free such formulas from all abuse and vice, and inculcate and preserve at all times their right use, which we indeed believe may be done profitably, if three things are kept before ones eyes and carefully observed.

First, if no authority that is ἀνυπέυθενα, that is, unquestionable and beyond all exception, is granted to these formulas in the church, nor allowed to be granted, by whatever title, pretext or species, either directly or indirectly, in matters pertaining to religion, so that the consciences of any should be tied to them as either primary or secondary rules of faith. That this may be easily avoided is beyond all doubt, if only they are held to that place and degree which they deserve, namely, for bare expositions of our belief, or for such formulas which do not define or establish what is to be held for true or false, what is to be believed or not to be believed, by what method something is to be expressed or mentioned, but which only may make known and testify what they hold for true and false; what they believe, or do not believe, and in what manner they express the understandings of the minds of those whose formulas or declarations they are. For if they are given no other place nor greater esteem, there is no danger that their authority should be equaled (God forbid), still less preferred to the Scriptures, but not given even any place, however so low, in the church. For, as we have already said before, they can and should not be held for squares and rules of faith by which truth or falsity, heresy or error may and ought to be known, and which are published for that end, that by them what is true

datur; sed pro nudis tantum testeris ac symbolis, quæ indicent solum ac declarent, qui ii ad quos eæ pertinent, de hisce & illis Religionis Christianæ articulis ac sensibus crediderint ac statuerint.

Et sane si priscos Ecclesiæ annales consulamus, non aliud fuit consilium, non alius scopus aut finis eorum, qui primi ejusmodi Symbola, Cannones Ecclesiasticos, Confessiones ac Declarationes fidei suæ ediderunt, quam ut per eas testatum facerent, non quid credendum esset, sed quid ipsi crederent; idque ut Symbola ista, &c. vel pharorum instar essent, quæ incautis & imprudentibus errorum vada ac brevia pietati & saluti noxia indicarent & ostenderent, vel etaim contra calumniantes, pro apologiis servirent, ex quibus intelligere unicuique daretur, quam longe abessent ab erroribus, blasphemiis & criminibus illis, quæ per calumniam ipsis à maleferiatis quibusdam hominibus impingebantur. Et certe si intra hanc metam Declarationes & Confessiones omnes semper constitissent, utique nullo unquam tempore dignitatem authoritatemque ullam dictatoriam, nedum majorem, aut æqualem Scripturis in Ecclesia consecutæ fuissent. Quare ut hoc imprimis fixum ratumque semper teneat Ecclesia, etiam atque etiam adlaborandum est, ac propterea subinde per occasiones omnes Ecclesis inculcundum, & in ipsis Confessionum ac Declarationum formulis accurate exprimendum: Eas scilicet, ne quidem pro certis indicibus, nedum pro judicibus verorum sensuum, sed tantum pro indicibus sensuum illorum, quos authores earum pro veris habuerunt, recipi debere, eoque fine in lucem editas esse.

Id enim si fiat, tum hæc tria vitia sufficienter ac facile vitabuntur. I. Nemo ad formulas illas confugiet, ut ex iis certa fide, veluti ex fontibus hauriat ac depromat ea, quæ credenda sunt. Proinde nec in dubiis Scripturarum sensibus recurret ad eas, tanquam recti & obliqui indices: nec obscuros aut controversos sensus ad eas tanquam ad lapidem Iydium probabit aut explorabit. II. Nemo ad earum sensus

or false may be discerned or recognized, but only for bare signals and symbols, which only indicate and declare what those to whom they belong believed and judged of these and other articles and thoughts concerning the Christian religion.

And certainly if we consult the ancient annals of the church, they who first published such symbols, ecclesiastical canons, confessions and declarations of their faith, had no other counsel, nor other aim or end, than that they might testify, not what was to be believed, but what they themselves believed. And that these symbols, etc. instead should be even lighthouses to indicate and point out to the incautious and imprudent the shoals and shallows of errors that were harmful to piety and salvation, or also to serve as an apology against slanderers, by which it was given to understand how far they were from the errors, blasphemies, and crimes which were thrust upon them through the slander of evil men. And certainly if all declarations and confessions had always kept within this limit, they would not have obtained some dictatorial dignity or authority, still less one greater than or equal to the Scriptures in the church. Wherefore, in the first place, special effort must be made that the church hold this to be fixed and ratified, and therefore inculcated in every occasion in the churches, and carefully pronounced in the formulas of the confessions and declarations themselves, namely, that they are not to be held as certain indices, much less for judges of the true senses [of the Scriptures], but only ought to be received as indices of those senses which were held to be true by their authors, and which were published for that purpose.

If this is done, these three abuses will sufficiently and easily be avoided. 1. No one will flee to these formulas as if they were a fountain worthy of faith, that he might draw and take from them what must be believed. Thus he will not run to them with doubtful interpretations of Scripture, as indices of what is straight and crooked; nor probe and examine dark and controverted interpretations by them, as if by a

adstringetur aut adstringi se patietur alia lege, quam quatenus & quamdiu ipse certo deprehendit atque in conscientia sua convincitur, eas cum Scripturam sensibus convenire. III. In disputationibus, collationibus, examinibus ad illas nunquam provocabitur, neque ad illarum incudem revocabuntur fidei controversiæ, sed ad solum verbum divinum, tanquam ad regulam unicam, omni exceptione majorem & veram sanorum sermonum ὑποτύπωσιν, quam unicus Magister noster Jesus Christus & Apostoli ipsius nobis reliquerunt, omnes omnino sine metu aut periculo exigentur & exprendentur. Et sic quidem nihil erit, quod ad divinam authoritatem iis derogandam & Scripturis Sacris in solidum adserendam desiderari jure poterit. Neque tum metuendum erit, ne ex iis idola fabricentur, quæ juxta Scripturas in Ecclesiæ Jesu Christi erigantur & in pari gradu collocentur, aut simili aliquo honore adficiantur, aut ne vincula ex iis nectantur, quibus hominum conscientiæ innodentur, aut denique ne venena ex iis præparentur, quibus fidei sinceritas inficiatur, aut doctrinæ veritas teretur.

Hoc itaque fundamento semel rite jacto, hocque principio firmiter supposito, semper in Ecclesia Jesu Christi sarta tecta manebit libertas, qua sine periculo in formulas istas inquirere, iisque sine scrupulo contradicere (salvis semper modestiæ, charitas & prudentiæ Christianæ legibus) licebitut hac ratione inter illas & verbum divinum discrimen semper manifestum exstet, cui uni illud privilegium sanctum atque inviolatum constare debet, quod solum supra & extra omnem controversiam & contradictionem positum sit, quodque ei soli conscientiæ fidelium obligandæ sint.

Neque tamen libertas hæc eo usque extendenda est, ut in dissolutam & enormem licentiam abeat, qua cuique, quod libet, effutire liceat. Tam enim libertas abutitur, qui ejus fibulam nimis licenter laxat, quam qui nimis arcte astringit. Extrema omnia vitanda sunt, & mediocritari litandum, quæ tyrannidem inter

touchstone. 2. None will be bound, nor suffer himself to be bound, by their meanings as if by law, than so far and so long as he himself certainly finds and is convinced in his conscience that they are consistent with the meanings of Scripture. 3. One may never cite them in debates, conferences [and] examinations, nor will controversies of faith be brought to their anvil. But without any fear or danger, they will all be solicited and examined by the Word of God alone, as the only rule beyond all exception, and the true ὑποτύπωσιν of sound words, which our only Master Jesus Christ and his apostles have left to us. And thus indeed there will be nothing which rightly detracts divine authority from them, but gives it solidly to the sacred Scripture. Neither must it be feared, lest idols be made of them to be raised up in the church of Jesus Christ, and placed in an equal degree with the Scriptures, or granted similar honor, or chains be bound from them, whereby the men's consciences are bound, or finally, lest venoms be prepared from them, by which the sincerity of faith might be poisoned, or the truth of doctrine infected, or the truth of doctrine expended.

Therefore, once this foundation is rightly laid, and this principle firmly placed, liberty will be maintained whole and protected, and one may without danger examine formulas, and contradict them without scruples (always without violating the laws of Christian modesty, charity and prudence), that by this means there may always be a manifest difference between them and the divine Word, to which alone that privilege ought to remain sacred and inviolate, that it alone is placed above and beyond all controversy and contradiction, and that to it alone the consciences of believers are obligated.

And yet this liberty is not to be extended so as to turn into a dissolute and irregular license, by which anyone is permitted to babble what he pleases. For he who loosens the buckle impudently abuses liberty as much as he who ties it exceedingly tight. All extremes are to be avoided, and must gain the middle ground which

atque vagam & effrenem licentiam media consistit. Idcirco prudentia & charitas semper in consilium adhibenda sunt, quææ facile dictabunt, quando & quomodo libertas hæc utiliter, & sine piorum scandalo, in usum possit deduci. Prudentiæ est, ponderare res, & circumspicere idonea tempora & loca, quibus hoc aut illud dogma sive ore sive calamo commode proponatur. Charitatis est, personarum rationem habere, ne offendantur aut turbentur, quos ædificatos oportebat. Prudentis & pii ac charitate vera præditi non est, libertate contradicendi ex qualibet occasione, apud omnessive ubique cum ita collubitum est animo ipsius, promiscue uti, imo nec aliorum contradictiones omnes semper & ubique æquo animo fere. Habenda sæpe est ratio & rerum seu dogmatum, quibus contradicitur, & personarum, apud quas contradictiones hujusmodi proponuntur. Quædam enim res tanti sunt ponderis atque momenti, ut iis sine summo salutis nostræ periculo contradici nequeat. Hisce libere contradicere, aut æquo animo pati, ut aliis contradicatur, à prudentia & charitate foret alienissimum. Quædam res ejus indolis sunt, ut sine periculo salutis cujusquam contradictionem quidem ferant, sed quibus tamen contradicere publici boni causa necesse non est, & contradici ubique & semper non expedit. Non enim omne, quod licet, statim etiam expedit aut ædificat. Sæpissime infirmitas aliorum libertati nostræ legem ponere debet: non raro etiam aliorum improbitas, qui ad lites, rixas, & contradictiones pruriunt, & quibus occasio litigandi & contendendi ex quavis ocasione placet. Ilis offendiculum dandum non est, ne cadant: his fomenta subtrahenda sunt, ne sibi & aliis noceant. Ita enim evitanda simper sunt pericula omnia fidelium, præsertim infirmorum, ne libertate nostra abutamur ad ullius destructionem, sed recte & ad omnium ædificationem ea utamur. At in rebus non omnino necessariis, interque eos, quos perfectos appellat Scriptura, quique exercitatos sensus in Scripturis habent ad directionem veri & falsi, aut qui alioquin veritatis etiam abstrusioris summopere studiosi sunt, libertas hæc locum habere semper sine

stands between tyranny and wild and unbridled license. Therefore prudence and charity are always to be summoned to council, which will easily dictate when and how this liberty may be useful profitably, and without scandalizing the godly. It belongs to prudence to ponder a matter, and consider well suitable times and places in which this or that doctrine may be proposed by word, mouth or pen. It belongs to charity to have regard for persons, that those who ought to be edified are not offended or troubled. It does not belong to a prudent and godly man, and truly gifted with charity, to use indiscriminately the liberty of contradicting, upon every occasion, with all people or in all places, whenever he thinks fit, nor always and everywhere patiently to bear with all the contradictions of others. One must regard both the reasons and circumstances of the doctrines by which one is contradicted, and of the persons by whom such contradictions are proposed. For there are some things of such weight and importance that they cannot be contradicted without greatest danger to our salvation. To contradict these freely, or patiently suffer them be contradicted by others, would be most alien to prudence and love. There are some things of the nature that they may receive contradiction without danger to anyone's salvation, but to contradict is not necessary for the cause of the public good, and it is not expedient to be contradicted everywhere and always. For not every thing permissible is at the same time expedient and edifying. Most often the weakness of others ought to impose upon our liberty, and likewise, not rarely the importunity of others, who lust for quarrels, brawls, and contradictions, and the opportunity of strife and intention upon every occasion. To the first we must not give offence, lest they fall. From the second must be withheld all incitement, lest they hurt themselves and others. For thus we must always avoid all peril to believers, especially the weak, lest we abuse our liberty to the destruction of anyone, but use it rightly and to the edification of all. But in things entirely necessary, and among those whom the Scripture calls mature, and who have

scandalo aut periculo potest. Quippe acuitur industria ipsorum contradictionibus moderatis, quæ veluti cotes veritatis sunt, & ex quibus non aliter, quam ex silicum inter se attritu & collisione, hic fructus elicitur, ut vel errorem antea latenter clare videant, vel in veritate, quam tenent, solidus confirmentur. Qui fructus non potest non deinde in ecclesiam totam redundare, idque ad eximiam veritatis promotionem & divini nominis gloriam. At contradictionibus ex pulpito in templis coram populo digladiari, & publicarum formularum vellicationibus, atque obtrectationibus apud imperitam plebem ex ambone tumultuari velle, aut publicis scriptis traducere & contumeliose lacessere atque infectari, res foret insaniæ simillima, & scandali & periculi plenissima. Neque vero unquam tantum prodesse potest non necessariæ veritatis notitia, quantum publice privatimque nocere atque obesse potest importuna & inverecunda ejus inculcatio. Atque hæc de prima cautione in Confessionibus diligenter observanda.

Secundum, quod ad rectum formularum usum observandum est, ex primo fluit: si videlicet ex formulis Confessionum ac Declarationum spiritualia quædam vincula, numellæ, & compedes non fiant, quibus declarantium conscientiæm linguæ & calami ita adstringantur & affigantur, ut ab earum phrasibus, modo loquendi, ordine, methodo, &c. recedere nemini liceat, quin & in suspucionem aut criminationem ἑτεροδοξίας protinus vocetur, qui Scripturam divinam, suæque mentis sensa, aliis phrasibus, aliove ordine methodo, quam quæ in iis expressæ sunt, interpretari deprehenditur. Hæc enim ratione non tantum eliminatur & proscribitur ex Ecclesia libertas illa, quæ salva manente ipsorum sensuum veritate, unicuique fidelium in Scripturam interpretatione pro arbitrio suo, ad maximam veritatis promotionem,

their senses exercised in the Scriptures to discern between true and false, or who are desire very much to learn truths which are difficult to understand, liberty may always have a place without scandal or danger. Their diligence is naturally sharpened by moderate contradictions, which are like whetstones of truth, and from which no less than by striking or beating flints against each other, this benefit is elicited, that either they clearly see a previously hidden error, or are more solidly confirmed in the truth they hold. This benefit cannot but afterward overflow to the whole church, and that to the excellent promotion of truth and the glory of the divine name. But to wave the sword by debating in the church before the people from the pulpit, and by the fault-finding of public formulas, and to want to create a disturbance by malicious attacks before the common people, or to publicly display writings in order to insultingly attack and criticize, would be something insane, and most scandalous and dangerous. Nor can the knowledge of an unnecessary truth truly do as much good, as the harm and prejudice done by the troublesome and impudent pressing of it both publicly and privately. For this reason the first caution concerning confessions must be diligently observed.

The second thing that must be observed for the right use of formulas flows from the first, namely, formulas of confessions and declarations must not become spiritual chains, stocks and shackles by which the consciences, tongues and pens of the declarers be bound and fastened, so that no one is permitted to recede from their phrases, manner of speaking, order, method, etc., and that no one who is found to interpret the divine Scripture, and express the opinions of his own mind, in other phrases, or other order or method, than what are expressed in them is immediately being suspected and accused of heterodoxy. For by this means that liberty, which can remain wholly and completely safe only as long as each of the believers may interpret the true meaning of the Scripture at will for the greatest promotion of the truth and the

& ecclesiarum ædificationem, sarta tecta constare debet; sed etiam divini verbi authoritas clanculum & quasi per uniculos suffoditur ac labefactatur. Etenim fieri aliter vix potest, quin, ubi phrases formulatum pluris fieri incipient, quam ipsius divini verbi, ibi paulatim divini verbi authoritas evilescat, & infra formularum pretium subsidat. Et sane si animum ad vertere velimus præcipuus & forte primus gradus, per quem ad fastigium usurpatæ authoritatis majestatisque prope divinæ conscenderunt humanæ formulæ, hic fuit, quod earum phrasibus, verbis, ordini ac methodo, plus quam par est, principio attributum fuit; tanquam si illis sensus omnes credendi, sperandi & faciendi clarius, brevius, solidiusque exprimerentur, quam iis, quæ in Scripturis occurrunt. Hinc enim paulatim existimatio earum aucta, Scripturarum vero imminuta est: adeo ut ex verbis phrasibus, imo syllabis fere ac literis formularum, exque methodo & ordine earundem proprio de veritate aut falsitate dogmatum ac sententiarum prope omnium statui & pronuntiari cæptum fuerit, tanquam si verum esse non posset, nisi quod examussim & per omnia cum ipsis conveniret, & quasi ab hæresi, aut saltem errore & falsitate immunis non esset, qui iis (licet modestissime) contradiceret, aut ab iis vel latum culmum discederet, imo in verba ipsorum tantum non juraret.

Cui pernicioso abusui tamque manifesto vitio atque incommodo ut in tempore occurratur, enixe atque unice fere inculcandum semper est, formulas Declarationum eo fine non cudi ut doceatur, quod isto ordine, ista methodo, istis phrasibus, & non aliis quam commodissime enunciandi sint, aut omnino enuntiari debeant sensus Religionis Christianæ; sed quod illis sat recte & commode enuntiari possint, aut judicio ipsorum confitentium, quam rectissime enuntientur. Sic enim iis uti, non erit præcisæ necessitates, sed meræ libertatis; & qui iis utitur,

edification of the churches, is not only eliminated and prohibited from the church, but also the authority of the divine Word is secretly undermined and shaken almost as if by bombs. For it can hardly be otherwise, but that where the phrases of such formulas begin to be of higher value than the divine Word itself, there the authority of the divine Word little by little becomes despised and sinks beneath the value of formulas. And indeed if we are willing to think about it, the principle and perhaps first step by which human formulas ascended to the peak of usurped authority and almost divine majesty was this, that at the first they attributed to their phrases, words, order and method more than was appropriate, as if all their ideas for believing, hoping and acting were more clearly, briefly and substantially expressed than by those which occur in the Scriptures. For from this their esteem was increased little by little and that of the Scriptures diminished, to such a degree that according to the words, phrases, almost in fact the syllables and letters of formulas, and according to their method and peculiar organization, they began to establish and declare concerning the truth and falsity of almost all doctrines and opinions as if nothing could be true which did not exactly and in everything agree with them, and almost as if one was not immune from heresy, or at least error and falsity, who would contradict them (however so modestly), or depart even a straw's breadth from them, indeed if they did not swear by their very words.

In order that this pernicious abuse and so manifest corruption and detriment be prevented, it must always be earnestly and almost singularly stressed that formulas of declarations are not for the purpose of teaching by what order, method, phrases the thoughts of the Christian religion are to be most suitably enunciated, and by no other, nor that they ought only to be so enunciated, but that by them [these thoughts] may be rightly and agreeably enough enunciated, or that in the judgment of those so confessing, how they may be most accurately

recte quidem faciet, attamen non male censebitur facere, qui iis non utitur, maxime si summam doctrinæ salutaris in iis traditæ ultro admiserit, neque dissentients, hac in parte damnaverit.

Tertium, quod ex hisce jam dictis emergit ad rectum formularum usum, necessarium, istud est, ne formulæ istæ unquam habeantur pro limitibus & terminis, intra quos Religio & salvifica Dei cognitio consistere credatur, tanquam si ii, qui istis accedere, aut suffragari per conscientiam nequeunt, à salute æterna & regno cœlorum ea propter excluderentur ac separarentur. Absit id à nobis, qui Christianos in multis imprudenter errare posse sine salutis suæ jactura, firmiter credimus, quique pauca admodum esse arbitramur, quæ præcise ad æternam salutem obtinendum scitu creditu necessaria sunt. Quare ut superbam hanc crudelitatem à nobis quam longissime abesse demonstremus, palam testamur, non esse habendas Confessionum & Declarationum formulas alio loco, quam pro erectis quibusdam signis ac vexillis, quibus declarant ii, qui eas in lucem dant, se judicare, sensus illos, qui formulis istis continentur, ad veritatem quam proxime accedere, ac proinde, nisi melius erudiantur, ex animo optare ac cupere, ut istos alii omnes veritatis & pacis studiosi amplectantur, non quidem proprie hoc fine, ut ita demum salventur, sed ut à periculo errandi quam possunt longissime se removeant. Nec enim satis videri debet homini Christiano, quacunque ratione & via ad salutem æternam contendere: omnium tutissima & certissima eligenda est, nisi forte justus alicujus in ecclesia majoris periculi aut scandali metus obstet. Tanti enim debet apud eum esse æterna fælicitatis atque immortalis vitæ bonum, ut omnia pericula, quæ animum illius ab eo amplexando avertere, aut abducere possent, odisse debeat & sollicite fugere. Neque est quod metuat, schismati se propterea, quod opus carnis appellat Apostolus, patrocinari atque

expressed. For to use them thus will not be of absolute necessity, but of mere liberty, and while whoever uses them well certainly does rightly, nevertheless he who does not use them will not be thought badly, especially if he receives that which they relate which is absolutely necessary for salvation, and does not condemn those who dissent in this part.

The third thing necessary, which emerges from that which has already been said regarding the right use of formulas, is this, that these formulas are never to be held for the limits and boundaries within which religion and the saving knowledge of God is believed to consist, as if those who for conscience's sake cannot assent to them or publicly support them were therefore excluded and separated from salvation and the kingdom of heaven. Far be it from us, who firmly believe that Christians may imprudently err in many things without the loss of their salvation, and who judge that there are few things which are absolutely necessary to be known and believed for obtaining eternal salvation. In order that we may demonstrate that this proud cruelty is most far removed from us, we openly testify that formulas of confessions and declarations are not to be given any position, except for erecting certain signals and banners by which those who publish them may declare what, in their judgment, is contained in those formulas which comes near to the truth, and therefore, unless they are taught better, wish and desire from the soul, that they would be embraced by all others who are zealous for truth and peace. Not indeed properly for the purpose that at length they might be saved, but that they might to the greatest distance remove themselves from the danger of erring. For neither ought it appear adequate to a Christian man to contend for eternal salvation by whatever means and way. The safest and surest way is to be chosen, unless perhaps a just fear of some greater danger or scandal in the church should hinder. For the good of eternal happiness and of immortal life ought to be so important to him, that he ought to hate and carefully to flee all

opera, dare. Non enim si ab hisce cœtibus ad alios forte discedat, protinus eos, quos deserit, contemnit, aut à spe salutis exclusos judicat, sed tantummodo ab impurioribus ad puriores se confert, ut veritatem omnem saluti nostræ aliquatenus servientem sibi curæ & cordi esse ostendat, & Deo ac Jesu Christo Domino suo conscientiam suam probet. Interea nihilominus operam dat, ut pacem & concordiam cum omnibus vere piis, quantum fieri potest, sedulo colat, & moderationem, sive τῆς ἐπιεικῆς suum bonis omnibus testatum faciat.

Et hisce quidem recti usus & quasi sacris limitibus si circumscribantur Confessionum ac Declarationum formulæ, non modo non illicitæ aut noxiæ, sed contra utilissimæ ac Christianæ Reipub. Maxime salutares, imo etiam interdum necessariæ censendæ erunt. Unde, qui eas non modo non necessarias, sed inutiles, adeoque illicitas & noxias esse volunt, illiberale convitium illis facere censendi sunt. Tantum enim abest, ut eæ per se Scripturarum majestati, id est, earundem perfectioni aut claritati, quicuquam derogent, ut contra potius per eas, non minus quam per prophetias, aut Scripturarum interpretationes, vera earum authoritas confirmetur ac stabiliatur. Cum enim earum veritas, tum quoad sensum, tum quoad phrases, tum quoad methodum, ex ipsis Scripturis adserenda sit & vindicanda, imo quum id ipsum fieri libere posse ac debere ab omnibus & singulis, ipsæ formulæ profiteantur, adeoque à seipsis ad Scripturas nos remittant, atque ad eas solas in omni controversia provocari expresse jubeant; utique non ad convellendum aut labefactandum, sed contra ad constabilendum Scripturarum authoritatem facere videri debent. Nec libertati etiam ecclesiarum ulla in re præjudicant, cum ad eas nemo præcise obligetur, imo quum eas ad divini verbi trutinam expendere liberum unicuique concedatur; denique quun iis sine periculo, aut metu ullo contradicere citivis

dangers which may turn his mind from embracing it. Nor should he fear that he himself sponsors and promotes schism, which the Apostle calls a work of the flesh. For if by chance he withdraws from some congregations for others, he does not immediately condemn those which he left, or judge them as excluded from the hope of salvation, but only carries himself from the impure to the pure, that he may show that he has a concern and heart for the truth of our salvation, and examines his conscience before God and our Lord Jesus Christ. Nevertheless, in the interim, he works to carefully cultivate peace and unity with all the truly godly, as far as he is able, to testify his τῆς ἐπιεικῆς or equanimity with all who are good.

And indeed if formulas of confessions and declarations are restricted to these right uses and almost sacred limits, they will not only by no means be judged unlawful or hurtful, but on the contrary most profitable and wholesome to the Christian republic, if not sometimes necessary. From this, those who want them to be not only unnecessary, but useless, and consequently illicit and hurtful, will be judged to treat them with bigoted reproach. For they are so far in themselves from detracting anything from the majesty of the Scriptures, that is, from their perfection and clarity, that to the contrary, their true authority is no less confirmed and established by them than by preaching, or the interpretation of the Scriptures. For when their truth, whether of meaning, phrases or method, is asserted and vindicated from the Scriptures themselves, indeed when the very formulas themselves declare that all and every one may and ought freely to do the same, and consequently [these confessions] send us back from themselves to the Scriptures, and so expressly command [us] to appeal to them alone in all controversies, certainly they ought to be seen, not as overthrowing or undermining the authority of the Scriptures, but rather establishing [it]. Nor do they at all prejudice the liberty of the churches, since no one is precisely obligated to them, what is more, when it is freely

liceat, si modo prudentiæ, charitatis & modestiæ tantum ratio diligens habeantur. Schismatis vero & secessionibus fenestram nullam per se aperiunt. Nec enim schisma facere credendus est, qui iis de adjungit cœtibus, in quibus majorem doctrinæ puritatem, & vitæ sanctitatem, vigere credit, si modo superbe non contemnat alios cœtus, nec cælo, aut vitæ æternæ spe protinus exclusos judicet, quos à cœtu suo alieniores videt. Potest enim salva manere pax & concordia Christiana, imo debet etiam, inter cœtus opinionibus divisos distinctosque, si modo per nos stet, quominus omnes sit, qui necessaria omnia ad salutem adhuc retinent, & dogmata pietati noxia præfracte non urgent, in unum coeant, & mutua charite atque amore fraterno sese invicem in Domino Jesu complectantur. At si per nos stet, quo minus ecclesiæ illæ coalescant & in unum corpus consolidentur, quæ coalescere ac consolidari possunt & debent, aut si unitas conjunctasque, sine necessitate discindamus, ac in partes dividamus tum vero schismatis reos nos facimus, & turbatæ pacis ac concordiæ apud Deum postulari meremur: quod adeo verum est, ut Apostolus non minus eos etiam schismatis reos agere videatur, qui se Christi esse gloriabantur, non minus certe, quam cæteros, qui se Pauli, aut Apollo, aut Cepha esse dicebant, propterea quod illi hosce præ se contemnerent, & quasi secum non conferendos dedignarentur, imo tanquam alienos à Christo respuerent. Adeo non excusat quemquam à crimine schismatis, saltem coram ipso Deo, veritatis, licet optimæ & saluberrimæ, studium, nisi comitem sibi habeat verum pacis & concordiæ amorem, mutuæque benevolentiæ studium. Quippe tanti apud Deum est vera Ecclesiæ pax & concordia, ut displiceat etiam veritas seditiosa, seu schismaticus & turbulentus ejusdem propagandæ modus.

permitted to every one to weigh them in balance of the divine Word, and finally, seeing that every one is permitted to contradict them without danger or fear, if only they are diligent to do so in a prudent, charitable and modest manner. Nor do they open a window for schisms and secessions. For neither should one be credited with making a schism, who joins himself to those congregations in which he believes thrives a greater purity of doctrine, and holiness of life, if he does not in a proud manner condemn other congregations, or immediately judge those whom he sees alienated from his own congregation [as] excluded from the hope of eternal life. For Christian peace and unity may and indeed ought to continue safe among congregations divided and separated by opinions, so that we do not hinder all those who do not agree together, but nevertheless retain everything necessary to salvation, and do not obstinately press doctrines harmful to godliness, from coming together, and embracing each other in mutual charity and brotherly love in the Lord Jesus. But if by our doing fewer churches grow together and are consolidated into one body which could and ought to grow and be consolidated together, or if being united and joined together, we unnecessarily tear them apart and separate them into parties, then truly we make ourselves guilty of schism and deserve to be arraigned before God as disturbing peace and unity. This is so true that the Apostle is seen to make those who gloried that they were of Christ certainly no less guilty of schism than others who said that they were of Paul, or Apollos, or Cephas. Because they despised them, and almost did not think them worthy to be compared with them, indeed they rejected them as foreign to Christ. So then, zeal for the truth, be it the best and most wholesome, does not excuse anyone from the crime of schism, at least before God himself, unless it is accompanied by a true love of peace and unity, and zeal for mutual good will. For true peace and the unity of the church is so valued before God that he is even displeased with a truth that is seditious, or a

Neque tamen inficias imus, fieri posse ac solere aliquando, ut tractu temporis, majorem, quam par sit, honorem ac venerationem formulæ hujusmodi consequantur, ac tandem nisi diligenter prospiciatur, & malum glicens sedulo caveatur, facili momento degenerent in idola quædam inque conscientiarum vincula & schismatum insignia: attamen quia totum hoc per accidens evenire solet, ex eo utique judicium de formulis faciendum non est: cum id vitium non sit ipsarum formularum, sed eorum, qui illis pro ingenii sui præpostera industria, aut potius malitia, pro re nata abutuntur: & cum ex recto aut pravo usu æstimanda non sint vera rerum precia. Optimis enim rebus nonnunquam pessime abuti potest, qui vel malus vel imprudens est, sicut ex adverso, re per se mala noxiaque vir bonus & prudens recte uti & pro remedio salutari usurpare eam aliquando potest. Accedit deinde, quod fieri vix possit, quin si formulæ hujusmodi Declarationum aliquando non edantur, aliis vitiis atque incommodis, si non gravioribus, saltem paribus & æqualibus, fenestra lata aperiatur, atque ad dissolutam quidvis effutiendi licentiam, tyrannide certe non meliorem, via facile sternatur: Denique cum vitiis hisce atque incommodis, quæ nonnulli hinc oritura metuunt, ea, quam diximus, ratione in tempore commode possit occurri. Etenim si intra illum usum semper stetissent ii, quibus Confessiones & Declarationes fidei suæ edere consultum visum fuit, nunquam excessivæ earum authoritanti in Ecclesia locus datus fuisset. At postquam ejus ratio accurata haberi desiit, paulatim ac veluti per gradus attolli cœpit earum authoritas, adeo ut ex illis tandem non aliter, quam ex stateris quibusdam, atque indubitatis fidei regulis, conscientiæ, oculi linguæ & calami mortalium pendere cœperint. Unde factum deinde est, ut quidam per eas, tanquam speciales quasdam literas, aliis omnibus cœtibus bellum indixerint, & ne spes redeundi in amicitiam reliqua fieret, iis Christianorum cœtus, non aliter quam imperia schismatic and turbulent manner of propagating the same.

Yet still we do not deny that it may be and usually happens that with the passing of time, formulas achieve greater veneration and honor than is suitable. And in the end, unless they are diligently watched and the growing evil carefully guarded, they very easily degenerate into idols and chains of conscience and badges of schism. Yet because all this usually occurs by accident, for this reason one must not judge the formulas, when it is not the fault of the formulas themselves, but of those who, because of the nature of their preposterous diligence (or better, malice), abuse them, and at the same time, the true value of things must not be taken from the correct or perverse use of them. For the best of things may sometimes be the most badly abused by one who is evil and imprudent, just as on the contrary, a good and prudent man may use well something that is defective and harmful in itself, and seize it as a wholesome remedy. Besides this, it often happens that if such formulas of declarations are not sometimes published, a wide window is opened to other evils and inconveniences, if not more grave, at least alike and equal, and a way is easily laid out to a dissolute license of irresponsible babble, certainly no better than tyranny. Finally, for the reasons which we have said, one may profitably withstand those defects and inconveniences which some fear will arise from this. For when those who considered it prudent to publish confessions and declarations of their faith limited themselves to this use, never was there given a place of excessive authority to them in the church. But afterwards, when an exact reckoning of them ceased to be had, their authority began to be advanced by little and little as if by steps, to the point that the consciences, eyes, tongues and pens of mortals began to depend on them as weigh-scales, and unquestionable rules of faith. From this it then happened that through them, they were treated as specific letters for the declaration of war against all other congregations, which were left

olim limitibus, & castra adversaria vallis atque aggeribus, à se invicem divisi fuerint ac disseparati: denique, quæ suprema tyrannidis linea est, ut in eos, qui formulis istis contradicerent, vi ac gladio animadversum fuerit, idque tanto zelo fervore, imo furore, ut, cum profanis, impiis Scripturam contemporibus atque atheis levi momento venia fieret, hisce solis carceres, equulei, rotæ, furcæ, cruces, rogi & exquisitissima quæque suppliciorum ac tormentorum genera destinarentur, idq., hoc solo fine, ut authoritas harum formularum à contradictione vindicaretur, & à contemptu adseretur, atque ita scilicet externa Ecclesia pax, & Reipub. tranquilitas imperturbata conservaretur. Quæ quidem agendi ratio uti Christianis omnibus meritissimo jure invisa atque exosa esse debet, ita nobis quam maxime semper displicuit, quippe quibus Religio est, humanis ullis scriptis, decretis aut statutis, authoritatem ullam vel directivam vel coactivam in rebus fidem & conscientiam attinentibus eo usque deferre, aut ut deferatur permittere.

Ex hisce facile intelligens, pie Lector, quis finis scopus nobis in hujus Declarationis editione fuerit propositus. Nempe, illi ipse quem supra diximus, & nullus alius. Non enim eò editur hæc declaration, ut novus conscientiarum laqueus hinc paretur, aut immota fidei norma seu doctrinæ regula per eam cuiquam præscribatur, quæ scilicet conscientias hominum coram Deo præcise obliget, & proinde à qua nemini unquam vel lecissime discedere liceat, puta neque in rebus neque in phrasibus, imo neque in methodo aut modo docendi. Absit hæc superba vanitas a nobis, qui honorem istum nullis hominum scriptum, quantumvis accuratis, ac diligenter, diu multumque perpensis, sed soli Dei verbo, S. literis comprehenso, competere novimus: quique ex abusu talium scriptorum, nimium sane crebro nimiunque proclivi, nova subinde schismata, sectas, damnationes, persecutiones, aliaque id genus scandala, sæpius orta fuisse & scimus, &

without any hope of restoration of friendship. These congregations of Christians were divided and separated from one another like empires [divided] by boundaries, and enemy camps with trenches and ramparts. Finally, they punished with power and sword those who contradicted these formulas, which is the supreme line of tyranny, and that with such great fervor and fury that while the profane, ungodly, despisers of the Scriptures and atheists were lightly pardoned, these alone are destined to prisons, racks, wheels, gallows, crosses, pyres and the most bizarre punishments and torments. And all for one purpose only, that the authority of these formulas could be vindicated from contradiction, and protected from contempt, that of course the outward peace of the church, and tranquility of the Republic might be preserved undisturbed. Just as this method of action ought to be most justly detested and hated by all Christians, so it has always been most displeasing to us, for whom it is a point of religion never to grant to any human writings, decrees or statutes, any authority either directive or coercive, in matters relating to faith and conscience, or to permit that it be conferred.

From this, godly reader, you may easily understand what was the end and scope which we proposed to ourselves in publishing this declaration. Indeed, it was this very thing we did, and no other. For this declaration is not published so that by it a new snare of consciences is prepared, or an immovable square of faith and rule of doctrine be prescribed to any, which clearly would absolutely obligate the consciences of men before God, and so no one would ever be permitted to depart from it even in the least, neither in thought, nor substance, nor in method or manner of teaching. Far be this proud vanity from us, who know that this honor does not belong to any writings of men, however accurate, and diligently, lengthily and excessively weighed, but only to the Word of God contained in holy letters, and who both know and seriously grieve that from the abuse of such writings, far to frequent and far too prone,

serio dolemus. Scopus autem nobis præcipuus hic fuit: Crebis eorum flagitationibus satis facere, qui officium hoc Ecclesie simul & Reipub. nostre a nobis deberi judicabant, & quidem publici boni promovendi caussa, hoc est, tum divinæ veritatis amplius illustrandæ, tum pacis in utraque illa felicitus procurandæ & quaquaversum propagandæ. Accessit alter, ut orthodoxiam & innocentiam nostrum adversus iniquas eorum criminations hac ratione commodius assereremus, qui quum ipsi graves & valde noxios errores, tum alios, tum imprimis de fatali prædestinatione, aliisque annexis capitibus (uti etiam de hæreticidio) jamdudum sequantur, soli tamen orthodoxi, & puri puti Reformati videri volunt, nobisque non errores tantum, sed & hæreses, & blasphemias impingere non verentur, imo qui dum novum in Ecclesia dominatum ipsimet exercent, nec schismata modo & sectas faciunt, sed & diras adversus innoxios persecutiones ac proscriptiones passim excitant, de nobis tamen, (quos in conciliabulo suo Dordraceno citatos quidem ex partem, sed inauditos atque indefensos nuper admodum injuste damnarunt) tanquam de veris scilicet omnium scandalorum, & turbarum in Ecclesiis Belgicis hactenus datarum auctoribus, plusquam calumniose conqueruntur. Ad hos igitur manifestæ calumniæ, & multiplicis injustitiæ, huc usque in nos exercitæ, coram Deo & toto orbe Christiano plenius convincendum, & simul ad pios omnes divinæ veritatis ac pacis Ecclesiasticæ studiosos rectius informandum, publicam hanc unanimenque sententiæ nostræ de tota pene Religione Christiana declarationem edendam esse, non sine gravi justaque ratione putavimus. In qua quidem concinnanda id imprimis operam sedulo dedimus, ne quod vel necessarium vel admodum utile dogma in ea omitteretur, neque aut falsum, aut confulsum, aut denique ociosum ac superfluum quid ibidem contineretur: sed ut ipsam ὑποτύπωσιν sanorum, vel potius sanitium verborum, que fidem ac pietatem Christiana abunde nobis exprimunt, breviter simul ac perspicue, nec minus methodice in se comprehenderet, & velut in synopti totam

new schisms, sects, condemnations, persecutions, and other kinds of scandals have more often arisen. Moreover, our principal aim was this, to satisfy the repeated demands of those who judged that we owed this duty both to the church and our republic, and indeed to the cause of promoting the public good, first for the greater illustration of divine truth, then for the more happy search and universal propagation of peace in them both. Another purpose may be added, that we might by this means the more suitably assert our orthodoxy and innocence against the unjust accusations of those, who themselves at the same time follow grave and very hurtful errors. Foremost among others is fatal predestination and other points annexed to it (such as the killing of heretics). Yet they want to be seen as the only orthodox and the altogether pure Reformed who do not fear to fasten upon us not only errors, but also heresies and blasphemies, while they indeed exercise a new domination in the church, and do not only make schisms and sects, but also everywhere incite dire persecutions and banishments against the innocent. Nevertheless they slanderously deplore us (who, although they summoned us to have a part in their counsel at Dort, they recently condemned, yet unheard and without defense) as the true authors of all the scandals and disturbances that have been made up to now in the Belgian churches. Therefore, for the fuller demonstration before God and the entire Christian world of the manifest slander and multiplied injustice exercised by these men against us to this point, and at the same time for the truer information of all that are godly and zealous for divine truth and ecclesiastical peace, we have thought, not without grave and just reason, that we must publish this public and unanimous declaration of our opinions concerning almost the whole Christian religion. In the first place, we dedicated ourselves in its preparation so that no necessary or useful doctrine would be omitted from it, nor anything false or confused be contained, nor anything idle and superfluous, but that it might contain

omnibus spectandam exhiberet: idque ex unanimi fratrum omnium (ne iis quidem, qui in ergastulis conclusi teneantur, exceptis) consensu, qui omnes & singuli diligenter eam ante legerunt, in timore Domini expenderunt, ad normam S. Scripturæ, quatenus per temporum inquitatem fieri potuit, sedulo examinaverunt, tandemque uno corde unoque ore omnes approbarunt.

Eam vero non Confessionem fidei tantum, sed & Declarationem sententiæ nostræ vocavimus, ea quod Declaratio talis amplius & prægnantius quid promittat, quam nuda solius fidei confessio: Quippe satis facere voluimus spei & exspectationi eorum, qui uberem, plenam, ac dillucidam sententiæ nostræ de plerisque omnibus Christianæ Religionis articulis expositionem desiderabant: & simul etiam pessulum obdere ori eorum, qui cum non habeant, quod merito carpant in nobis, id populo hactenus persuasum voluerunt, nunquam futurum, uti in communem, claram atque uniformem aliquam de præcipuis Religionis capitibus sententiam consentiamus: premere nos nonnulla, de quibus sententiam nostram dicere in publico erubescamus, eaque talia, quæ ipsa Religionis Christianæ præcipua capita & quasi ἀκροθίνια evertant: aut si interdum ista etiam proferremus, obscuris dubiis atque incertis phrasibus, vel generalibus & lubricis quibusdam verborum velaminibus ea tagere atque operire.

Huic illorum criminationi, licet jam pridem à nobis alibi aliquoties detectæ satisque refutatæ, publica tamen etiam & generali fidei nostræ Declaratione obviam ire maluimus, quam aliis calumniæ magis obnoxiiis modis. Adeo secura est recta conscientia & bonæ caussæ fiducia, quam ut ista etiam occasione publice testaremur, operæ duximus. Et hæc etiam inter alias caussa fuit, cur eam Scripturæ meris verbis non

healthy ὑποτύπωσιν, or better, healing words, which abundantly express to us Christian faith and godliness, briefly and at the same time clearly, and no less methodically, and exhibit a synopsis of what must be seen by all. And [this was done] by the unanimous consent of all the brothers (excepting only those who are held shut up in prison workhouses), who each and every one diligently read it beforehand, and in the fear of the Lord weighed it by the rule of the Holy Scripture, and carefully examined it, to the degree that they were able, given the iniquity of the times, and finally with one heart and one mouth, they all approved it.

For truly we have not called it just a confession of faith, but also a declaration of our opinions, for such a declaration promises something more full and pregnant than a bare confession of faith alone. Naturally we wanted to satisfy the hope and expectation of those who desired a rich, full and clear exposition of our opinions concerning the greater part of all the articles of the Christian religion, and at the same time, to put a bolt upon the mouth of those who, having nothing of merit to carp at in us, even now want to persuade the people that we would never consent to some common, clear and uniform opinion on the chief articles of religion, who oppress us not a little, that we were ashamed to speak our opinions in public, and that they were such that they would overthrow the very principle articles, and as it were, the treasures of the Christian religion. Or, if we did sometimes also mention them, that we hid and covered them by obscure, doubtful and uncertain expressions, or some general and deceitful veil of words.

This accusation of theirs, although long since elsewhere often exposed and sufficiently refuted by us, still we would rather prefer to meet it by a public and general declaration of our faith, than by other means more liable to slander. So secure is a good conscience and the confidence of a right cause, that we consider it useful that we testify publicly in this opportunity. And this among others was the reason why we did not

conceperimus, ne scilicet suspicionem illam aleremus, quod latibula quæramus, & sub æquivoco, ut quidem nonnulis videtur, Scripturæ S. verborum cortice sensus tetros ac profanos celemus: utque ita calumniandi novam materiam præcideremus iis, quibus id solemne studium isque perpetuos labor est, ut Remonstrantium famam atque existimationem sub quovis prætextu atrocibus opprobriis, aut saltem sinistris suspicionibus, maculent & contaminent.

A quæstionibus autem spinosis & nimium subtilibus, quæ Academiarum & Scholarum fere propriæ sunt, quæque nec scientem juvant, nec ignoranti nocent, consulto abstinuimus, relinquentes eas otiosis & nimium curiosis, quæque insanabile disputandi cacoethes tenet, ingeniis, quibus volupe est acumen suum ostentare, atque ex isto mustaceo laureolam sibi quærere. Soli illi veritate, quæ secundum pietatem est, & quidem cum ingenua atque aperta simplicitate conjuctæ, operam dedimus, quam sine magno labore & indoctus capere potest, & eruditus fastidire non debet. Intra necessaria denique, & nostro judicio utilia, consistere, cæteris omnibus data opera omissis, optimum ac tutissimum putavimus, & quidem ad utrumque extremum, excessum scilicet & defectum, commodius vitandum. Neque enim eorum nobis sententia placuit, qui Confessionibus & Declarationibus nil, nisi præcise necessarium scitu ac creditu, contineri volunt. Utilium ratio jure nobis habenda etiam videtur, præsertim eorum, quæ in hoc genere cæteris præcellunt, & quasi familiam ducunt. Hæc enim calcarium instar ac stimulorum sunt, quæ voluntatem valide incitant atque impellunt, ut in eorum, quæ omnino necessaria sunt, amorem & observationem libentius atque alacrius incumbat: Hinc fieri sæpe videmus, ut quædam, quæ præcise quidem necessaria non sunt ad salutem, magnos tamen post se trahant animorum motus, & vehementer in hanc aut illam partem affectus nostros ac totam voluntatem pondere suo inclinent. Adeo ut qui in illis pedem minus recte aut parum firmiter forte figit, levi momento à statu recte mentis

frame it in mere words of Scripture, lest we indeed feed the suspicion that we sought dens and hid offensive and profane meanings under an equivocal covering of the words of Sacred Scripture, as indeed it is appears to some, and that we might by this means cut off all new material of slander from those whose solemn zeal and perpetual labor it is to spot and stain, under any pretence, the fame and esteem of the Remonstrants with atrocious reproaches, or at least with sinister suspicions.

As to thorny and excessively subtle questions which are appropriate for universities and schools, but which neither help the knower nor hurt the ignorant, we have purposely abstained [from them], leaving them to the idle and overly curious, and those who have an incurable disease of disputing, to whom it is pleasurable to show their acumen, and from this laurel-cake they seek for fame in trifles. We have dedicated this work only to that truth which is according to godliness, and indeed together with a frank and open simplicity, which even the unlearned may be able to master without great labor, and the learned ought not to disdain. Finally, we have thought it best and safest to stay within the necessary and, in our judgment, profitable, conveniently avoiding both extremes, namely, of too much and too little. For neither do their opinions please us who want to have nothing contained in confessions and declarations unless what is absolutely necessary to be known and believed. It appears useful to us to have regard for those [things] which are also profitable, especially those which in this kind excel the others, and as it were lead the family. For these are like spurs and goads which powerfully incite and impel the will, that by them one may willingly and eagerly press on to the love and observation of all things which are necessary. From this we see that it frequently happens that some things which are not indeed absolutely necessary for salvation nevertheless draw after them great motions of minds and vehemently bend our affections and whole will to one side or the other by their weight, to such a degree that

dejiciatur, & facile, vagi fluctus instar, huc atque illuc impellatur. Quare etsi ea scire omnibus absolute non sit necessarium, nescire tamen velle, aut interdum etiam simpliciter ignorare, periculosum est, & non raro vehementer noxium.

Ad praxim autem Christianæ pietatis omnia direximus. Quippe veram Theologiam credimus mere practicam esse, non autem vel simpliciter, vel maxima & potiore sui parte speculativam, & proinde quæcunque in ea traduntur, eo unice referenda, ut ad officium suum sedulo faciendum, & mandata Jesu Christi observandum acrius aptiusque homo inflammetur, atque animetur. Arida enim, effœta, sterilis, & proinde spuria est Theologia, quæ intra inanem speculationem, & contemplationem meram consistit, quæque, postquam diu multumque vigilantissimi cujusque industriam fatigavit, atque ingenium solum operose exercuit, ad voluntatem tamen non penetrat, & debitum Deo obsequium in ea non gignit; eoque nec veram ac salutiferam Dei Christique notitiam in nobis efficit. Qui enim dicit, se Deum nosse, & mandata ejus non servat, mendax est, & in eo veritas non est. Prima igitur ac præcipua Theologiæ laus in eo sita est, animum hominis in obsequium Dei flectat, & eam nostram partem, quam libertate naturali donavit Deus, & quasi sui juris atque arbitrii fecit, ita inclinet, ut Deo sese totam sponte sua iterum subjiciat, & abdicato pristino libertatis suæ abusu ductum divinæ tantum voluntatis sequatur. Cætera omnia, nisi ad hunc scopum dirigantur, coram Deo vana sunt ac frivola, & per se nimini precii, adeoque pene nihili ducenda. Eorum itaque scientia ulterius, neque necessaria, neque utilis est, quam quatenus huic principali scopo servire potest & solet.

Hac ipsa etiam de caussa, quæ ad quinque, quos vocant, articulos, de prædestinatione, scilicet, eique annexis capitibus pertinent, paulo

he who sets his foot less correctly or less firmly in them, is thrown from a right state of mind by a light push, and like a restless wave, is easily driven this way and that way. Wherefore even if it is not absolutely necessary for all to know them, yet to want not to know, or sometimes to be simply ignorant, is dangerous, and not rarely powerfully hurtful.

For we have directed all things toward the practice of Christian godliness. Clearly, we believe true theology is merely practical, and not either simply, or for its greatest or better part speculative, and therefore whatever things are delivered in it must have this one reference, that a man may be more sharply and suitably inflamed and animated to carefully doing his duty and observing the commandments of Jesus Christ. For it is a dry, decayed, sterile and consequently spurious theology which consists in empty speculation and mere contemplation, and which, after it has for long time greatly wearied the diligence of even the most vigilant, and painfully exercised his genius alone, yet it does not penetrate to the will and bring forth a due obedience to God, and thereby does not effect either a true or saving knowledge of God and Christ. For he who says that he knows God and does not keep his commandments is a liar, and the truth is not in him. Therefore, the first and principle praise of theology is centered in this, that it bends the soul of man in obedience to God and so inclines that part of us which God has granted natural liberty, and made as it were to be at its own pleasure and dispose, that it again of its own accord subject itself wholly to God, and renouncing the former abuse of its own liberty, follows the leading of the will of God. All other things, unless they are directed to this aim, are vain and frivolous before God, and in themselves of the least value, and so considered almost nothing. Thus knowing them is neither any more necessary nor useful than so far as it may and ought to serve to this principal aim.

It is also for this very reason that we have expounded somewhat more fully on those things which pertain to the five articles (as they call

copiosius exposuimus atque hic illic sedulo miscuimus. Si qui enim sunt fidei nostræ articuli, qui ad praxim, sive observationem mandatorum Jesu Christi, inculcandam & ingenerandam perutiles sint, ac tantum non absolute necessarii, certe hi tales censendi sunt. Etenim per universum Theologiæ corpus passim ac varie disperse sunt, veluti nutrimenta quædam, imo quasi nervi, fibræ, arteriæ ac venæ, quibus spiritus noster ad exercitium pietatis efficaciter instigatur, inque eodem continetur, alitur ac fovetur, imo indesinenter rapitur ac concitatur: atque adeo ad profectum ejus continuum impellitur Quæ causa etiam fuit, cur contrarios articulos nuper in Synodo Dordracena perperam stabilitos, passim & sparsim, ubi res ita tulit, additis etiam rationibus, palam rejecerimus, tanquam infelix quoddam lolium & zizania veræ pietati & sanctimoniæ perquam noxia, imo ut foedas Religionis Christianæ maculas ac vibices, quos pii omnes non aliter aversari debeant, quam abscessus & apostemata, probitatis omnem succum, sanguinem & vigorem penitus exugentia, & ex anima nostra, ad sese alendum, attrahentia. Nihil enim tam inimicum Religioni, quam fictitium illud prædestinationis fatum, & inevitabilis parendi ac peccandi necessitas.

Accessit tamen ad hanc alia etiam facti nostri causa, ut nimirum hac ratione universo orbi Christiano testatum faceremus, quam justæ gravesque causæ nos impulerint, cur sententiam eorum, qui prædestinationem illam fatalem, tanquam Religionis suæ, uti revera est, præcipuam basim, seu στῦλος και ἑδραίωμα, præfracte & præcise urgebant, & dissentientes de ea Fratres tolerare recusabant, in Belgio nostro impugnaverimus, quod videlicet Religioni & pietati eam, si quidem per se quoad genuinam suam indolem consideretur, vehementer noxiam esse videremus: & ut judicandum deinde piis omnibus relinqueremus, an ullo pacto meriti fuerimus ea propter tam indignis modis, tamque

them) regarding predestination, and the heads annexed to it, as well as carefully considering it throughout. For if there are any points of our faith which are very profitable, and in a manner absolutely necessary to practice, for the inculcating and engendering the observing of the commands of Jesus Christ, these certainly must be considered as such. Therefore, these are everywhere dispersed throughout the whole body of theology, as certain nourishments, like nerves, fibers, arteries and veins, by which our spirit is effectually moved to the exercise of piety, and by it kept, fed and warmed, indeed continually seized and stirred, and so impelled to their continual progress. This also was the reason why here and there throughout [the Confession], where the subject required and with reasons added, we have openly rejected the contrary articles recently and unhappily established by the Synod of Dort, as some unproductive tares and cockles which are harmful to true godliness and holiness, evem worse, like ugly blots and spots on the Christian religion, which all godly people ought to detest no less than abscesses and pus pockets, wholly sucking up all moisture, blood and inner vigor of uprightness and drawing them out of our souls to nourish themselves. For there is nothing more hostile to religion than the fictitious fatalism of predestination, and the inevitable necessity of obeying and sinning.

_et another reason for what we have done is that by this means we may make indisputable testimony to the entire Christian world of how just and grave causes impelled us, why we impugned their opinion who harshly and absolutely pressed fatal predestination as the principle base, the pillar and support of their religion. And they refused to tolerate their brothers in our Belgium who dissent with them about this. [We dissented] because, if indeed considered in itself and according to its genuine disposition and tendency, we saw that it was powerfully harmful to religion and godliness. Then we leave it to all godly men to judge whether we in any way deserved to be treated in

ignominiose à Dordracena Synodo tractari, cum probro dimitti, muneribus nostris ex authorari, & ab Ecclesiis nostris, quantumvis invitis, separari ac violenter divelli, quin etiam postmodum ab Illustr. D. D. Ordd. Magnam partem insolenti more paulo ante passim mutatis, patria ejici, & æternum proscribi, eo quod, religione & conscientia sola adducti, promittere non possemus, nos sententiam illam nostram æterno silentio pressuros, & nusquam, qua clam, qua palam, qua directe, qua indirecte, seu quæsita, seu oblata occasione, eandem disseminaturos, aut Ecclesiis nostris inculcaturos; parati alioquin omnia bonorum civium ac subditorum munia cum aliis popularibus præstare atque exequi: de uno utroque processu, Ecclesiastico simul ac Politico, haud dubie Deus & Ecclesia suo tempore longe aliter judicabunt, quam adversarii nostri aut cupient aut sperant.

Denique, nusquam dira personarum anathemata & nimis, proh dolor! tritum illud, Damnamus, huic exomologesi nostræ apposuimus; sed ubique sententiam nostram nude tantum, sive simpliciter, sive cum addita errorum quorundam moderata rejectione, diximus: Non quod religio nobis sit, anathema illic dicere, ubi sanctus Dei Spiritus exemplo suo nobis præit. Cum Apostolo enim Paulo,[a] Angelis atque hominibus anathema dicere non dubitamus, si aliud quid evangelizent, quam quod evangelizatum est. Quin imo cum eodem, Anathema, maranatha,[b] dicimus omnibus, qui non amant Dominum Iesum Christum, id est, impiis, profanis atque atheis. At ubi spiritum Dei præeuntem non habemus, ibi jure merito ἐπέκομεν, & veniam petimusque damusque vicissim, memores illius, quod Servator monet: Ne judicate, ne judicemini: & quod Apostolus, ne ante tempus quicquam judicate, usque dum venerit Dominus, qui & illustraturus est occulta tenebrarum & manifesta faciet consilia cordium: ac tunc laus unicuique erit à Deo. Hinc nunquam facile anathema dicimus ei, quem errore puro

a manner so shameful and disgraceful [as] by the Synod of Dort, to be dismissed with insults, put out of our ministries, separated and violently torn away from our churches, however unwillingly, and then afterward to be ejected from our country and banished forever by the most Illustrious Lords of the States General, the greater part of which had but a little [while] before been insolently overthrown throughout, because, being moved only by religion and conscience, we could not promise that we would keep our opinion in eternal silence, and that nowhere would we disseminate the same, whether privately or publicly, whether directly or indirectly, whether offering or offered an opportunity, or press it upon our churches. Otherwise in all other respects [we were] ready to perform and pursue both the ecclesiastical and civic duties of good citizens and subjects, with the rest of our people. No doubt God and his church in their due time will judge far differently than our adversaries desire or hope.

Finally, we have opposed adding to this our public confession the direful anathemas of persons, and even less (Oh, the sorrow!) that worn-out "We condemn ...." Instead, we have everywhere stated our opinions, anadorned, simply, or with the addition of moderate rejection of certain errors. It is not that we scruple to speak an anathema where the Holy Spirit of God precedes us by his own example. For with the Apostle Paul, we do not hesitate to anathematize angels and men if they preach some gospel other than what was preached. Indeed, what is more, we say "Anathema Maranatha"[b] to all who do not love the Lord Jesus Christ, that is, to the ungodly, profane and atheists. But where we do not have the Spirit of God going before us, there we rightly stand fast, and ask and grant mutual pardon, remembering that which the Savior commanded, "Do not judge, lest you be judged," and which the Apostle [commanded], "Do not judge anything before the time, until when the Lord comes, who will bring to light the hidden things of darkness, and make manifest the counsel of hearts, and then praise will be to

puto teneri credimus, si alioquin pius, sit. Dei timens & rectæ conscientiæ ac veritatis divinæ studiosus, id est, si Dominum Jesum amare nobis videatur, & Evangelium ejus in pretio habere, ut ex solo errorem suum, quem nescius errat, tueri velit. Novimus enim, quam proclive sit, in tanta opinionum multitudine, tanta errantium turba, ingeniorum varietate, impedimentorum ac scrupulorum copia, judiciorum infirmate, in talibus labi atque errare: quamque facile sit argumentis in speciem veris decipi, ac falli: quam item innoxium per se sit, in pluribus errare atque hallucinari: quanta etiam clementia & benignitate usus sit Deus circa simpliciter errantes, qui peccata ipsa voluntaria pænitentibus condonat ac remittit, quamque sit alienum à miti & mansueto Domini nostri Jesu ingenio, errantium non misereri: quam denique tristes & tragicos motus omni tempore dederit illa damnandi & præceps & superba confidentia: Quippe anathemata anathematis provocari solent, & ubi alea ista semel jacta est, ilico de remedii omni sper in posterum actum & conclamatum est: Nempe seccedunt dira partium odia, & laxatis odiorum habenis, tandem fere ruitur infestis animis in mutuas cædes ac lanienas, & fructus extremus harum damnationum ac anathematismorum sit, æterna remedii desperatio. Hæc igitur mala ut evitaremus, ab anathematis studiose & data opera abstinuimus, rati sufficere, si verum ingenue diceremus, & errorem indicaremus: Liberum interim judicium de quolibet errore, errorisque gravitate aliis relinquentes, sed imprimis ei, qui solus juste judicat, & corda ac renes hominum scrutatur.[c] Satis litatum hactenus est intempestavis anathematis, & diris illis carminibus: damnamus, execramur, &c. Tempus est, ut Christianæ concordiæ, mansuetudini & charitati sacra faciamus.

everyone from God." From this we do not easily speak an anathema to him who we believe is held by a pure simple error, if otherwise he is pious, God-fearing, and zealous for a good conscience and divine truth, that is, if he appears to us to love the Lord Jesus, and hold the gospel in esteem, by which alone he is willing to recognize his error, through which he errs unknowingly. For we know how easy it is, in view of the multitudes of opinions of the deceived, of various intellectuals, of abundant hindrances and scruples, of weakness of judgments, in such to slip and err, and how easy it is to be deceived by arguments which appear true, and beguiled, likewise how harmless it is in itself to err and wander in many things. Also, [we know] how great a clemency and kindness God is will use concerning those who err simply, who pardons and remits even voluntary willful sins to those who repent, and how alien it is from the gentle and tender nature of our Lord Jesus not to pity those who err. And finally, [we know] how sad and tragic disturbances the rash and proud confidence of condemning has given at all times. For anathemas usually provoke anathemas, and where this die is once cast, immediately the hope of any later remedy is ended. The dire hatreds of parties certainly result, and the reins of hatreds being loosened, with festered minds they usually, commonly rush upon one another with the slaughter and butchery, and the last fruit of these condemnations and anathematizings is the despair of ever [finding] a remedy. Therefore, that we might avoid these evils, we have studiously and painstakingly abstained from anathemas, deeming it sufficient to openly speak truth and indicate error, meanwhile leaving to others free judgment on whatever error, and the gravity of the error, but principally to him who alone judges justly, and searches the hearts and innermost parts of men.[c] There has already been sufficient sacrifice to unseasonable anathemas, and to those dire incantations, "we condemn," "we execrate," etc. It is now time that we sacrifice [these things] to Christian unity, gentleness and charity.

a. Gal. 1:8.
b. 1 Cor. 16:22.
c. 1 Pet. 2:23, Rev. 2:23.

Post tot tristes & funestas diras, quibus hinc inde atrocitas odiorum & feralium irarum irritata & exasperata est, ponamus inimicos & exulceratos animos, & mansuetudine, lenitate, benignitate, Sancto Christi Spiritu, charitate non simulata, sermone veritatis, virtute Dei, armis justitiæ à dextris & sinistris, ad exemplum Domini nostri Jesu Christi ejusque Apostolorum pugnemus contra errores, ut errantes pro virili nostra salvemus, & ex æterna perditionis periculo eripiamus.ᵃ Ne simus multi magistri: unus enim est Magister noster:ᵇ Accedamus sanis sermonibus Domini nostri Jesu Christi, & ei, quæ secundum pietatem est,ᶜ doctrinæ: fugiamus inanes quæstiones, ac verborum pugnas, ex quibus nascitur invidia, lis, maledicentia, suspiciones malæ, perversæ exercitationes hominum mente corruptorum, & qui privati sunt veritate, & quæstui habent pietatem: Ne damnemus, aut ab Ecclesiæ communione excludamus, quod Christus non damnat, nec excludit ex regno suo. Ne fiamus iterum servi hominum, sed nec dominemur alienæ fidei. Moderatio nostra innotescat omnibus,ᵈ & per modestiam mutuamque charitatem alii alios toleremus, certi ac persuasi, neminem facile damnandum, aut à censu Christianorum expungendum, qui fidem in Christum arcte tenet, & præceptis ejusdem, sub spe promissorum ab ipso bonorum, obedire ex animo studet, licet in multis interim aberret, quæ Religionem quoquomodo concernunt: Quam sanctam & merito laudabilem ἐπιείκειαν, ubi Deus Opt. Max. aut eorum omnium, aut certe plerorumque cordibus insparaverit, qui Ecclesiis & Rebus-publicis præsunt, tum demun veritas Evangelii ubique folrebit, & sancta in Domino pax, atque concordia inter omnes vere pios stabilem sedem fixura est. Quod ut brevi fiat in universo mundo, præsertim in orbe Christiano, & maxime Reformato, supplices à Deo Patre nostro pre Jesum Christum in spiritu & veritate precamur. Hisce ita præmissis, recta nunc ad Declarationis nostræ capita ac cedemus, quippe

After so many sad, dark, dire [cursings], whereby on every side ferocious hatreds and deadly rages have been irritated and exasperated, let us lay aside inimical and ulcerated minds, and follow the example of our Lord Jesus Christ, and of his apostles, by gentleness, longsuffering, kindness, the Holy Spirit of Christ, unfeigned charity, the word of truth, the power of God, the amour of righteousness on the right and on the left. Let us fight against errors, that with manliness we may save those who err, and snatch them from the danger of eternal perdition.ᵃ Let us not be many masters, for we have one Master.ᵇ Let us agree with the wholesome words of our Lord Jesus Christ, and to that doctrine which is according to godliness.ᶜ Let us shun "vain questions and disputes about words, from which are born envy, strife, evil speaking, evil suspicions, perverse disputings of men of corrupt minds, and who are destitute of the truth, who hold godliness for gain." Let us neither condemn nor exclude from the communion of the church whom Christ does not condemn nor shut out of his kingdom. Let us not again become servants of men, but neither let us dominate the faith of others. "Let our moderation be known to all,"ᵈ and tolerate one another in modesty and mutual charity, certain and persuaded that none is to be easily condemned, or blotted out of the register of Christians who holds fast to faith in Christ, and in hope of the good things promised by him, seek from the heart to obey his commands, granted in the meanwhile that he strays in many things which in some way concern religion. We humbly beseech God through Jesus Christ in spirit and truth, that gentleness, holy and worthy to be praised, be inspired by the most high God in the hearts either of all, or at least of the majority, of those who preside in churches and republics, and then at last the truth of the gospel will flourish everywhere, and holy peace in the Lord and unity will fix its abode among all that are truly godly, and that this may shortly take

quæ cum hac ipsa Præfatione individuo semper nexu cohærere volumus.

place in the whole world, especially the Christian world, but most of all amongst the Reformed. These things thus premised, we now pass directly to the chapters of our declaration, which we always want to be joined with this preface.

a. Ja. 2:1.
b. Matt. 6: 24.
c. 1 Tim. 6:4, 5.
d. Phil. 4:5.

CONFESSIO, sive DECLARATIO,
Sententiæ Pastorum, qui in Fœderato Belgio
REMONSTRANTES vocantur,
Super præcipius articulis Religionis Christianæ.

The Confession or Declaration of the Pastors
which in the Belgian Federation
are called the Remonstrants,
on the principle articles of the Christian Religion.

Chapter 1

CAPUT I:
De S. Scriptura, ejusque authoritate, perfectione & perspicuitate.

1. Quisquis Deum ritè colere, & æternam salutem certo atque indubie consequi vult, ante omnia ei necessum est, ut credat,[a] Deum esse, & præmia largiri quærentibus ipsum: ac proinde ad eam normam ac regulam se componat,[b] quam ab ipso vero Deo, legistatore supremo, traditam ac præscriptam, vitæque æternæ promissione sanctam esse indubia fide constat.

a. Heb. 13ff.

2. Deum esse,[a] eumque multis vicibus, multisque modis, olim Patribus per Prophetas locutum esse; tandem verò postremis temporibus per unigenitum Filium suum nobis ultimam voluntatem suam plenissime declarasse ac manifeste,[b] tot tantisque argumentis, signis prodigiis, virtutibus, Spiritus S. distributionibus, ac mirandis aliis effectis, certisque prædictionum eventibus, ac testimoniis hominum fide dignarum, comprobatum est, ut ad fidem ei rei faciendam, & dubitationem omnem justam eximendam, certiora, solidiora, & perfectiora ulla dari, aut jure nequeant.

a. Heb. 13, John 1:18;

3. Universa divinæ voluntatis, quæ quidem ad Religionem pertinet, declaratio comprehensa est libris V. & N. Testamenti, & quidem illis sois authentice, qui Canonici dicitur, sive quos ab illis hominibus,[a] qui Spiritu Dei Sancto adflati, instructi ac directi fuerunt, scriptos approbatosve fuisse, nulla justa de caussa dubitari potest: quales sunt in V. Testamento,[b]

Chapter 1
On the Sacred Scripture, its authority, perfection, and perspicuity.

1. Whoever desires to duly honor God, and certainly and undoubtedly obtain eternal salvation, before all else it is necessary that he believe that God is,[a] and that he is a generous rewarder of those who seek him. Therefore, he must conform himself to the rule and square which was given and prescribed by the true God himself,[b] the supreme legislator, and stand firm upon the promise of eternal life through undoubting faith.

b. Matt. 7:21, Gal. 6:16.

2. That God is,[a] and that he has spoken to the fathers through the prophets many times and in many ways, and that he has finally in the last times most fully declared and manifested his final will through his only-begotten Son,[b] has been attested by so many and so great proofs, prodigious signs, mighty works, distributions of the Holy Spirit, and other wonderful effects, and the certain predictions of events, and the testimonies of men worthy of belief, that no more certain, solid or perfect reason for faith can be given, or justly desired.

b. Heb. 2:3-4, Deut. 29 throughout, Acts 2:22, 1 Thess. 1:5, 1 John 2:1, 3.

3. The entire declaration of the divine will pertaining to religion is contained in the books of the Old and New Testaments, and indeed authentically only in those which are called canonical. And there is no just reason to doubt that they were written and endorsed by those men who were inspired,[a] instructed and directed by the Spirit of God. Those in the Old Testament[b] are the five

quinque libri Mosis, liber Iosuæ, Iudicium, Ruth, 2 libri Samuelis, 2 Regum, 2 Chronicorum, sive Paralipomenon, Esdras, Nehemias, Esther. Item Iob, Psalmi Davidis, Proverbia, Ecclesiastes, Canticum Canticorum, Prophetæ majores, nempe Esaias, Ieremias cum ejusdem Threnis, Ezechiel & Daniel: 12 Prophetæ minores, nempe Oseas, Ioel, Amos, Obadias, Ionas, Micha, Nahum, Hæbacuc, Zephonias, Haggæus, Zacharias & Malachias.

a. 2 Tim. 3:15-17, 2 Pet. 1:20-21;

4. In N. Testamento sunt quatuor Evangelistæ,[a] Matthæus, Marcus, Lucas & Ioannes; Acta Apostolorum; Epistola Pauli,[b] videlicet, ad Romanos, prior & posterior ad Corinthios, ad Galatas, ad Ephesios, ad Philippenses, ad Colossenses, duæ ad Thessalonicenses, ad Timotheum duæ. ad Titum, ad Phileminem: item Epistola ad Hebræos: Epistola Iacobi una,[c] Petri duæ, Ioannis tres, Iudæ una, denique Apocalypsis.[d]

a. Luke 1:1-3, John 19:35, 20:31, Acts 1:1.
b. 2 Pet. 3:15-16, 1 Thess. 2:2, Heb. 3:17.

5. Hosce omnes libros a viris divinis, & omni exceptione majoribus, scriptos approbatosve esse, tot tamque certis & evidentibus testimoniis ac documentis olim deprehensum, & clare comprobatum est, ut jure merito desiderari nihil ultra potuerit. Etsi enim de paucis quibusdam aliquando nonnihil dubitandum fuit, an scilicet ab ipsis, qui dicebantur, authoribus scripti, aut approbati essent, tandem tamen re proprius explorata, & veritate indagata, eos a viris divinis, quorum apud omnes fideles infallibis authoritas, & fides indubitata erat, revera scriptos aut approbatos fuisse, abunde compertum est.

6. Præter eos, quos diximos V. T. Libros, sunt & alii jam olim apud multos in pretio habiti, vulgo dicti Apocryphi; qui tametsi ad confirmandum fidei dogmata non valent, utiliter tamen (licet alii magis, alii minus) ad fidei vitæque profectum in Ecclesia legi possunt, ac

books of Moses, the book of Joshua, Judges, Ruth, the two books of Samuel, two of the Kings, two of the Chronicles (or *Paralipomena*), Ezra, Nehemiah, Esther. Likewise Job, the Psalms of David, Proverbs, Ecclesiastes, Song of Songs, the four major Prophets, namely, Isaiah, Jeremiah, with his Lamentations, Ezekiel, and Daniel; the twelve minor Prophets, namely, Hosea, Joel, Amos, Obadiah, Jonah, Micah, Nahum, Habakkuk, Zephaniah, Haggai, Zechariah and Malachi.

b. Luke 16:29, 24:27, 45-47, Acts 17:2-3, 24:14, 16:22-23, Rom. 1:2.

4. In the New Testament are the four Evangelists,[a] Matthew, Mark, Luke, and John; the Acts of the apostles, the Epistles of Paul,[b] namely, Romans, the former and latter to the Corinthians, Galatians, Ephesians, Philippians, Colossians, two to the Thessalonians, two to Timothy, to Titus, to Philemon; also the Epistle to the Hebrews, one Epistle of James, two of Peter,[c] of John three, of Jude one: lastly the Revelation.[d]

c. 2 Pet. 3:1, 1 John 1:1-4.
d. Rev. 1:2, 22:18-19.

5. That all these books, and without any exceptions for the majority, were written or approved by inspired men, has been recognized in the certain and evident testimonies and documents, and was so clearly proven, that nothing more can be justly or reasonably desired. For even if there were doubts about a few of them, that is, whether they were written or approved by those who are said to be their authors, nevertheless after the matter has been explored and the truth sought, it has been abundantly proven that they were truly written or approved by inspired men of infallible authority and whose credibility was undoubted by all believers.

6. Besides these books called the Old Testament, there are also others which for a long time have been held in esteem by many, commonly called the Apocrypha. Although they are not valid for confirming doctrines of faith, still they are useful (some more, some less), and are

solent, quales sunt Tobias, Iudith, Baruch, Sapientia, Ecclesiaticus: iii & iv Esdræ tres libri Macchabæorum, & quædam additamenta ad Estheram & Danielem, quæ vulgo sunt nota.

7. Doctrinam libris N. T. Comprehensam (qua & doctrinæ V. T. Veritas ac divinitas abundè stabilitur, atque asseritur) plane veram ac divinam esse, non tantum inde liquet, quoda divinis illis viris, quos suprà nomina vimus, scripta est vel approbata, & Ecclesis tradita; quodque[a] variis & innumeris miraculis, omnemque humanam & Angelicam sapientiam, ac potentiam excedentibus operibus, signis ac prodigiis, quin &[b] ipsius primi Authoris, D. N. Jesu Christi, gloriosa è mortuis suscitatione, & irrefragabilibus testimoniis ac documentis adsertâ exaltatione, confirmata est ac stabilita; sed ex eo vel imprimis, quod præcepta talia continet,[c] quibus perfectiora, æquiora & sanctiora excogitari nequeunt; & promissa tanta,[d] quibus excellentiora, Deoque magis digna, nec humana, nec Angelica mens concipere potest. Quibus non leve momentum addit doctrinæ ipsius admirabilis[e] efficacia, quod videlicet ea, licet carni inimical atque ingrata, per admodum paucos Apostolos, eosque simplices, infirmos, fingendi non modo crimine, sed & suspicione alienissimos, nullo eloquentiæ mundanæ præsidio instructos, nullo authoritatis humanæ titulo claros; sine vi, sine armis, sola rationum persuasione, & spiritus demonstratione, mera item innocentia vitæque sanctitate & patientia armatos, brevissimo tempore, ubique locorum, (obstante licet toto regno satanico & universo fere mundo) mirabiliter disseminata est, atque ita se quaquaversum dissudit, ut innumeræ hominum myriades, omnis ordinis, generis & conditionis, non idiotæ tantum, sed & doctissimi & sapientissimi non pauci, relictis antiquis suis ritibus & religionibus, in quibus nati fuerant & educati, sine ulla terreni commodi spe (imo cum certa crucis, ignominiæ & periculorum omnium expectatione) constantissime ei adhæserint: imo ut religiones aliæ omnes, quamvis humanis

usually read in the church for the perfecting of faith and life; such are Tobit, Judith, Baruch, Wisdom, Ecclesiasticus, third and fourth of Esdras, the three Books of Maccabees, and some additions to Esther and Daniel, which are commonly known.

7. That the doctrine contained in the books of the New Testament (by which also the truth and dignity of the Old Testament is abundantly established and confirmed) is completely true and divine, is not only proven by being written or approved by those inspired men whom we named before, and delivered to the church, nor from its being confirmed and established by various and innumerable miracles,[a] and by deeds, signs and wonders exceeding all human and angelic wisdom and power, and even more by the glorious resurrection from the dead of its first author,[b] our Lord Jesus Christ, and his exaltation asserted by many irrefutable testimonies and documents. But primarily because it contains commandments more perfect,[c] just and holy than anyone could have contrived, and such excellent promises[d] that neither a human or angelic mind could conceive of anything more worthy of God. It adds no small weight to the admirability and efficacy of its doctrine[e] that such an unaccommodating enemy of the flesh was [written] by so few apostles, simple, weak men, free not only from the crime of forgery, but also unworthy of suspicion, with no protection of worldly eloquence, no renown from writs of human authority; without force, without arms, only by the persuasion of reasons and arguments and the demonstration of the Spirit, likewise men armed merely with innocence, holiness of life and patience. In the shortest time and in all places (although opposed by the whole satanic kingdom and almost the whole world) it was amazingly disseminated, and so spread itself wherever one might turn, so that innumerable myriads of men, of all ranks, classes and conditions, not only of ignorant men, but also not a few of the most learned and wise, leaving their ancient and rites and religions into which they were born and educated, without any hope of any earthly advantage (indeed with a certain expectation of

præsidiis undique firmatæ, sola Iudaica excepta, quia hæc divina erat, tantum non ad hujus exorientem fulgorem evanuerint, atque exstinctæ sint.

a. Acts 5:11, 13-15, Heb. 2:3-4; Acts 10:37-39.
b. Acts 2:14, 5:29-32.
c. Matt. 5:6-8.

8. Etsi vero Ecclesia primitiva, quæ temporibus Apostolorum fuit, certissime resciscere potuit, & indubie etiam rescivit,[a] libros istos ab Apostolis scriptos esse, vel saltem approbatos, nobisque istius rei scientiam quasi per manus tradidit, ac veluti depositum quoddam reliquit: non tamen idcirco sacri hi libri à nobis pro veris ac divinis habentur, quod eos veros esse, sive divinos continere sensus Ecclesia primitiva judicio suo irrefragabili censuerit, utque pro talibus habeantur, cum infallibi authoritate statuerit. Primo enim necessarium non erat, ut Ecclesia judicio suo desiniret, & cum authoritate statueret, veros ac divinos esse libros illos, qui ab Apostolis scripti vel approbati erant: id enim & ante, & citra omne ejusmodi judicium, planè certum atque indubitatum erat apud omnes & singulos Christianos: adeo ut, simulatque horum aliquis resciceret, scriptum aliquid vel approbatum esse ab Apostolis,[b] eo ipso verum ac divinum id esse, credere jure posset ac deberet; nulloque alio judicio, aut statuto hac in parte opus haberet. Deinde nec sufficere quidem potuisset ejusmodi Ecclesiæ judicium, quum ne quidem id ipsum, quod Ecclesia aliqua sit, cui authoritas talis competere dicitur, constare cuiquam vel probabiliter queat, nisi prius certum ei atque exploratum sit, libros illos, in quibus illa authoritas Ecclesiæ adsignata esse dicitur, veros ac divinos esse: quamque certo sciri ac statui non possit, Ecclesiam aliquam veram Christi Ecclesiam esse,[c] nisi jam ante certum atque indubium sit, verum ac divinum esse, quidquid libris hisce continetur: quia per eam fidem, qua Ecclesia amplectitur id omne tanquam verum, ipsa demum id habet, quod vera Ecclesia sit. Quod si vero ipsi primitivæ Ecclesiæ, seorsim ab Apostolis acceptæ, hujus-

cross, dishonor, and all dangers) most persistently adhered to it. Thus all other religions, although everywhere supported by human protection, faded at the rising of its refulgence, Judaism alone excepted because it was of God.

d. 2 Pet. 1. 4, Heb. 8. 6, 2 Cor. 7. 1.
e. Rom. 10:18, 1 Cor. 2:3-4; 2 Cor. 3 *in passim*, 2 Cor. 4:2-5, Col. 1:6, 23, Acts 5:14, 19:11.

8. Even if the primitive church which was in the time of the apostles, could most truly, most certainly know and undoubtedly did know that these books were written or at least approved by the apostles,[a] and almost hand-delivered the knowledge of this matter to us and left it as a trust, nevertheless we do not hold these books to be true and inspired because the primitive church has decreed them true by its unbreakable judgment, or that they contain in them inspired meanings, and has by its infallible authority decreed that they be held as such. For first, it was not necessary that the church by its judgment should define and by its authority establish that those books which were written or approved by the apostles were true and inspired. For both before and after all such manner of judgment, this was altogether certain and undoubted by all Christians, both in general and particular, precisely in that as soon as any one of them knew that anything was written or approved by the apostles,[b] he could and ought to have known that it was true and inspired. He had no need for any other judgment or decision in the case. Consequently, neither indeed could such a judgment of the church suffice, when indeed the church is not something that has such authority to make the judgment itself, unless first one was certain and convinced that those books by which the authority of the church is said to be bestowed, were true and divine. And it cannot be known or established for certain that any church is the true church of Christ,[c] and unless whatever is contained in these books is already previously certain and beyond doubt. Because it is through that faith which the church embraces as wholly true that she herself finally holds that she is a true church. For if truly the primitive church itself did not receive such an authority from the apostles, certainly much less is it to be believed that any church received it, much less ought we to

modi authoritas non competit; multo certe minus hodiernæ eam, aut primam illam sequenti ulli Ecclesiæ, competere credendum est.

a. Luke 1:12, Col. 4:16, 1 Thess. 5:27, 2 Thess. 3:17.
b. Eph. 2:20, Acts 2:41, 1 Thess. 2:13.

9. Doctrina itaque hisce Canonicis libris comprehensa, ex semet ipsa prorsus est authentica, & quidem authoritatis divina,[a] atque irrefragibilis: ac proinde propter infallbilem Dei veracitatem, omnino fidem meretur indubiam, & propter $αὐτόκρατορκήν$, sive absolutam ac supremam ejusdem potestatem, humillimum à nobis obsequium. Quæcumque autem[b] doctrina vel traditio hoc supremæ & divinæ revelationis privilegio caret, ea nec eandem, nec parem cum illa authoritatem habere ullo jure potest; nedum illa, quæ vel aliud quid, (sive contrarium, sive diversum) idque cum usurpatâ authoritate,[c] tanquam creditu necessarium statuit, vel aliter saltem, quam hisce libris scriptum extat, sub periculo amittendæ salutis enunciari, aut enunciantum credi jubet: quum nec sibi ipsi adversari possit Deus; nec divinæ authoritati vel humana ulla, vel Angelica æquari debeat.

a. Is. 1:2-3, Heb. 1:2.
b. Deut. 4:2, 12:32, 2 Tim. 3:15, 2 Pet. 1:21.

10. Cæterum quia solis hisce libris divina hujusmodi authoritas competit, necessum etiam est, ut ad eos[a] solos, tanquam ad lydios lapides & immotas regulas, controversiæ & lites omnes ad Religionem pertinentes exigantur, & ex iis solis disceptentur: sicque soli Deo & Iesu Christo, tanquam unico, supremo atque infallibili[b] Judici, peremptorie decidendæ reliquantur. Dirimi enim eas jure judiciali, aut potestativâ, per judicem aliquem visibilem ac ordinarie loquentem in Ecclesia, Deum minime coluisse censendum est: quum normam tantum dirigentem,[c] sive directivè duntaxat, non etiam coactive jundicantem, nobis in verbo suo relinquere voluerit: judicem vero infallibilem, semper in Ecclesia loquentem, esse debere, nusquam significaverit: neque quis ille perpetuo futurus esset, in verbo suo designaverit; sed contra omnibus & singulis ex æquo[d] scrutari leges, seu

believe that it belongs to any other church which succeeded that church, or any church today.

c. Rom. 10:14-17, John 10:3, 4, 27, 1 Pet. 1:23-25, 2:1-3.

9. Therefore, the doctrine contained in these canonical books is of itself altogether authentic and indeed of divine authority,[a] and unquestionable, and by reason of the infallible veracity of God, entirely deserves undoubted faith, and by virtue of its $αὐτόκρατορκήν$ or absolute and supreme power, most humble obedience from us. Any other doctrine or tradition,[b] however, lacks this privilege of supreme and divine revelation, and so cannot by any right have equality with that authority, much less that which either decrees something else (whether contrary or different) and that by a usurped authority,[c] or at least commands it to be declared otherwise than is on record in writing in these books, or being declared to be believed, upon the pain and peril of the loss of salvation, since God can neither contradict himself, and no authority, either human or angelic, ought to be equaled to the divine.

c. Matt. 15:9, 16:6, Gal. 18-9.

10. Because such divine authority as this belongs to these books alone, it is therefore necessary that controversies and all debates pertaining to religion be examined by them alone,[a] as touchstones and firm and unmovable rules, and to be disputed from them only, and so leave them to be decided by God and Jesus Christ alone as the one supreme and infallible judge.[b] For it must not be supposed that God wanted in the least that they should be decided by any judicial or authoritative right, by some visible judge, and one ordinarily speaking in the church, since it has pleased him to leave us, not forced judgment, but a rule in his Word so direct or even directed.[c] But he nowhere indicated that there ought to be an infallible judge always speaking in the church, nor has he designated in his Word who that would perpetually be. But he has expressly commanded all and every one alike to examine his laws,[d] or judgments and

judicia ac statuta sua,[e] probare spiritus, an ex Deo sint, imo[f] omnia probare, quodque bonum est retinere expresse mandaverit; quum etiam scrutantibus[g] leges suas, & quærentibus intelligentiam earum, gratiam suam, & Spiritum Sanctum promiserit;[h] eosque, qui Scripturas scrutati sunt, ex iisque fidei controversias examinarunt, imo quæ ab ipsis etiam Apostolis proferebantur, diligenter ad Scripturæ normam ac regulam expenderunt, singularibus elogiis commendaverit ac laudaverit.

a. Isaiah 8:20, Acts 17:11.
b. John 4:12; Matt. 23:8.
c. Ps. 19:8-9, 119:105, Luke 16:29, 21.
d. Deut. 6:6-7, 11:8.
e. 1 John 4:1.
f. 1 Thess. 5:21.
g. Prov. 2:2-4, 3:13.
h. Acts 17:11, 2 Pet. 1:19.

11. Quocirca ij, qui authoritatem hanc irrefragabilem, lites & controversias, vel omnes, vel aliquas, de fide aut Religione peremtorie dirimendi, certæ alicui vel Ecclesiæ, vel Doctorum Synodo, aut cuicunque hominum societati, vel singulari cuipiam personæ, quæ etiam impia ac prophana esse possit, tanquam visibili & loquenti judici,[a] ultro deferunt, vel deferri sinunt; istaque decisione conscientias teneri atque obligari volunt: nulla firma ratione, nedum authoritate aliqua divina, nituntur; imo contra hanc pariter & illam, id facere credendi sunt:[b] præterquam quod Christianum Scripturas indagandi, spiritus explorandi, & omnia probandi &c. officium, præcationemque piarum, pro adsequenda Scripturarum intelligentia, necessitatem simul & utilitatem, ea ratione magnoperè labefactant, imo prorsus elevant.

a. Is. 8:20.

11. Therefore those who wantonly bestow, or allow to be bestowed, the unquestionable authority to peremptorily judge debates and controversies concerning faith or religion, whether all or some, either to some certain church, or synod of the learned, or to any human society, or to any single person, who also may be ungodly and profane, as to a visible and speaking judge,[a] and who want to hold and bind consciences by this decision, they are not supported by firm reason, still less by any divine authority. Indeed, they are to be understood as acting equally against both the one and the other. Beyond this, on this account they greatly undermined and wholly diminish the Christian duty of searching the Scriptures, testing the spirits, examining all things,[b] etc., which is both necessary and useful for the prayers of the godly and understanding the Scriptures.

b. Ps. 119:33, Eph. 1:16, 3:14-15, Matt. 7:7-8, Ja. 1:5.

12. Ob hanc igitur gravissimam certè simul & justissimam causam, non patimur nos, in controversiis quidem religionis, vel sacris causis, urgeri nudis hominum authoritatibus, puta Patrum, qui vocantur, glossis ac sententiis, Conciliorum, aut Synodum determinationibus, Confessionum articulis, Theologorum placitis, aut Academiarum conclusionibus; multo vero minus receptis jam olim consuetudinibus, aut splendore ac numero, seu multitudine hominum idem sententium, vel longi denique temporis

12. Therefore, on account of this most weighty and most just cause, we do not suffer ourselves in controversies of religion or sacred concerns to be pressed by the bare authorities of men, such as the glosses and opinions of those called the "fathers," the determinations of councils or synods, articles of confessions, the opinions of theologians, or the conclusions of universities, much less with ancient practices, or with the splendor and number or multitude of men of the same opinion, or lastly by some long-observed rule, etc. For neither ought we

præscriptione, &c. Neque enim hæc attendere debemus, quid hic aut ille Ecclesiæ Doctor, aut Doctorum cœtus, quantumvis doctrinæ, aut sanctimoniæ opinione clarus, neque quid hæc vel illa Synodus, aut particularis Ecclesia; sed qui ante omnes est, quique solus nec fallere, nec falli potest Dominus noster Iesus Christus, in verbo suo dixerit, aut præscripserit.

13. Nec mirum: hisce enim libris sacris perfectè continetur plena, & plus quam sufficiens revelatio omnium fidei mysteriorum; imprimis eorum, quæ universis & singulis hominibus simpliciter,[a] ad æternam salutem consequendam, scitu, creditu, speratu, factu necessaria sunt: adeo ut nullus sit vel minimus ad fidem, aut vitam Deo placentem, recte informandum, requisitus articulus, cuiquam Christiano præcise tenendus, qui his ipsis abunde non contineatur.[b] Necessaria autem ad salutem ea tandem esse intelligimus, sine quibus fieri nullo modo potest, ut quis vel præceptis Christi recte & prout oportet, obediat, vel divinis ejusde promissis firmiter confidat: quæque proinde talia sunt, ut sine manifesta hominis culpa negari, ignorari, aut in dubium vocari nequeant.

a. 2 Tim. 3:15-16, 1 Pet. 1:23-25, 2 Pet. 1:19-21.

14. Præterea eorundem librorum, licet alicubi (præsertim indoctis & minus exercitatis) satis obscuri sint, tanta est[a] claritas, ac perspicuitas; in sensibus inprimis ad æternam salutem intellectu necessariis, ut omnes lectores, non docti tantum, sed & idiotæ (communi quidem sensu ac judicio præditi) quantum satis est, mentem eorum adsequi possint: modo præjudicio, vana confidentia, alijsve pravis affectibus, sese occæcari non sinant: sed scripturam hanc pie ac sedulo scrutentur (quod ipsum non modo omnibus licitum,[b] licet alioqui rudibus, idiotis ac laicis; sed præceptum atque injunctum à Deo esse credimus) & phrases Scripturæ proprias, istoque tempore quo libri hi scripti, eodemque adhuc vigente idiomate, clarissimas & significantissimas, familiares sibi reddere studeant: ut hi tales, inquam, omnia ad

to attend to what this or that teacher of the church or assembly of teachers [has said], however famous for their learning or holiness, nor this or that synod or particular church, but what he who is before all and who alone can neither deceive nor be deceived, our Lord Jesus Christ, has said and prescribed in his Word.

13. Nor is this astonishing, for in these books is perfectly contained a full and more than sufficient revelation of all the mysteries of faith, especially those which are simply necessary for each and every man to know, believe, hope, and do in order to obtain eternal salvation,[a] so that there is not one article, not even the least, required for a right understanding of faith, or a life pleasing to God, and absolutely necessary to be held by any Christian, which is not abundantly contained in them.[b] However, for things necessary to salvation we only understand those things without which it would be utterly impossible for any man either to obey the commandments of Jesus Christ rightly and as he ought, or firmly confide in his divine promises, and are such that they cannot be denied, unknown or called in question without a man's manifest guilt.

b. Rom. 10:9, Matt. 5:6-7, Heb. 5:9, Gal. 5:6, 6:15, 1 John 5:1.

14. Furthermore the clarity and understandability of these books,[a] although they are obscure enough in some places (especially to the unlearned and less exercised) is so great, especially in meanings necessary to be understood for salvation, that all readers, not only the learned, but also the ignorant (who are gifted with common sense and judgment), as much as is sufficient, may be able to follow their meaning, if they do not permit themselves to be blinded by prejudice, vain confidence, or other corrupt affections, but piously and carefully search the Scripture[b] (which we believe is not only permitted for all, though untaught, ignorant or lay people, but also commanded and enjoined by God), and study to become familiar with the very phrases of Scripture, and which were most clear and meaningful in the time and language in which these books were

veram fidem ac pietatem pertinentia, non solum quæ necessaria sunt, sed etiam sub ipsa necessitatis ratione, quod scilicet & quatenus necessaria sint, ex iis abunde percipere possint: probi vero,^{c} dociles, & Dei ex animo timentes, reipsa etiam facillime percipiant.

a. Ps. 19:8, 119:105, 130, 2 Cor. 3:14-15, 4:3-4, 2 Pet. 1:19.
b. John 5:39-40, 2 Pet. 1:19, Luke 16:29, 1 Thess. 5:20.

15. Quia verò permulti sunt, etiam inter Christianos, qui vel sacros hosce libros omninò non legunt,^{a} vel non satis attentè, nec cum cura ac judicio id, quos leguntur, perpendunt; vel divinum auxilium subinde, uti decet, piè non implorant; vel^b alioqui præjudicio, confidentiâ odio, invidiâ, ambitione, aliisve pravis affectibus imbuti, in horum librorum lectione versantur; deinde verò, quia in ipsis etiam hisce libris non rarò, hic illic, tum res^c tum phrases antiqui istius seculi propriæ, itemque tropicæ & figuratæ locutiones occurunt, quæ hoc tempore nobis obscuritatem & difficultantem aliquam pariunt; quæques tales sunt, ut nisi quis solidè de istis omnibus instruatur, aut alioqui animum valdè docilem, probum, & ab affectibus vacuum, ad eorum dijudicationem adferat, facilè in sensum alienum, imò pravum, & saluti noxium, detorqueri possint; hinc non una justa ratio emergit (ne de pluribus aliis nunc agamus) cur Scripturarum^d interpretationi & explicationi & locus suus in Ecclesia concedi utiliter possit, imò semper debeat.

a. John 3:18-19, 5:39-40, 12:39-40.
b. 2 Pet. 3:16, 2 Cor. 3:14.

written. We say that such [people] as these, truly honest, teachable and fearing God from the heart,^{c} are able to perceive everything which pertains to true faith and godliness, not only those things which are necessary, but also the very reason of their necessity, namely, they really do easily perceive that they are necessary and for what purpose.

c. Ps. 25:12, 14, John 7:17, 8:47.

15. But because there are very many even among Christians who either do not read these books at all^a or not with sufficient attention, nor consider what they read with care and judgment, or do not frequently and piously ask for divine aid, as is proper, or else being drenched with prejudice, confidence, hatred, envy, ambition, or other depraved feelings,^{b} are busy in the reading of these books, and then next, because not rarely even in these books themselves they meet with some antique matter or phrase from the time period of the Scriptures,^{c} and likewise tropes and figurative speech, which in the present time produce for us some obscurity and difficulty, and which are such, that unless one be solidly instructed in all these, or bring with him to the interpretational process a very teachable, honest mind, and not bring emotions, they may easily be twisted to a wrong meaning, indeed to [one that is] perverse and prejudicial to salvation. From this emerges but just one reason (lest we deal with many others now) why the interpretation and explication of the Scriptures may usefully be allowed its place in the church, and indeed always ought to be.^{d}

c. Acts 8:30-31, 18:24-25.
d. 1 Cor. 12:7-8, ch. 14, 1 Thess. 5:20-21.

16. But the best interpretation of Scripture is that which most faithfully expresses the native and literal sense thereof, or at least comes nearest to it. Obviously, it alone is the true and living Word of God,[a] and by it, just as by incorruptible seed, we are reborn to the hope of eternal life. We call, however, the native and literal sense not so much that which the words properly taken bear (as indeed most often occurs), but that which, even if not favorable to a rigid understanding of the words, yet is most agreeable to right reason, and the very mind and intention of the one who uttered the words, whether it was enunciated properly or figuratively. Because this can and ought to be discerned from the scope and occasion of whatever passage,[b] likewise the subject matter, the things which precede and follow, likewise from comparison with similar passages, and from palpable absurdities likely to result from it and other arguments of that kind, or from the judgment of such things.

a. Heb. 4:12-13, 1 Pet. 1:23-25, Ja. 1:18-21.

b. Matt. 4:4-5, 22:19, 2 Pet. 1:20-21, 2 Cor. 3:13-15.

17. But to desire to beg an exposition from some other source, namely, from any creed of human fabrication or analogy of faith received in this or that place, or any public confession of churches (which we also warned before in our Preface, which we never would want at any time to be separated from this our declaration) or from the decrees of councils, or of this or that father, though even the most or greatest part of them, is very uncertain and often dangerous.

18. And yet do we not therefore easily despise the pious, probable or ancient received interpretations of others, especially the Greek or Latin Fathers. Much less do we proudly or arrogantly reject their unanimous consent. But we do eventually, and then modestly, recede from them if we discover in our conscience that they convey something alien to the true meaning of Scripture, or contrary to it. Nor do we think that by this reasoning to subject them to some injury, since not only every of them individually, but also the greater part of them jointly, indeed all of them taken

omnes simul sumpti, errare in multis potuerit; ipsique etiam uno ore de seipsis id ultrò agnoscant: eoque diserte prohibeant, scriptis suis simpliciter fidem adhiberi, sed eatenus demum sua probari à nobis cupiant, quatenus cum S. literis consentiunt; contraque libere improbarim quatenus ab iisdem dissentiunt.

together, may err in much. For they themselves voluntarily admit this with one accord, and eloquently prohibit that their writings be simply believed, but desire that in the end they be tested by us to what degree they agree with the Sacred Scriptures, and to the contrary, that we freely reject them to the degree that they disagree with the same.

• Chapter 2 •

CAPUT II.
De Cognitione Essentiæ Dei,
sive Naturæ divinæ.

CHAPTER 2
On the knowledge of the essence of God,
or the divine nature.

1. Porrò Religio nostra universa, sacris hisce libris comprehensa, summatim cosistit in rectâ unius veri Dei, &, quem ille misit, Iesu Christi mediatoris cognitione;[a] & legitimo utriusque cultu, sub spe vitæ æternæ atque immortalis, post mortem, in cælis, ex gratuita ejusdem promissione, certo consequendæ.

1. Furthermore, our entire religion contained in these sacred books can be summarized in the correct knowledge of the one true God and Jesus Christ the mediator whom he has sent,[a] and in a legitimate worship of both, under the hope of life eternal and immortal after death, to be certainly obtained in heaven according to the free promise of the same.

a. John 17:3, 1 John 2:23, 5:11-12, 2 John v. 9.

2. Ut autem Deus recte agnoscatur & pie colatur, idque juxta Scripturas,[a] tria nobis consideranda & necessario tenenda veniut: Natura, Opera, & Voluntas ipsius. Natura quidem Dei, ut recte intelligatur, hunc ipsum ex sese dignissimum esse, qui à nobis colatur: Opera vero, ut sciatur, eum jure meritò cultum, qualemcumque vult, à nobis exigere posse: denique Voluntas, ut evincatur, velle eum à nobis coli; & simul cognoscatur, qua ratione coli velit, ac coli debeat, ut æterna salus certo ab ipso sperari possit. Veruntamen, de Natura, atque Operibus Dei, non necessario tenenda sunt ea omnia, quæ ad divinam essentiam, & omnes operandi modos atque operationum species, quacunque tandem ratione, pertinent: nedum ea

2. But that God may be rightly known and piously worshipped according to the Scriptures,[a] three things must be considered and necessarily held by us: his nature, works, and will. By the nature of God, we may rightly understand that in and of himself he is most worthy to be worshiped by us. By by his works, we may truly know that he may rightfully and deservedly demand of us whatever manner of worship he desires. Finally, by his will, we may be convinced that he wills to be worshipped by us, and at the same time it may be known after what manner he desires, and ought to be worshipped, that one may certainly hope for eternal salvation from him. However, it is not necessary to hold everything concerning the nature and works of God in every respect (at least

whatever pertains to the divine essence and all the modes of its working and kinds of operations, much less all those things, which either according to the hypothetical and specious opinions of the schools, or the probable discourse of reason, are customarily affirmed by them, but those only, without which the divine will, revealed in the Scriptures, either cannot be rightly understood or attended to by us[b]), since it is said throughout Scripture that only those who obey the divine will and serve his commandments truly know God, and on the contrary, they who do not obey him do not know God. Indeed, that alone deserves to be called the saving knowledge of God which is joined with the practice of godliness. To be sure, other things pertaining to this are more or less useful, either for promoting godliness or for better understanding and successfully settling whatever religious controversies may occur, yet they should not be held as necessary doctrines of faith which cannot be ignored without the loss of salvation.

b. Job 28:28, Jer. 2:8 & 22:16, hos. 6:6, tit. 1:16, 1 John chs. 2-4, and 3:6.

3. [Concerning] what pertains to the nature of God, the Scripture presents God to us under a twofold consideration: 1. absolutely and generally in his essential attributes, namely, by which it unfolds to us his spiritual nature and glorious majesty common to distinct persons,[a] so far as is sufficient for our faith and salvation in this life; 2. distinctly and relatively in the mystery of the Holy Trinity,[b] which concerns the internal and mutual condition of the persons among themselves, and their proper division.

b. Matt. 28:19, 2 Cor. 13:14, 1 John 5:7.

4. The following are those attributes, so far as they necessarily pertain to [his nature].

5. 1. God is one,[a] in that he is alone, without associate, most supreme and high, who has neither any before him, nor above him to whom he depends for being, willing, or acting, but he has his deity and divine sovereignty over all from himself. There neither is nor can be another who can compete with all his the attributes of a true deity.

tant: ideoque[b] authoritatis prorsus absolutæ, sive potestatis est irrefragabilis, ut creaturis bonisque suis omnibus statuere possit, quidquid vult: puta[c] donare, auserre, conservare, destruere, vivificare, mortificare; mandare, prohibere, permittere, punire, remittere; augere, imminuere, commutare, transferre & c. prout gloriæ suæ & saluti suorum conducere noverit; & prout sapientiæ, bonitati, ac justitiæ suæ congruere viderit.

a. Deut. 6:4, 31:39, Ps. 86:10, 1 Cor. 8:6, 1 Tim. 2:5.
b. Gen. 14:18, Deut. 6:17, Is. 4:4, 44:6, 45:6-7.

6. II. *Eternus est*,[a] quia semper fuit, semperque est & erit idem: omni principio & fine, omnique innovatione carens: imo solus per naturam necessario vivens, sive à se ipso vitam & immortalitatem habens: ac proinde in se ipso semper *invariabilus*,[b] *incorruptibilis*, omnique modo *immutabilis*: denique ipsius etiam vitæ[c] æternæ, gratiose nobis in J. Christo promissæ, sumpremus author, ac largitor unicus.

a. Rev. 1:4, Ps. 90:2, 1 Tim. 1:17, 6:15-16.
b. Ja. 1:27, Rom. 1:20, 23, Mat. 3:6, Ps. 102.26-27.

7. III. *Infinita* atque *immensus* est[a]: quia cœlum & terram ita implet, ut nullis certis locorum spatiis circumscribi, nullis finibus comcludi possit; sed omnibus ubique locis, licet abditissimis & remotissimis, generali & incomprehensibili modo præsens adsit. Tametsi[b] peculiari quodam modo tum in cœlo beatorum gloriose habitat, tum in sanctis suis specialem, quamvis inæqualem,[c] gratiæ efficaciam exserit. Unde varii præsentiæ divinæ gradus, in diversis rebus creatis, non difficulter intelligi possunt.

a. 1 Ki. 8:27, Ps. 139:8-9, Jer. 23:24, Is. 66:1, Acts 7:48-49.
b. Ps. 2:4, 11:4, 33:13-14, 115:3, Matt. 6:9.

8. IV. *Omniscius* est, & quidem scientiæ infallibilis:[a] quia non tantum omnia omnino, quæ entitatem aliquam habent, penitissime cognoscit, prout singula in se ipsis sunt: sive bona sint sive mala; præterita, præsentia, futura, item eventa possibilia & verisimilia; imo etiam arcanissima cordis cogitata, secretissima dicta, occultissima facta, (sub quibus etiam ea, quæ omittuntur; comprehensa volumus) sed etiam

Because of this utterly absolute authority or irresistible power,[b] he can decide whatever he wants for all of his creatures and goods, namely, to give, take away, preserve, destroy, make alive, kill, command, prohibit, permit, punish, pardon, increase, diminish, change, translate, etc.,[c] as he knows is fitting for his glory and the salvation of those that are his, and sees it to agree with his wisdom, goodness and justice.

c. Job 9:43, Deut. 32:39; 2 Chron. 20:6, 1 Sam. 3:11-13, Dan. 2:28, Ja. 4:12, Ma. 20:15, Prov. 16:4, Is. 42:6, 48:11.

6. 2. He is eternal,[a] because he always was, ever is, and likewise will be, without any beginning or end, or any alteration. Indeed [he is] the only [being] who is necessarily living by nature, or having life and immortality from himself, and therefore in himself [is] forever unchangeably incorruptible,[b] and in every way immutable. Finally, [he is] the supreme author and only bestower of eternal life,[c] graciously promised to us in Jesus Christ.

c. 1 John 5:11, 1 Tim. 4:10, Tit. 1:1.

7. 3. He is infinite and immense,[a] because he so fills heaven and earth that he cannot be limited to any certain space of places, nor confined within any boundaries, but he is present everywhere in all places, although most hidden or remote, in a general and incomprehensible manner. Even so, in a certain specific way he especially, gloriously inhabits the heaven of the blessed,[b] then exerts the special efficacy of his grace in his saints, however unevenly.[c] From this the various degrees of divine presence is understood without difficulty by the diverse things of creation.

c. 2 Cor. 6:16, John 14:23.

8. 4. He is omniscient, and certainly of infallible knowledge,[a] because he not only intimately knows absolutely everything which has being, just as they are individually in themselves, whether good or evil, past, present, future, likewise possible and hypothetical, indeed even the most intimate thoughts of the heart, the most secret words, the most hidden deeds (under which also we will include matters of omission), but also because he keeps them most

quia[b] præsentissima semper memoria tenet, & quasi oculus posita videt, quæcunque recte aut secus a nobis unquam sint: ita ut nec ignorantia, nec oblivione, deliri scientia ista, nec fraude, aut astu, aut dolo ullo falli unquam possit: denique quia[c] sapientissime omnia ordinare, disponere, dirigere ac dispensare novit, ad reipsa perpetuo solet.

a. Job 42:2-3, Ps. 139, 147:5, Prov. 15:11, Is. 41:22-23.
b. Jer. 17:9-10; 1 Sam. 16:7, Ps. 10, 94:11, 1 Cor. 4:2, 5,

9. V. Liberrima voluntatis est,[a] qui nec intrinseca naturæ suæ necessitate, nec extrinsecâ ullis sive potentiæ vi, sive objecti efficacia determinatur ad volendum, aut nolendum, aut permittendum ea, quæ extra ipsum sunt, aut fiunt: sed pro liberrimo arbitrio suo, sive mero voluntatis suæ consilio, ac beneplacito, sese extendit ad ea omnia vel volendum, vel nolendum, vel permittendum. Et bona quidem omnia ita vult,[b] ut ea etiam approbet ac procuret: quædam etiam jubeat, suadeat, optet, desideret, & suo semper modo efficiat, Mala vero culpæ[c] sive peccata (id est, non tantum malitiam ipsam, sed actus etiam vitiosos, quatenus quidem iis necessario, vel per se vel posita lege, malitia sive culpa adhæret) revera non vult; sed odit, aversatur, prohibet, dissuadet, punit, & sæpe inhibet; nunquam vero efficit, vel procurant. Permittit hæc tamen volens, & permittere vult:[d] non quod ea fieri a nobis velit, aut ut fiant efficaciter ordinet, vel decernat; sed quia nostram in iis actionem progredi sinit, nec, ut potest, impedit: idque ne ordinem semel à se constitutum evertat, quam creaturæ dedit libertatem, ne destruat ac rescindat.

a. Ex. 33:19, Ps. 115:3, 135:6, Mat. 20:15, Rom. 9:15, 18.
b. Ps. 11:5, 7, 81:14, Is. 5:1-2, Mic. 6:7-8, 2 Cor. 5:20, Heb. 13:18.

10. VI. *Optimus* est[a], tum in se ipso, tum erga creaturas suas: quia modo per naturam summe perfectus eoque summe amabilis; sed etiam erga creaturas suas, licet inæqualiter, etiam interdum erga peccatores, admodum

present in memory, and sees whatever is done by us, correctly or otherwise, as if set before his eyes,[b] so that this knowledge cannot be erased either by ignorance or oblivion, nor fraud or trickery, nor any deceit or deception. Finally, he most wisely knows how to order, dispose, direct and manage all things, and so perpetually.[c]

    Heb. 4:13, 1 John 3:20.
c. Is. 40:13-14, Rom. 16:27, 1 Tim. 1:17.

9. 5. His will is completely free,[a] because he cannot be forced to will, reject or permit [anything] either by the inward necessity of his nature, nor by external power either of some force or the efficacy of an object which either are outside himself, or will be. But according to his most free judgment or the mere counsel of his will, or good pleasure, he extends himself either to will, reject or permit them all. And indeed everything good he so wills them that he also approves and seeks them. Some things also he commands, counsels, wishes, desires and always in his own way effects.[b] But he truly does not will evil things of guilt or sins (that is, not only the wickedness itself, but also vicious acts, so far indeed as wickedness or guilt necessarily adheres to them, either in themselves or established law), but hates, recoils, prohibits, dissuades, punishes and often inhibits them, but never causes or seeks them.[c] Yet he willingly permits them and wills to permit them, not because he wills them to be done by us or efficaciously ordains that they be done, but because he permits and does not hinder our actions to proceed as he might.[d] And [he does] this not to overthrow the order once constituted by himself, that he might neither destroy nor rescind the freedom he gave to his creature

c. Ps. 5:5-6, 11:5-6, Ex. 20:5, 34:7, Deut. 25:16, 28:65.
d. Ps. 81:13, Acts 24:2, 6.

10. 6. He is most good,[a] first in himself, then towards his creatures. Because he is not only completely perfect by nature, and so completely lovely, but he is also very kind and liberal toward his creatures,[b] although unequally, indeed

benignus ac liberalis est: erga fideles vero suos[b] maxime gratiosus, clemens, longanimis, ac misericors est; imo propensissime adfectus ad communicandum iis summum eternum que bonum, hoc, est, quo melius ullum, aut, majus, ab iisdem nec desiderari, nec haberi unquam potest.

a. Ps. 10:1-2, 25:8, 36:5, 103:8, 145:8-9, Joel 2:13.

11. VII. *Iustissimus & æquissimus* est,[a] & quidem justitiæ & æquitatis inflexibilis: non tantum quia in nobis id, quod rectum & æquum est, perpetuo amat, & iniquitatem omnem odio habet: quo etiam nomine *sanctus* in scriptura dicitur: sed etiam quia nemini ipse injuriam[b] unquam facit; inque omnibus operibus ac judiciis suis (inprimis autem in legibus ferendis, præmiis distribuendis, & pænis infligendis) rectitudinem & justitiam, qua suum cuique tribuitur, semper exactè servat & jus æquissimum exercet: denique quia in verbis suis *verax*,[c] *sincerus*, minimeque simulatus est, inque pactis suis ac promissis exsequendis summe *fidelis* ac *constans* est.

a. Gen. 18:23, Deut. 32:4, Ps. 11:5, 6:7, 145:17.
b. Ez. 18:23, 33:17, Matt. 20:13, 2 Thess. 1:5-7, Rev. 19:2.

12. VIII. *Omnipotens* est, sive potentiæ invictæ atque insuperabilis:[a] quia facere potest quidquid vult, invitiis licet omnibus a rebus creatis: imo plura semper potest, quam licet reipsa unquam vult: adeoque simpliciter omnia potest, quecunque contradictionem non involvunt, hoc est, quæ nec certæ rerum veritati, nec divinæ ipsius naturæ necessario ac per se repugnant.

a. Gen 17:1, 2 Chron. 20:6, Ps. 115:3, Mat. 19:26, Mark 14:36, Luke 1:37, Rev. 1:8, 4:8.

13. IX. Denique *beatismus* est, seu *felicisimus*, & quidem beatudines[a] perfectæ & incomprehensibilis: quia & naturam omnibus numeris absolutam, & majestatem summe gloriosam possidet, bonorumque omnium thesauris unde quaque adfluit: nec mali quicquam à quoquam sibi metuit, nec boni ullius extra se unquam indiget; sed de suo, prout placet, omnibus omnia largitur, quippe fons omnium bonorum primus, & semper inexhaustus.

sometimes also toward sinners. Toward his believers, he is truly most gracious, gentle, longsuffering, and merciful. Indeed, he is most eagerly disposed to communicate to them the highest and eternal good, of which there is nothing better or greater which can either be desired or had by them.

b. Rom. 2:4, Eph. 2:4, Ja. 1:17, 1 Tim. 2:4, 4:10.

11. 7. He is most just and impartial,[a] and indeed of inflexible justice and equity, not so much because he always loves that in us which is right and equal, and hates all iniquity. It is for this he is called "holy" in Scripture. But also because he never causes injury to any,[b] and in all his works and judgments (especially in making laws, distributing rewards and inflicting punishments) he always exactly preserves uprightness and justice, by which he gives every one his due, he exercises a most impartial justice.[c] Finally, because he is true, sincere and in no way deceiving in his words, and most faithful and constant in following his covenants and promises.

c. 1 Sam. 25:29, Rom. 3:4, 2 Tim. 4:8, 2:13, Tit. 1:2, Heb. 6:10, 1. John 1: 9.

12. 8. He is omnipotent, or of invincible and insuperable power,[a] because he can do whatever he wills, even though all creatures be unwilling. Indeed he can always do more than he really wills, and therefore he can simply do whatever does not involve contradiction, that is, which are not necessarily and of themselves repugnant to the truth of certain things, nor to his own divine nature.

13. 9. Finally, He is most blessed or happy, and indeed of perfect and incomprehensible blessedness,[a] because he possesses both a nature in all respects absolute and a majesty glorious in the highest degree and abounds with the treasures of all good. Neither does he fear any evil from anyone, nor require any good outside himself at any time, but bountifully grants of his own as he pleases, since he is the foremost and ever inexhaustible fountain of good.

a. Ps. 5:12, Mat. 11:25, Acts 17:24, 1 Tim. 6:15-16, Ja. 1.7, Acts 14:15-17.

14. Et tantum de *Attributis Dei essentialibus*, huic quidem pertinentibus: quæ omnia & singula scitu utilissima, imó & necessaria hactenus esse credimus, quatenus sine horum notitia Deum recte colere non possumus; per eam vero possumus. Nam quia Deus unus est, æquum omnino ac necessarium nobis est, ut ut ab eo uno[a] & solo, tanquam primo salutis nostræ authore, toti anima & corpore pendeamus, inque eum unum vicissum universus noster cultus terminetur & desinat.

a. Deut. 6:4, Matt. 4:10, 1 Cor. 8:5-6.

15. Quia *irrefragabilis potestatis & summa authoritatis* est, ut ei, quicunque & ubicunque tandem simus, veluti Regi Regum[a] ac domino dominantium, nulli uspiam jurato, neque cuiquam obnoxio, in omnibus humillime nos submittamus: pro beneficijs[b] nobis aliisque necessariis, aut certe utilibus, ipsum indesinenter oremus, pro acceptis gratias ei agamus: adversa etiam omnia, quæcunque immittit, patienter & quod animo fereamus, fecundis autem nunquam abitamur, aut insolescamus.

a. Gen 13:27, 2 Sam. 15:25-26, Lam. 3:25-26.

16. Quia *æternus, & imutabilis est*,[a] ut æternæ vitæ præmium, ab eo gratiose nobis in Christo promissum, certa fide expectare ac firmiter sperare audeamus; idque nullo unquam tempore aut ab ipso immutatum, aut per alios nobis eruptum iri, certo credamus.

a. Rom. 16:25-26, Tit. 1:2, Ja. 1:17-18.

17. Quia *immensus omnipræsens* est, ut ubique locorum circumspectè reverenter & sollicite, veluti in[a] conspectu ejus, ambulemus; preces etiam & supplicationes nostras, cum omni humilitate & submissione, certaque exauditionis fiducia, semper ad ipsum fundamus; nihilque nisi serium, grave, ac tanti Numinis præsentia dignum, unquam cogitemus, loquamur aut faciamus.

a. Ps. 139:7-8, Amos 9:2, Mat. 6:1-2.

14. And so [we conclude with] what pertains to the essential attributes of God, about which the knowledge of each and every one we believe to be most useful, and indeed to this extent necessary, insomuch that without their knowledge we cannot correctly worship God, but by it we may. For because God is one,[a] it is entirely just and necessary for us, that in every way we depend upon him alone with soul and body as the foremost author of our salvation, and again likewise, that our entire worship terminate and stop in him alone.

15. Because he is of irresistible power and supreme authority, let us submit ourselves to him in all humility as to the King of kings and Lord of lords,[a] whoever or wherever we are, sworn nowhere to anyone, nor subject to any. Let us pray continually to him for his benefits and other necessities,[b] or certain things useful for us. Let us give him thanks for things received, also patiently bear with a quiet mind all adversity whatever he sends, and never abuse our prosperity nor grow proud.

b. Phil. 4:6, Ja. 5:1-2, 1 Pet. 3:17.

16. Because he is eternal and immutable,[a] with resolved faith let us dare to expect and firmly hope for the prize of eternal life, graciously promised to us by him in Christ, and certainly believe that he will never at any time either overthrow it himself, nor [allow it] to be violently taken from us by others.

17. Because he is immense and omnipresent, let us everywhere walk circumspectly, reverently, and carefully, as in his sight.[a] Let us always pour out to him our prayers and supplications, with all humility and submission, and a firm confidence of being heard. Let us not think, speak or do anything unless it is serious, grave and worthy of the presence of so great a deity.

18. Quia *scientiæ infallibilis* est, ut coram eo integrè ac sincere viviamus ac provide ambulemus; cogitationes,[a] sermones, & actiones nostras ei semper probare studeamus; causam nostram bonam ei perpetuo commendemus; preces nostras, gemitus ac suspiria nostra ei fidenter offeramus; & nos denique nostraque omnia, semper ei curæ esse, persuasissimum habeamus.

a. Ps. 34:16-17, 94:7-8, Mat. 6:4, 6, 18, Rom. 8:17, Heb. 4:11-13, 1 Pet. 3:12.

19. Quia *liberrimæ potestatis ac voluntatis* est,[a] ut quæcunque habemus, sive cum aliis communia, sive præ aliis hominibus aut populis peculiaria bona, (quâ corporalia, quâ spiritualia) ipsius unius spontaneæ liberalitati, ac liberrimæ munificentiæ, accepta feramus: gratiam & favorem ejus sedulo & serio semper ambiamus, ac sollicitè retinere studeamus: pœnas contra ac minas ejus humiliter deprecemur: & quacunque vel ipse facit,[b] vel ab aliis fieri sinit, vel denique a nobis fieri vult, ea ex sensu nostro proprio ne metiamur, sed, ut ab optimo simul & liberrimo ipsius arbitrio profecta, religiose semper adoremus.

a. Gen. 32:10, Deut. 4:4-5, 7:6-7, Ps. 18:1-2, 116:12, 1 Cor. 4:7.

20. Quia *optimas, & beneficus* est,[a] ut eum toto corde, tota anima, & viribus omnibus amemus & diligamus; ejus promissis animose fidamus, gratiam & misericordiam fidenter imploremus, ipsiusque benignissimæ voluntati lubenter & alacriter, etiam sub cruce, nos conformemus, eique semper & ubique paræmus.

a. Deut. 32:6-7, Ps. 18:1, 145, 2 Cor. 1:3-4.

21. Quia *æquitatis* &[a] *justitia,* itemque veritatis inflexibilis est, ut contra præcipientem, tentantem, visitantem, punientem, mala permittentem &c. nunquam murmuremus: & de promissis, ac commintionibus, aliisque adsertionibus ejus, nullo unquam tempore dubitemus. Et quia summe sanctus est, ut[b] nos quoque serio sanctimoniæ studio ipsum imitemur.

a. Ps. 36:6-7, 73:2, Rom. 9:14, 11:33.

18. Because he is of infallible knowledge, let us live blamelessly and sincerely and walk prudently before him.[a] Let us desire to test our thoughts, words and actions by him. Let us continually commend our good cause to him. With confidence, let us offer our prayers, groans and sighs to him. And finally, let us be thoroughly persuaded that he always cares for us and all our concerns.

19. Because he is of most free power and will,[a] whatever good things we have, either in common with others or in private before other men or people (physical or spiritual) let us attribute it to his alone spontaneous liberality and most free generosity. Let us always diligently and seriously seek his grace and favor and carefully seek to retain the same. Let us humbly intercede against his punishments and threats and not judge by our own perceptions whatever he either does himself,[b] or permits to be done by others, or wills to be done by us, but let us always religiously respect it as proceeding from his best and most free will.

b. Rom. 9:18, 11:33, Job. 1, 2, throughout.

20. Because he is the best and most generous,[a] let us love and delight in him with all our heart, soul, and all strength. Let us boldly confide in his promises and confidently implore his grace and mercy. Let us willingly and eagerly conform ourselves to his most kind will, even under the cross, and always and everywhere obey him.

21. Because of his unbending fairness and justice,[a] and also truth, let us never murmur against his commands, trials, visits, punishments, permitting of evils, etc., and let us never at any time doubt concerning his promises and threats and his other sayings. And because he is most holy let us also imitate him in a serious pursuit and exercise of holiness.[b]

b. Lev. 19:2, 20:7, 1 Pet. 1:15-16.

22. Quia *potentia insuperabilis* est, ut timeamus illum, qui corpus & animam[a] in gehennam mittere potest, iramque ejus terribilem reformidemus: & mala quidem, quæ comminatur, ferio metuamus; bona vero, quæ promittit, firma & indubitata fide exspectemus; denique[b] nec diaboli, nec mortis, nec inferni, nec tyrannorum, nec aliorum ullorum hostium vim ac potentiam, quamdiu Christo servimus, nimium pertimescamus: aut in gratiam illorum quicquam indignum Christi nomine unquam committamus.

a. Matt. 10:28, Deut. 32:39, Jer. 5:12, Job. 40:1.

23. Quia *beatissimus* & quidem perfectæ beatitudinis ac gloriosæ majestatis est, ut ad gloriam gaudiumque ipsius, pro modulo nostro participandum, sedulo adspiremus; eoque perfectè uniri cum ipso post hanc vitam, ipsum que coram videre, & plenitudine domus ipsius, bonorumque omnium cælestium, beari ac satiari desideremus: istoque desiderio ac spe inconcussa fulti, sincerè omnia faciamus, quæ nobis mandat; studiose fugiamus, quæ vetat; fortiter denique feramus, quæcunque ferre nos vult; etiamsi acerbissimæ ac ignominiosissimæ mortis supplicia pro ipsius nomine perferenda forent. Atque hæc de natura Dei communiter & absolute considerata.

22. Because he is of insuperable power, let us fear him who is able to cast body and soul into Gehenna,[a] and let us dread his terrible wrath, and let us seriously fear the evils indeed which he threatens. Let us look for the good things which he promises, with a firm and undoubting faith. Finally, so long as we serve Christ,[b] let us not greatly fear the force and power either of the devil, or death, or hell, or tyrants, or any other enemies, nor for their sakes ever commit anything unworthy of the name of Christ.

b. Ps. 2:3, 27, 46, John 10:29, Rom. 8:31.

23. Because he is most blessed, and indeed of perfect blessedness and glorious majesty, let us carefully aspire to participattion in his glory and joy according to our measure, and therefore desire to be perfectly united with him after this life, to see him face to face, and let us desire to be blessed and satisfied with the fullness of his house and of all the goodness of heaven, and being supported with this desire and unshaken hope, let us sincerely do all that he commands. Let us carefully flee those things which he forbids. Lastly, let us bear with courage whatever he will have us bear, even if they be the most bitter distresses and most shameful deaths borne for his name. And thus the nature of God has been considered commonly and absolutely.

• CHAPTER 3 •

CAPUT III:
De S. S. Trinitate.

1. Cæterum *distinctè ac relatè* consideratur Deus sub trina[a] hypostasi, sive tribus personis: sub quibus videlicet ipse Deitatem suam, œconomice nobis atque ad seipsam respective

CHAPTER 3
On the holy and sacred trinity.

1. But God is considered distinctly and relatively under a three-fold hypostasis,[a] or under three persons, under which indeed he himself has made known his own deity in his Word, to be

meditandam, in verbo suo patesecit. Esique hæc Trinitas *Pater*,[b] *Filius*, & *Spiritus S.* prout Deitatis hypostasis alia prorsus ἀναίτια, hoc est, improducta & ingenita est: alia vero per generationem a Patre producta, sive Patris unigenita: alia denique à Patre & Filio peculiariter procedit, sive a Patre per filium emanat.

a. Matt. 28:19, John 14:16, 26, 15:26, 1 Cor. 12:4-6, 2 Cor. 13:14.

2. Est enim *solus Pater* originis omnis expers, seu prorsus ingenitus, &[a] nullo alio procedens: sed qui Deitatem tamen suam, tum[b] *Filio unigenito*, non quidem per creationem[c] (cujus respectu angeli dicuntur filii Dei) neque per gratiosam[d] adoptionem (per quam nos fideles etiam sumus filii Dei) neque per solam divinæ potestatis, ac gloriæ supremæ, qua Mediator est,[e] gratiosam communicationem; sed etiam per veram, attamen arcanam & ineffabilem,[f] generationem; tum etiam *Spiritui Sancto*, ad utroque precedenti,[g] per similiter arcanam emanationem, sive spirationem, ab æterno communicavit: eoque Pater fons & origo totis Deitatis optimo jure cesentur.

a. 1 Cor. 8:6, Eph. 4:6.
b. John 1:18, 3:16, Rom. 8:32.
c. Job 1:6, 2:1, 38:7.
d. John 1:11-12, Gal. 3:26.

3. *Filiius* ergo & *Spiritus Sanctus*, licet quoad & hypostasin & modum ordinem que habendi deitatem, à Patre vere distincti; ejusdem tamen cum Patre Deitatis, seu divinæ essentiæ ac naturæ absolute ac communiter consideratæ, vere consortes sunt: prout inter alia maximè probatur ex divinis[a] nominibus, seu titulis;[b] item, ex divinis proprietatibus, & operationibus, quæ utrique in sacris literis apertè passim tribuuntur. Atque huc redit summa totis symboli Apostolici, in quo profitemur, nos credere in unum Deum Patrem omnipotentem &c. Et in Filium ejus unigenitum &c. & denique in Spiritum Sanctum.

a. John 1:1-2, 20:28, Rom. 9:5, Col. 1:15, Heb. 1:2, Rev. 1-4.

considered by us economically and with respect to itself. And this trinity is the Father, Son, and Holy Spirit.[b] One hypostasis of the deity is ἀναίτια, that is, unproduced and unbegotten. _nother is produced of the Father by generation, or the only begotten of the Father. Finally, another in a peculiar manner proceeds from the Father and the Son, or emanates from the Father by the Son.

b. 1 John 5:7.

2. For the Father alone is void of all origin, or entirely unbegotten and proceeding from no other,[a] but who nevertheless has from eternity communicated his own deity, whether to his only begotten Son,[b] indeed not by creation[c] (respecting which the angels are called the sons of God) nor by gracious adoption[d] (by which we believers are also the sons of God) nor only by the gracious communication of divine power (or authority) and supreme glory, by which he is the mediator,[e] but also by a true yet secret and ineffable generation;[f] and also to the Holy Spirit, proceeding from both by a mysterious emanation or spiration.[g] And so the Father is most justly considered the fountain and origin of the whole deity.

e. John 3:35, 5:22.
f. Ps. 2:7, Heb. 1:2, John 1:18.
g. John 15:26, Gal. 4:6, 1 Cor. 2:11-12.

3. Therefore, the Son and the Holy Spirit, although both are divine with respect to their hypostasis, manner, and order, are truly distinct from the Father; yet they are truly partakers with the Father of the same deity or divine essence and nature absolutely and commonly considered, just as is certainly proved from the divine names[a] or titles,[b] likewise from the divine properties and operations which are clearly attributed to them both throughout the Sacred Scriptures, among other things. And here is the sum total of the Apostles Creed, by which we profess that "we believe in one God the Father Almighty," etc. "And in his only begotten Son," etc. And lastly, "in the Holy Spirit."

b. Is. 11:1, 63:10, 1 Cor. 2:10, 3:16, 6:19-20, 12:4, 11, Acts

4. Atque hæc de isto etiam mysterio satis: quod quidem admodum sobriè, prudenter, ac religiose tractare, omnino necessarium; & quantum fieri potest, propriis & expressis Spiritus S. phrasibus enunciare, quam tutissimum arbitramur: quum ipse Dei Spiritus, sese quam[a] optime noverit, & quam rectissime naturam suam exprimere potuerit, imo etiam quantum necesse ac fatis est, exprimere nobis in suo verbo voluerit: quem tantisper reverenter, & cum summa religione, nos sequi decet, donec Deum ispum aliquando coram[b] videamus, & perfectè cognoscamus: prout ipse scilicet clarissime se videndum, ac cognoscendum, nobis in glorioso illo seculo futuro dabit. Et hactenus quidem de ipso Deo.

a. 1 Cor. 2:10, John 1:18, Matt. 11:27.

4. And these are sufficient for this mystery, which indeed is completely necessary to treat soberly, prudently and religiously, and as far as possible, to enunciate the same in the proper and express phrases of the Holy Spirit, which we judge to be most safe,[a] since the Spirit of God himself best knows and is most correctly able to express his own nature. Indeed, as far as is necessary and sufficient, he willed to express [it] to us in his word, whom it is fitting reverently and most religiously to follow for the present, until we see God himself in person, and know him perfectly.[b] Then indeed, in that glorious world, he will grant that he may be most clearly known by us. And thus far indeed [is sufficient] regarding God himself.

b. 1 John 3:2, 1 Cor. 13:12.

• CHAPTER 4 •

CAPUT IV.
De Cognitione Operum divinorum.

1. Secundo loco consideranda veniunt *Opera Dei*, per quæ gloriam ipse suam patefacit, & bona quædam sua nobiscum communicat, seseque aliquatenus cognoscendum nobis exhibet: quæque proinde fundamentum quoddam sunt, cui superstruitur jus & authoritas Dei,[a] ex qua justè postulare à nobis potest & solet cultum, quem & qualem vult: item justitia atque æquitas, secundum quam nos obligamur, talem ex esse cultum ei deserre,[b] qualem ipse exigit pro jure suo.

a. Exos. 20, Deut. 32:6, Ps. 136, Acts17:24, Rev. 4:11.

2. Hujusmodi opera dupliciter[a] consideranda veniunt. I. quatenus ante secula, seu jacta mundi fundamenta, divinitus præscita & præordinata

Chapter 4
On the knowledge of the works of God.

1. In the second place we come to consider the works of God by which he revealed his own glory and communicates what is good to us, and to some degree exhibits himself to be known to us. Consequently these are a certain foundation built upon the right and authority of God[a] by which he can, and usually does, justly impose our worship, what and how he pleases; likewise justice and equity, by which we are obliged to yield to him wholly and entirely such worship as he himself demands according to his right.[b]

b. Mal. 1:6, 2:10.

2. These works come under a twofold manner of consideration:[a] 1. as they were foreknown and foreordained by the deity before the ages, or before the

sunt, quæ uno nomine *decreta* vocari solent, 2. quatenus in tempore manifestantur, seu juxta modum, & ordinem, jam olim in decreto illo divino (seu generali, seu speciali, seu absoluto, seu conditionato) sapientissime constitutum, *exsecutioni* mandantur. Ex hac autem *exsecutione*,[b] ejusque ratione & modo, judicium faciendum est de decretus ipsis, Talia enim omnino sunt decreta, qualis est eorundem exsecutio: neque citra notam inconstantiæ fieri potest, ut exsecutio decreto non respondeat, nedum ut decreto repugnet, aut contraveniat.

a. Acts 15:18, Eph. 1:4, 1 Cor. 2:7, 2 Tim. 1:9, 1 Pet. 1:20.

3. Opera ejusmodi exsecutionis, principalia quidem, *duo* sunt: puta opus creationis,[a] cum homo nondum esset: & *Recreationis*, sive *Redemptionis*,[b] cum homo jam lapsus, & per peccatum morti atque condemnationi æternæ, cum posteris suis omnibus, obnoxius factus esset, Utrique operi adhæret continua Dei providentia,[c] seu rerum conservatio, & gubernatio; eaque naturis & proprietatibus rerum creatarum (nisi cum extra ordinem quid fi, uti in miraculis &c.) semper accommodata.

a. Gen. 1.
b. 2 Cor. 5:17.

foundations of the world were laid, which are customarily in one word called "decrees;" 2. as far as they are manifested in time, or their most wisely established mode and order, now long since commissioned by that divine decree (whether general or special, whether absolute or conditional). The decrees themselves must be judged from this execution and its method and manner.[b] For the decrees are entirely such as their execution, nor could the execution not correspond to the decree without a mark of inconsistency, much more that it should fight or oppose the decree.

b. Ps. 33:11, Is. 14:26-27, 46:10, Jer. 18:7.

3. There are two principal [works] of this execution, namely, the work of creation,[a] when man did not yet exist, and of re-creation or redemption,[b] when through sin man was made liable to death and eternal condemnation, together with all his descendants. The continual providence of God,[c] or his preservation and control of all things, adheres to both these works and is always appropriate for the natures and properties of created things (unless something should happen out of the ordinary, such as miracles, etc).

c. Eph. 1:10, Col. 1, Ps. 104.

• CHAPTER 5 •

CAPUT V.
De Creatione Mundi, Angelorum,
& Hominum.

I. Creatio mundo est prima[a] & potentissima rerum omnium è nihilo facta productio: nempe primæva illa formatio cœli, terræ, maris, & omnium, quæ in iis sunt, spatio sex dierum perfecta: de qua etiam in Symbolo Apostolico mentio sit, cum dicimus, *credo in Deum Patrem*

CHAPTER 5.
On the creation of
the world, angels and men.

1. The creation of the world is the initial and most powerful production of all things made from nothing,[a] namely, the primeval, perfect formation of heaven, earth, sea and all things which are in them in the space of six days, which is also mentioned in the Apostles Creed when we say, "I believe in God

omnipotentem, creatorem cœli & terra.

a. Gen. 1, Ex. 20:11, Is. 40:12, Ps. 104, 136, Acts 17:24, Rev. 4:11.

2. Inter creaturas maxime excellentunt, Angeli[a] & Homines: illi cœlorum, hi terræ incolæ: illi invisibiles, hi visibiles Angelis sunt ministratorii Spiritus,[b] in cœlis supramundanis ordanirie degentes, ibique coram Deo, veluti apparitores, sive famuli & nuncii adsistentes: tum ad laudes ipsius assidue prædicandum, tum ad jussa ejusdem in toto mundo vel annunciandum, vel etiam potenter exsequendum.

a. Col. 1:16.

3. De horum essentia, ordinibus, gradibus, numero &c. multa subtiliter extra Scripturas definire, nec necessaruim, nec utile, imo periculosum arbitramur. Sufficit autem nobis, ut, quod de iis Scripturæ clare asserunt, pie credamus. Quod videlicet eorum alii originem seu principatum suum retinentes, Deo creatori Domino suo constantes adhæserint, qui idcirco[a] Sancti, electi & lucis Angeli dicuntur: variis quidem ordinibus, in thronos, potestates, dominationes &c. distincti; sed quos nemo hominum in hac mortalitate, facile definiverit. Alii,[b] contra Deuam peccantes, in veritate non perstiterint: sed originem primævam ac domicilium officiumque suum jam olim deseruetint sideoque de cœlo beatorum in tartarum detrusi, & catenis tenebrarum vincti, passim in hoc inferiore mundo sub[c] principe suo (qui serpens ille antiquus, draco magnus, item Deus & princepshujus seculi, tentator ille, diabolus & satanas appelolatur) per aerem vagantur: malique dæmones & spiritus impuri, suam ipsorum culpa facti, gloriæ Dei & saluti piorum semper & ubique adversantur: in impiis vero, & contumaciter divinæ voluntati auscultare nolentibus,[d] potenter per seductiones, sive errores, perque scelera, flagitia cupiditates mundanas, variasque artes, fraudes, vim, idolatriam, tyrannidem, aliaque mundi propria opera, domminantur & regnat: omnes olim una cum impiis hominibus, in[e] ignem æternum præcipitandi.

the Father Almighty, Creator of Heaven and Earth."

2. Among the creatures, angels and men are the most excellent,[a] the first of the heavens, the second of the Earth, the first invisible, the second visible. The angels are ministering spirits,[b] ordinarily dwelling in the heavens beyond the world, and standing there before God as officers or servants and messengers, first to proclaim continually his praises and then either to announce or powerfully execute his orders throughout the whole world.

b. Heb. 1:14, Dan. 7:9-10, Rev. 5:11, Mat. 18:10, Ps. 103:20-21, 104:4.

3. But we judge that it is neither necessary nor useful and even dangerous to go beyond the Scriptures to define minutely their essence, orders, degrees, number and many other things. It is sufficient for us that we piously believe what the Scriptures clearly assert about them. Evidently some of them, retaining their principality and steadfastly clinging to God their Lord Creator, are called holy, elect and angels of light, distinguished indeed by various orders into thrones, powers, dominions, etc., but which no man in this mortality can easily determine.[a] Others,[b] sinning against God, did not persist in the truth, but now long ago deserted their original, primeval estate, home and duty, and having been pulled down from the heaven of the blessed to Tartaros and bound under chains of darkness, they wander in the air throughout that lower world under their prince[c] (who is called that old Serpent, the great dragon, also the god and prince of the world, the tempter, devil and Satan).[b] By their own fault they are evil demons and impure spirits, everywhere adversaries to the glory of God, and the salvation of the godly. But they powerfully dominate and reign over the wicked and those who stubbornly refuse to obey the divine will through seductions or errors[d] and through wickednesses, shameful acts, worldly lusts and various tricks, deceits, power, idolatry, tyranny and other works proper to the world. In the future, all [these], together with ungodly men, will be cast into eternal fire.[e]

a. Mat. 25:31, 1 Tim. 5:21, 2 Cor. 11:14, Col. 1:16, 1 Pet. 3:22.
b. 2 Pet. 2:4, Jude 4, John 8:44.
c. Eph. 2:2, 6:12, Rev. 12:9, 1 Thess. 1:5, 2 Thess. 2:9.
d. 2 Cor. 4:4, 11:3, John 1:6, 2:1, Acts 5:3, 16:16, 19:12, 15, 1 Pet. 5:8, 1 Ki. 22:21.
e. Mat. 25:41, Rev. 20:10.

4. Homines initio tantum duos condidit Deus,[a] virum & fœminam: ac corpus quidem viri ex terra, fœminæ autem ex costa viri formavit: & utrumque spiritu rationali & immortali[b] donavit; imo ad *imaginem*[c] & *similitudinem* suam creavit; inque hoc mundo, velut regno pulcherrima, in gratiam ipsorum adornato; quinimo in mundi ipsius amœnissimo *paradiso*, veluti palatio quodam augusto, ut cæterarum creatarum rerum Dominos, Principesque collocavit, ac constituit.

4. In the beginning, God made two people, a man and a woman,[a] and he formed the body of the man from earth, but [that] of the woman from a rib of the man, and gave to them both a rational and immortal spirit.[b] Indeed, he created them in his own image and likeness[c] and placed them in this world, adorned like a most beautiful kingdom for them, even more, in the most pleasant paradise of this world, just as in some majestic palace, and appointed them as lords and princes over the other created things.

a. Gen. 1:26-27, 2:7.
b. Eccl. 12:7, Mat. 10:28.

c. Gen. 1:26, 9:6, Ja. 3:9, Ps. 8.

5. Intellectu vero etiam puro, animoque recto, &[a] libera voluntate, aliisque affectibus integris, ornavit eos Deus: quin & necessaria in isto statu sapientia, integritate, gratiaque varia, sufficientes instruxit, non solum ut glorioso in cæteras creaturas imperio, ac dominio recte uti scirent;[b] sed ut Dei etiam Creatoris sui erga se voluntatem imprimis recte intelligerent, suamque propriam voluntatem (qua alioqui libere non tantum cæteris creaturis, sed etiam propiis suis actionibus imperabant) Deo, utpote supremo suo Domino & legislatori, ultro subjicerent: eique constanter obediendo, non hic tantum ex voto viverent, sed & olim perpetua felicitate bearentur.

5. God also truly adorned them with unclouded understanding, an upright mind, a free will and other sound affections.[a] In fact in that state he sufficiently provided wisdom, integrity and a diversity of grace, not only that they might know correctly to use their glorious authority and dominion over the other creatures, but also that they could, above all, correctly understand the will of God their creator towards themselves and freely subject their own will (by which they would freely rule not just over the other creatures but over their own proper actions) to God as their supreme Lord and Legislator; and by constant obedience they would live not only as they wished but also in the future be blessed with perpetual happiness.[b]

a. Eccl. 7:29, Ecclesiasticus 15:24.

b. Chapters 2 & 3.

6. Quare opus hoc creationis eo potissimum pertinet, ut intelligat homo,[a] se, quicquid boni habet, id Deo omne in solidum debere; eique totum, si postulet, reddere ac consecrare teneri; denique ad gratias illi perpetuo agendas, summo jure obligatum esse, Qui[b] enim nihil boni habet à seipso, omnia debet ei, à quo habet, quicquid habet: eoque in hoc solo,[c] non in seipso gloriari perpetuo debet.

6. Thus this work of creation principally leads man to understand that whatever good he has,[a] he owes all solidly to God and that he is obligated, if he require, to render and consecrate the same wholly to him. Finally, he is obliged by highest right always to give thanks to him. For he who has nothing good of himself owes all to him from whom he has whatever he has, and he ought to glory in him alone and not in himself.[b]

a. Ps. 8, 104, 136, 145, Acts 14:15, 17:24.

b. Rev. 4:11, 14:17.

7. Qui vero huic operi præmittunt, non modo absolutam quorundam singularium hominum

7. But those who truly advance not only the absolute election of certain individual men to

electionem ad æternam salutem,[a] sed & similem aliorum plerorumque reprobationem ad æternos cruciatus: & quidem utramque peremptoriam, ac de singulis nominatim ab omni æternitate factam: ij non modo naturalem rerum ordinem invertunt, sed & verum creationis usum abnegant, & nativam ec opere hoc resultantem vim, obligandi scilicet hominem ab obendiendum Deo in omnibus, planè tollunt. Neque enim Deus jure postulare potest, ut homo seipsum exercitio suæ libertatis, quam per creationem acceperat, totum exuat, voluptatumque variarum usufructu privet, alteruisque voluntati, cum maximo suo labore ac molestia, per omnia subjiciat: si jam antea ei destinavit, nulla ipsius præeunte culpa, malum multo majus graviusque infligere, quam bonum illud est, quod per creationem eidem dedit: imo si idcirco ei bonum illud temporale ac leve per creationem impertivit, ut æternum vereque lamentabile malum, antea ipsi præcise destinatum, infligere aliquo prætextu eidem posset, Neque jam ullo jure tenetur homo ad obediendum ei, qui ipsum antequem inobediens esset, imo antequam obedire posset, fataliter ad æternum hoc malum destinavit. Accedit, quod auctores hujus sententiæ, Deum non tantum insipientem faciunt, qui nempe destinet eum, qui nondum est, (imo de cujus existentia nihildum decretum est) ad vitam, aut mortem eternam; sed etiam injustissimum, adeoque verum ac proprium peccari auctorem. Etenim si Deus creaturam innoxiam, ut illi volunt, prædestinavit ad æternum, vereque horrendum, exitium; necessum utique est, ut destinaverit eandem ad ipsum quoque peccatum:[b] quia ubi peccatum, vel transgressio non est, ibi locum habere non potest justa pœna, seu pœnalis perditio; eoque nec justa destinatio ad ullam pœnam, neum ad sempiternos cruciatus, ac perpetua & nunquam finienda lamenta. Itaque juxta[c] istos etiam Deus propriissimè, & ex prima intentione sua, peccati verissima caussa erit, quippe caussa unica destinationis ad exitium simul & peccatum. Neque jam homo juste ob tale peccatum poterit puniri, ad quod præcise divinitus est destinatus, eoque ad quod

eternal salvation[a] but also the reprobation of the greatest part of all others to eternal tortures, and both indeed peremptory, and did so concerning every individual person by name from all eternity, they not only invert the natural order of things but also deny the true use of creation and plainly take away the native ability resulting from this work, namely, of obligating man to obey God in all things. For God cannot demand that a man should wholly divest himself of the exercise of his liberty which he received by creation and deprive himself of the use of various pleasures, and in all things subject himself with the greatest labor and trouble, if he already, now before-hand, for no preceding guilt of his own, determined to inflict upon him a much greater and more grievous evil than the good which he gave him through creation, nor indeed, if he bestowed on him that temporal and lighter good in order that he might, under some pretence, inflict an eternal and truly lamentable evil absolutely destined to him before. And neither is a man now justly held to obeying him who before he was disobedient, indeed before he was able to obey, fatally destined him to this eternal evil. In addition, not only do the authors of this opinion make God foolish but also most unjust, who certainly destines him who does not yet exist (especially of one whose being is nothing but decreed) to eternal life or death, and consequently the true and proper author of sin. For if God, as they like to say, has predestinated his innocent creature to an eternal and truly horrendous destruction, it is also necessary that he destined him also to sin, because where there is no sin or transgression there can be no place for punishment or penal perdition,[b] nor a just destination or appointment to any punishment, much less to eternal torments and eternal, endless weeping. Therefore, according to them, even God himself most properly, and from his first intention, will be the truest cause of sin, for he is the sole cause of destination both for destruction and sin.[c] Nor can a man now be justly punished for such a sin to which he was absolutely divinely destined, and consequently to which, in the end, he was compelled by that most powerful will or decree and ordination of God.

potentissima Dei voluntate seu decreto ac ordinatione tandem est compulsus.

a. See Calvin's *Institutes*, 1.3.20-23.
b. Gen. 18:23-25, Ez. 18:4, Is. 50:1, 59:2, Rom. 3:5-6.
c. See Calvin on the said places.

• CHAPTER 6 •

CAPUT VI.
De Providentia Dei, seu rerum conservatione & gubernatione.

Creationem excipit immediate *actualis Dei providentia:* quæ interim se extendit etiam ad opus *Redemptionis*, ad omniaque tum secula, tum opera & res, quæ in mundo sunt aut fiunt. Est enim hæc aliud nihil,[a] quam seria & continua totius hujus universi, atque imprimis hominis (cujus bono, ad Dei gloriam, omnia condita sunt) inspectio, cura & regimen: seu conservatio & sustentatio omnium creaturarum, puta rerum simul & personarum: itemque gubernatio & directio actionum nostrarum, & eventorum omnium (sive bona, sive mala sint) quæ ipsis creaturis, imprimis autem homini, sed maximè pio, in tempore quoquo modo accidunt: & quidem instituta secundum exactissimam normam sapientiæ, justitiæ, & æquitatis divinæ.

a. Ps. 36:6-7, 94:7, 104, 105, 106, 107, Prov. 16:7, 9, 33, Is. 45:6, Amos 2:6.

2. Est igitur hæc partim *generalis*,[a] quoad omnes creaturas, partim *specialis*,[b] quoad Angelos & homines: maxime certo quoad pios & sanctos. *Generali* providentia curat & regit Deus omnia, quæcunque uspiam sunt:[c] dispari tamen modo & gradibus actionum diversis, idque pro suo unius æterno beneplacito ac verè admiranda sapientia. Neque enim conservat tantum eorum naturas, seu proprietates ac vires; sed iis etiam utitur pro arbitrio suo, sive in bonum, sive in pœnam hominis; communicando cilicet

CHAPTER 6.
On the providence of God, or his preservation and government of things.

1. Creation is immediately followed by the actual providence of God, which in the interim also extends itself to the work of redemption, first to all ages, then the works and things which are or will be in this world.[a] For this is nothing else than a serious and continual inspection, care and control of the entire universe, but especially of man (for whose good, to the glory of God, all things were composed), or the preservation and sustenance of all creatures, namely, of things and persons, likewise the governing and directing of our actions and of all events (whether they be good or evil) which happen in time by whatever manner to his creatures, but especially to men and most of all to the godly. And this was instituted according to the most exact rule of divine wisdom, justice and equality.

2. This therefore is partly general[a] with respect to all creatures, partly special[b] with respect to angels and men, but most certainly with respect to godly and holy people. By his general providence God cares for and rules all things, whoever and wherever they are, but in different ways and various degrees of action, and that for his own eternal good pleasure and truly admirable wisdom.[c] For he not only conserves their natures or properties and powers, but also uses them according to his will, either for the good or

eas, aut negando, auferendo, transferendo, concitando, sistendo, reprimendo, dirigendo, multiplicando, imminuendo, intendendo, remittendo, &c. prout vel bonitas, vel gratia seu misericordia & longanimitas; vel contra vindicta, seu ira & severitas Dei postulare videtur. *Specialis* Dei Providentia circa *Angelos*,[d] quatenus nobis quidem in Scripturis patefacta est, jam ante in creatione ipsorum satis indicata fuit. Utitur enim Deus illorum operâ, tum ad gloriam suam manifestandum, tum ad omnes mundi partes gubernandum; & speciatum eximia eorundem, tum sapientia, tum potentia, tum celeritate, tum numero, seu multitudine &c. nempe ut homines doceant, curent, observent, custodiant, solentur, aut etiam puniant, prout ipse sibi gloriosum, & suis salutare arbitratus. Circa *homines* autem, sive potius hominum liberas & imprimis religiosas operationes, variis modis versatur. Nam *primo* libertatem voluntatis ipsorum limitat & circumscribit, per legislationem:[e] ut non possit homo aut velle, aut facere, sine peccato, quicquid vult: imò hoc potissimum fine, ut non nisi recta ille & justa velit ac faciat: utque ita, velut imago viva, reflectatur in Creatorem suum, ipsique semper ultro subjectus maneat. *Deinde*[f] ut obedientiam illam homo libenter & alicriter præstet, legem, quam ei fert Deus, promissis & minis illustribus sancit: utque illam magis ac melius eliciat ac procuret, variis suasionibus, hortationibus, precibus, signis, prodigiis &c. circa hominem occupatur: eumque semper incitat, exstimulat, adjuvat, & corroborat; quantum quidem satis est, ut homo reipsa ei obediat, & ad finem usque in obedientia perseveret. Tertio[g] obedientiam ipsius, actionesque ex obedientia præstitas cum singulari cura, observat, approbat, iis delectatur, utque promissa gratiosa remuneratione dignas, fideli semper memoria tenet, atque ut tales ante oculos continuo positas habet.

a. Mat. 6:26, 10:29-30.
b. 1 Cor. 9:9, 1 Tim. 4:10.
c. Psal. 10 & 12.
d. Gen. 28:12, 32:1-2, 48:16, Ex. 14:19, 23:20-21, P. 91:12, 2 Ki. 16, 17, & 19.35, Is. 6:3-4, 37:36, Mark 18:20, Luke 22:43, Heb. 1:14.

punishment of man, especially seen by God denying, removing, transferring, agitating, stopping, repressing, controlling, multiplying, lessening, stretching, or remitting them, etc., either as [an act of] goodness or grace or mercy and longsuffering, or to the contrary, by his revenge or wrath and severity. The special providence of God about angels, so far indeed as is revealed to us in the Scriptures, was already sufficiently shown concerning their creation.[d] For God uses their service first to manifest his own glory, then to govern all parts of the world; and their excellent wisdom, power, swiftness, number or multitude, etc., certainly that they might instruct, attend, observe, guard [and] console men, or even also to punish them as he judges it by his own glory, or the salvation of his people. Concerning men, however, or rather about the free and especially religious operations of men, it moves in various manners. For first he limits and circumscribes the liberty of their will by legislation, that man cannot either will or do whatever he wants without sin,[e] and principally for this end, that he may not will nor do except that which is right and just, and this so that, just like a living image, he might reflect his creator, and always remain subject to him. Then, in order that man might willingly and cheerfully render that obedience, God consecrates a law which he makes with him by notable and great promises and threats.[f] And that he may the more and better elicit and seek the same, he employs various persuasions, exhortations, entreaties, signs, mighty works, etc. with regard to man. He always incites, stimulates, helps and strengthens him, as far indeed as is sufficient, that man might really obey him and persevere in obedience to the end. Thirdly, his obedience and actions obediently rendered, with singular care [God] observes, approves and delights in them and always faithfully holds them in memory as worthy of the promised gracious reward, and as such continually sets them before his eyes.[g]

e. Ex. 20:1. Deut. 20, Ps. 19, Gal. 3:19.
f. Ex. 19:9, Deut. 27 & 28, 2 Cor. 5:11, 7:1, 2 Pet. 1:3-4, 1 John 3:5, Rev. 3:18, Ez. 18:30, Acts 2:22, 10:38, Ps. 81:14, Is. 48:18.
g. Ps. 10:17, 18:20, 33:18, Rom. 12:1-2, Heb. 13:15, Mal. 3:16-17.

3. Ad inobedientiam,[a] sive peccata quod attinet: *primo* tametsi cum summo odio habet, sciens tamen ac volens permittit, non quidem permissione tali, qua posita, non potest non sequi inobedientia (sic enim necessario inobedientia sequeretur ex permissione Dei, tanquam effectus ex sua caussa: jamque Deus omnino peccari auctor esset: imo peccatum revera peccatum non esset, nedum pœna æterna dignum) sed qua posita homo duntaxat actu inobediens esse potest (etsi non impune) si quidem omnino ita velit. Permissio enim vera requirit, ut non tantum potentia voluntatis in se, sed usus etiam potentiæ liber sit, atque ad opposita indifferens: sive ut ab omni, interna simul & externa, necessitate maneat immunis. *Secundo*[b] actiones ex inobedientia profluentes varie dirigit, pro sapientia sua infinita, vel in hoc aut illud objectum, vel certum in finem, quem & qualem vult: homine ipso sæpe numero id nesciente, neque tale quid suspicante, imo interdum invito: easque ita determinat, ut nec semper reipsa fiant, quando diabolus & impii eas fieri vellent: neque tot, neque tam graves sint, neque tam diu durent, quam ipsi cuperent. *Tertio* factas[c] aut punit, aut remittit, prout ipsi bonum videtur. Nunquem vero actions malas decernit, ut fiant; neque approbat, neque amat;[d] neque unquam proprie jubet aut imperat: nedum ut eas efficat, aut procuret: aut ad eas quenquam incitet aut impellat: & propter easdem, ita à seipso procuratas, puniat aut plectat: sed serio semper eas odit &[e] aversatur; ac propterea etiam sancta prohibit ac vetat: & tandem peccatores propter eas, præsertim rebelles & obstinatos severiter punit.

a. Ps. 5:5-6, 11:5-6, Zech. 8:17, Ps. 81:15, Acts 14:16.
b. Prov. 16:9, 21:1, Ez. 21:20-22, Gen. 45:3, 50:20-21, 1 Cor. 10:13, Ps. 124 & 125, 2 Pet. 2:9, 2 Cor. 4:8-9.

4. Modus providentiæ hujus variat, tum *quantitate*, tum *qualitate*. Quantitate: quia primo curam & affectum suum ad omnia objecta non extendit æque *primo* nec æqualiter. Homines

3. Concerning disobedience or sin,[a] in the first place, although he has greatest hatred for it yet he knowingly and willingly permits it, but not with such permission, that being granted, disobedience cannot but follow. For thus disobedience would as necessarily follow from God's permission as an effect from its cause and God would be altogether the author of sin. Indeed sin would no longer be considered sin, much less worthy of eternal punishment. But being granted, man may become actually disobedient (yet not unpunished) if he indeed so wills. For true permission requires not just that the power of the will be free in itself, but also that the use of the power be free with the power of contrary choice, or that it remain immune to all necessity, internal as well as external. Second, the actions that flow from disobedience according to his infinite wisdom, he variously directs either to this or that object, and to some certain end, to whom and what he pleases.[b] Man himself often knows nothing about it nor suspects any such thing, indeed sometimes against his will. And he so determines them, that they do not always happen when the devil and wicked men would want them to be, neither are so many, nor so grievous, nor last so long, as they would desire. Third, being done, he punishes or forgives as seems good to himself.[c] But he never decrees that evil actions should happen, nor does he approve or love them.[d] Neither does he ever properly order or command them, nor cause or seek them, nor incite or compel them, nor does he himself administer it so that he could punish and revenge it. But he always seriously hates and refuses them, and for this reason also, in holiness, he prohibits and forbids them and in the end severely punishes sinners for them, especially the rebellious and obstinate.[e]

c. Exoc. 34:9, Rom. 9:18, Nahum 1:2-3, Ps. 11:6.
d. Ja. 1:13.
e. Ps. 5:5, Zech. 15:1, Ez. 14:14, Rom. 1:25, 2:5, 2 Thess 2:10-11.

4. The method of this providence varies, first in quantity, then in quality. Regarding quantity, because first it does not primarily nor equally extend its care and affection to all objects. For it

enim prius ac magis curat,^a quam cætera animantia; & inter homines magis pios,^b quam impios; & inter pios magis eximios, hoc est eos, qui vel virtutibus, vel^c muneribus, ac donis divinis, sive in Ecclesia, sive in Republicâ præ cæteris eminent. Quo etiam pertinet illud Apostoli: *Num boves cura sunt Deo? Secundo*, actiones internas, moraliter per se bonas, magis diligit & gratas habet, quam nudas personas.^d Non enim, quia persona utcunque placet, idcirco actiones tales placent: sed contra, quia actiones istæ placent, idcirco persona placet. *Tertio*, circa personas officium nondum facientes (sive propter crassam ignorantiam, qua vitio temporis adhuc laborant; sive propter habitum peccati, profundius forte radicatum, quem difficile est exuere) majori sæpe patientia,^e longanimitate & tolerantia occupatur, quam circa illuminatos, & contra illustratam conscientiam, vel assidue, vel subinde reluctantes, aut sæpius jam relapsos. *Quarto*: Circa vere pios & jam officium facientes, ordinarie majori^f affectu, voluptate, studio & cura occupatur, quam circa ullos alios. Unde etiam plura illis, & majora præstat gratiæ auxilia, Spiritus S. dona, & salutis media, quam aliis, imò majore tolerantiam & patentia, zeloque ardentiore illos, ex infirmitate labentes, ferre solet, quam reliquos. *Quinto*: Denique circa officium planè non facientes, & contumaciæ ac rebellionis diuturnæ reos, majore ferè odio & ira occupatur, quam circa alios quoscunque peccatores:^g immittendo scilicet eis non raro maledictiones graviores: aliquando etiam eos excæcando, indurando, tradendo in efficaciam erroris, in prava & propria desideria; inque mentem reprobam (quæ nec ipsa probat, quod rectum est, nec aliis ullis probari jure potest) imo in protestatem ipsius satanæ, qui potentar agit in filiis contumaciæ. Denique nonnunquam exemplariter ac palam,^h veluti in theatro mundi, coram sole, & in conspectualiorum, eosdem punidendo, justam iram, ad terribilem potentiam suam magnificè in ipsis ostendit.

attends first to men and then other animals,[a] and among men, to the godly more than the ungodly,[b] and among those that are excellent, that is, those who excel above others in virtues, or ministries, or divine gifts,[c] whether in the church or the republic, who belong to that saying of the Apostle, "Does God not care for oxen?" Secondly, he delights in and favors more internal actions which are morally good in themselves, than of just any persons.[d] For not because some person pleases him is he pleased about such actions. But to the contrary, because he is pleased with these actions, therefore he is pleased about the person. Third, he often employs greater patience, longsuffering and tolerance with people not yet doing their duty, whether because of crass ignorance due to the corruption of the times [in which] they labor, or because of a sinful habit, perhaps more profoundly rooted, which is difficult to put off, than with who are illuminated and resist against an enlightened conscience either constantly or repeatedly, or frequently relapse.[e] Fourth, concerning the truly godly and those already doing their duty, he ordinarily employs greater affection, pleasure, zeal and care about them than others.[f] Whence also he affords them more and greater assistances of grace, gifts of his Holy Spirit and means of salvation than to others. Indeed when they fall through infirmity he is accustomed to bear them with greater tolerance and patience and more ardent zeal than the rest. Fifth and finally, about those who plainly do not do their duty, and are guilty of prolonged defiance and rebellion, he almost employs greater hatred and wrath towards them than towards any other sinners, namely, not rarely sending upon them heavier curses, sometimes even by blinding, hardening or delivering them to the efficacy of error, to their own corrupt desires and to a reprobate mind (which can neither commend what is right, nor justly commend itself to any other), indeed to the power of Satan himself who powerfully works in the sons of defiance.[g] Lastly, sometimes he magnificently displays of his just wrath and terrible power in them by punishing them exemplarily and openly, just as in the theatre of the world in broad daylight and in the sight of others.[h]

a. 1 Cor. 9:9, Mat. 6:26-27.
b. Ps. 33:18, 1 Pet. 5:7, Ps. 105.5.
c. 2 Chron. 16:22, Acts 18:10, Ps. 73:1, Zech. 2:8, Ps. 91:11-12, Mat. 4:6.
d. Gen. 4:7, Prov. 16:7, Jer. 7:3, Heb. 11:5-6, John 14:22-23, 15:14, 16:27.
e. Acts 17:30, 1 Tim. 1:13, Rev. 2 & 3, Heb. 6:4,
f. Ps. 5:11-12, 18:20, Mat. 13:12 & 25:19, 1 Cor. 1:7, Phil. 1:6, Rev. 3:9-10.
g. Ps. 5:5, 109:17, Ex. 7 & 8, Lev. 16:14, Is. 6:9, John 12:40, 2 Thess. 2:11, Rom. 2:25, Eph. 2:2 & 4:17-19.
h. Ex. 9:16, Is. 14:4, Dan. 4:28-29, Acts 12:23.

10:26-28, 2 Pet. 2:20-21.

5. *Qualitate* variat: Quia, primò, circa quædam objecta, vel efficienda, vel impedienda, vel dirigenda, usurpat Deus absolutam & invictam omnipotentiam;^a circa quædam vero accommodatum rebus concursum & auxilium, naturæ nostræ quasi attemperatum. *Secundo*: Quædam immediate per seipsum agit; quædam mediate per Angelos, homines, aut alias creaturas. *Tertio*: Quædam quasi actione physica; quædam quasi morali vel ethica perficit: idque fit utrumque juxta naturas & facultates, rebus per creationem inditas: raro etiam supra. sed nunquam contra. Denique optime omnia administrat: hoc est, & suæ ipsius semper & rerum naturis ut plurimum convenienter.

a. 2 Chron 10:27-28, Is. 10:5-7, 46:10, Acts 7:51, etc.

5. It varies in quality, because, first, concerning some objects, either in effecting or impeding or controlling them, God uses his absolute and irresistible omnipotence; concerning others he uses concourse and assistance, truly accommodated to things, almost tempered to our own nature.[a] Second, some things he works immediately by himself, some things [he works] mediately by angels, men or other creatures. Third, some things he accomplishes by an almost physical action. Some he executes by an ethical or moral one. And both are done according to the natures and faculties implanted in things through creation, rarely above, but never against. Finally, he optimally administers all things, that is, almost always consistent to his own nature and the nature of things.

6. Quare licet *Providentia* divina[a] omnibus omnium hominum factis, dictis, cogitatis, semper interveniat; & per eam omnes externas actiones, atque omnium rerum eventa suo unius arbitrio Deus dispenset: naturalem tamen rerum *contingentiam*, atque innatam arbitrii humani[b] *libertatem*, olim semel in creatione datam, nunquam per ipsam tollit: sed rerum naturas ordinare salvas relinquit: atque ita cum hominis voluntate in agendo concurrit, ut ipsam quoque pro suo genio agere, & libere suas partes obire sinat: nec proinde præcisam bene, nedum male, agendi necessitatem eidem unquam imponat.

a. Prov. 16:4 & 21:1, etc.

6. Therefore, although divine providence always intervenes in all human deeds, words and thoughts,[a] and through it God manages all outward actions and events of all things according to his will alone, still, by it he never takes away the natural contingency of things and the innate liberty of the human will, once given long ago in creation, but ordinarily he leaves the natures of things safe.[b] And thus it concurs with the will of man in acting that he permits it also to act according to its own nature and freely performs its part, and therefore does not at any time impose on it the absolute necessity of doing well, much less of doing evil.

b. Deut. 30:15, 1 Chron. 21:10, Is. 1:19, Acts 5:4, 1 Cor. 7:32, 2 Cor. 2:11 & 9:7.

7. Nihil igitur uspiam *temere* aut *fortuito* fit in universo mundo: id est, Deo vel ignorante, vel non curante, vel ociose spectante; nedum omnino reluctante, vel prorsus invito ac ne permittere quidem volente. Nihil vero etiam ab hominibus vel boni vel mali, plane fataliter

7. Therefore nothing happens anywhere in the entire world rashly or by chance, that is, God either not knowing, or ignoring, or idly observing it, much less looking on, still less altogether reluctantly even unwillingly and not even willing to permit it. For truly there is nothing either good

atque incontingenter, seu præcise necessario fit: hoc est, Deo aut violenter huc illucve voluntatem ipsorum cogente, aut aliquam saltem vim ineluctabilem, decreto aliquo absoluto & semper efficare (sive id dixeris effectivum, sive permissivum, prout quidam inepte hic loquuntur (sic vel aliter agendi, cuiquam afferente.

8. Itaque nec cæcæ *Epicureorum* fortunæ ac brutæ temeritati, nec ferreæ ac fatali *Stoicorum*, *Manichæorum*, aut *Prædestinatorum* necessitati, locus in mundo ullus, per veram Dei providentiam utpote sapienter, sancte, justeque omnia moderantem) unquam relinquitur. Qui duo scopuli, utpoque summe noxii ac periculosi in hac materia, precipue cavendi sunt. Unde porro vere pii, de his omnibus recte informari, in adversis quidem patientes,[a] in secundis vero grati semper erga Deum redduntur; & præterea in futurum quoque optimam in Deo fidissimo Patre suo, spem libenter & assidue reponunt.

or evil which is fatally or not contingently done by man or by absolute necessity, that is, God either violently compelling their wills to this or that, by offering some irresistible power, some absolute and always efficacious decree (whether you will call it effective or permissive, as some foolishly say), or some other way of acting.

8. Therefore, through the true providence of God wisely and righteously governing all things in a holy manner, no place is ever left in the world either for the blind fortune and brute rashness of the Epicureans, nor for the unyielding, fatal necessity of the Stoics, Manicheans, or Predestinarians. These two rocks, extremely prejudicial and dangerous indeed in this subject, are especially to be avoided. Furthermore, those who are truly godly, being rightly informed about all these things and patient in whatever adversity, will always give thanks to God in prosperity, and in addition, in the future they will freely and continuously place their greatest hope in God, their most faithful Father.[a]

a. Job 1:21 & 2:10, Ps. 18 & 116:12-13, Matt. 6:25, 2 Tim. 4:17-18.

• CHAPTER 7 •

CAPUT VII.
De Peccato & miseria Hominis.

Hoc utriumque, quod diximus, opus divinæ bonitatis, *creationem* scilicet & *providentiam*, sequutum est singulare opus *gratiæ* & *misericordiæ*: sed cui occasionem quandam dedit ipsum peccatum,[a] &, quæ peccatum consecuta est, justa pœna, sive pœnalis & misera hominis conditio: unde credentes per Christum gratis liberantur: de quibus ex ordine deinceps agendum erit.

a. Rom. 3:20, 5:12, 6:20.

CHAPTER 7
On the sin and misery of man.

1. Both these works of the divine goodness about which we spoke, namely creation and providence, are followed by the special work of grace and mercy,[a] when sin itself was granted a certain occasion, and that which followed the sin, the just punishment or the penal or miserable condition of man, from which believers are freely delivered by Christ, concerning which things we will pursue later in order.

2. Peccatum hac ratione primitus inductum est in mundum.[a] Creato cum ejusmodi, quas diximus, facultatibus homini dedit Deus legem, *de non comedendo fructu arboris scientia boni & mali*, positæ in medio horti, sub pœna mortis æternæ & variarum præterea miseriarum. Eam vero legem transgressus est Adam,[b] una cum Eva uxore sua, seducta à Satana, & falsis persuasionibus decepta. Transgressus est, inquam, non spontanea tantum, sed prorsus libera[c] voluntate: quia nec per volentem ullam impulsionem externam, nec per secretam aliquam & occultam determinationem, aut necessetationem (sive à Deo, sive à diabolo profectam) ad fructum vetitum volendum, decerpendum & comedendum, addictus est: nec per ullius divinæ virtutis, aut actionis, ad evitandum peccatum necessariæ, aliquam substractionem, aut negationem, (quam alii imperite permissionem, sive decretum efficax permissivum appellant) in peccatum hoc incidit: nec denique per imperium, jussum, aut instinctum ullum, quantumvis arcanum & ocultum, ad transgrediendum à Deo impulsus ac commotus fuit: (ut haberet scilicet Deus occasionem exercendi misericordiam suam parcentem, & justitiam punientem) prout quidam perverse docent. Sic enim Deus vere, proprie, ac denique præcipuus, imo solus, peccati auctor esset: imo sic transgressio illa, verum peccatum non fuisset: neque per illam homo vere reus, aut jure miser fieri potuisset: proinde neque Deus veræ misericordiæ & veræ justitiæ exercendæ occasionem hinc consequtus fuisset. Sed pura puta arbitrii libertate, ab omni tum intentia tum externa necessitate prorsus immuni, homo peccatum hoc commisit, sola Dei permissione interveniente; solaque diaboli suasione, sed cui facile homo resistere & aures non præbere poterat, istic præeunte & fructus pulchritudine ac gratia extrinsecus alliciente.

a. Gen. 2:17.
b. Gen. 3:1, Rom. 5:12, 1 Tim. 2:13-14, 2 Cor. 11:3.

3. Per transgressionem hanc factus est homo, ex vi comminationis divinæ,[a] reus æternæ mor-

2. Sin was brought into the world on this account. God gave to the man, being created with such faculties as we have said, a law of not eating of the fruit of the tree of the knowledge of good and evil, placed in the middle of the garden, under the pain of eternal death and various other miseries.[a] That law was broken, however, by Adam, together with his wife, who was seduced by Satan and deceived by his false persuasions.[b] It was broken, I say, not so much by a spontaneous will, but by a truly free one. Because he was not forced either by any outward violent impulse or some secret and hidden determination or necessity (whether proceeding from God, or the devil) to will to pluck or eat the forbidden fruit.[c] Nor did he fall into sin through any subtraction or negation of some divine virtue or action necessary for avoiding sin (which some amateurishly call permission or an efficacious permissive decree). Finally, he was not impelled or moved to transgression by God through any command, order or instinct, however, secret or hidden (namely, that God might have an opportunity of exercising his forbearing mercy, and punitive justice), as some perversely teach. For God would truly, properly and especially, in fact solely, be the author of sin. Indeed, such a transgression would not be a true sin, neither could the man by that sin be truly guilty or justly miserable. Furthermore, God was not seeking from this an opportunity of exercising his true mercy or true justice. But the man committed this sin by the pure liberty of his will, immune to any internal or external necessity. On God's part, only his permission entered in, and on the devil's, only his persuasion, which the man could easily have resisted and not given ear, and the external beauty and grace of the fruit going before and enticing.

c. Ex. 7:29, Rom. 5:18-19, Gen. 2:1.

3. Through this transgression the man was made liable to eternal death and multiple miseries from

tis, ac multiplicis miseriæ: exutusque est primaveræ illa felicitate, quam in creatione acceperat, ac propterea ejectus[b] ex horto illo amœnissimo (cælestis Paradisi typo,) in quo alioqui feliciter cum Deo conversabatur: & perpetuo separatus ab arbore vitæ, quæ symbolum erat beatæ immortalitatis.

a. Gen. 2:17 & 3:16, Rom. 5:12, Gen. 3:21, Rev. 2:7 & 21:14.

4. Quia verò Adamus stirps ac radix erat totius[a] generis humani, ideo non seipsum tantum, sed omnes etiam posteros suos (qui quasi in lumbis ipsius conclusi erant, & ex ipso per naturalem generationem prodituri) eidem morti ac miseriæ involvit, & una secum implicuit: adeo ut omnes homines, sine ullo discrimine, excepto solo D. N. *Iesu Christo,* per hoc unicum Adami peccatum privati sint primæva illa felicitate, & destituti vera justitia, ad æternam salutem consequendam necessaria, adeoque morti illi, quam diximus, & multiplici miseriæ etiam nunc obnoxii nascantur. Atque hoc vulgo *peccatum originis* dici solet. De quo tamen tenendum est, Deum illum benignissimum, isti generali malo, quod nos ab Adamo derivatum est, gratuitum in Filio suo dilecto Jesu Christo, velut altero & novo Adamo, remedium omnibus præparasse. Ut vel hinc noxius illorum error[b] satis appareat, qui decretum absolutæ reprobationis, ab ipsis confictum, in isto peccato fundare solent.

a. Acts 17:26, Heb. 7:10, Rom. 5:12, John 14.

5. Præter hoc peccatum sunt & alia propria, seu actualia uniuscujusque hominis peccata:[a] quæ & reatum nostrum coram Deo revera multiplicant, & mentem in rebus spiritualibus obscurant, imo paulatim excæcant, denique voluntatem nostram magis ac magis adsuetudine ipsa peccandi depravant.

a. Gen. 6:5 & 8:21, 2 Cor. 4:3, Eph. 4:17-19, Jer. 13:23, John 8:24, Rom. 7:14, 2 Pet. 2:19.

6. Hujusmodi peccatorum species variæ sunt, variique gradus: prout ex variis ipsorum objectis, subjectis, causis modis, effectis, ac circumstantiis intelligi potest: puta aliud

the power of the divine threat[a] and was stripped of that primeval happiness which he received in creation. Thus he was ejected from that most delightful garden (a type of the heavenly paradise) in which he otherwise happily conversed with God, and was perpetually barred from the tree of life, which was a symbol of blessed immortality.

4. Because Adam was the stock and root of the whole human race,[a] he therefore involved and implicated not only himself, but also all his posterity (as if they were contained in his loins and went forth from him by natural generation) in the same death and misery with himself, so that all men without any discrimination, only our Lord Jesus Christ excepted, are by this one sin of Adam deprived of that primeval happiness, and destitute of true righteousness necessary for achieving eternal life, and consequently are now born subject to that eternal death of which we spoke, and manifold miseries. And this is customarily and vulgarly called original sin, concerning which it must also be held that the most kind God, in his beloved Son Jesus Christ, just as a second and new Adam, has prepared for all a remedy for this general evil which we derived from Adam. So even from this [original sin] sufficiently appears the hurtful error of those who are accustomed to lay a foundation for the decree of absolute reprobation in this sin.[b]

b. See the *Canons of the Synod of Dort*, chapter 1, at the beginning.

5. Besides this sin are the proper or actual sins of each and every man, which also really multiply our guilt before God and obscure our mind concerning spiritual matters. Indeed little by little they blind [us], and finally deprave our will more and more by the habit of sinning.[a]

6. Of this manner of sins there are various species and degrees, as may be understood from their various objects, subjects, causes, modes, effects and circumstances, namely, one of commission,

commissionis, aliud omissionis:[a] aliud carnis, aliud spiritus:[b] aliud ex ignorantia:[c] aliud ex subita passione, sive infirmate,[d] aliud ex destinata malitia proficiscens:[e] aliud contra conscientiam, aliud non contra conscientiam:[f] aliud regans, aliud non regnans:[f] aliud ad mortem, aliud non ad mortem:[g] aliud contra Spiritum S., aliud non contra Spiritum S. &c.[h] De hisce illud semper tenendum est, esse quædam peccata actualia, de quibus aut expresse scriptum, aut non obscure indicatum est, quod *qui ea facit, regni cælestis & vitæ æternæ particeps esse nequeat:* qualia sunt *opera illa carnis* omnia, quæ ad *Gal.* 5. 1 Cor. 6. & *Ephes.* 5. Tit. 3. & alibi describuntur, & quæ eis similia sunt:[i] sive ea cum contemtu Dei, & rationis rectæ manifesto abusu conjuncta sint: sive talia saltem,[j] quæ eum, qui æterna & colestia bona desiderat, minime decent: uti sunt, mundi & rerum mundanarum amor, & anxiæ ac perpetuæ fere de iis consequendis, possidendis ac retinendis curæ & sollicitudines, &c. Quædam vero sunt talia, *ut leviores Lapsus* potius dici mereatur, quam crimina:[k] per quæ, juxta gratiosum Dei fœdus & paternam benignitatem, non excluditur homo à spe vitæ æternæ:[l] licet se ab eorum aliquo nondum omnino exsolvat: si modo sciens prudens sibi ipse difficultatem non injiciat ab iis se exsolvendi, aut talia quacunque ratione in iis manendi: sed quod in illa incidat per solam incogitantiam, fragilitatem, inadvertentiam, aut subitam aliquam passionem contingat: sive ex naturæ aliquo temperamento, sive ex consuetudine mala, sive ex improviso aliquo casu &c. id oriatur. Itaque fere semper actus hic ab habitibus, &, in illo genre, imperfectiones ac fragilitates manifestæ ab iis actibus, qui contra dictamen naturalis rationis, aut supernaturalis revelationis expressum & præsens fiunt, & cum aperta præcepti alicujus transgressione, & injuria proximi sunt conjuncti (præsertim ex Novi Testam. Sensu) accurate distinguenda veniunt.

another of omission,[a] one of the flesh, another of the spirit;[b] one from ignorance,[c] another from sudden passion or infirmity,[d] and another originating from resolute malice;[e] one against conscience, another not against conscience;[f] one reigning, another not reigning;[g] one to death, another not to death;[g] one against the Holy Spirit, another not against the Holy Spirit,[h] etc. It must always be held concerning them that there are some actual sins of which it is either expressly written or not obscurely indicated that he who does them cannot share in the kingdom of heaven and eternal life, such as all the works of the flesh which are described in Galatians 5:1, 1 Corinthians 6 and Ephesians 5, Titus 3 and others, and those that are similar to them, whether they are accompanied with contempt of God[i] and a manifest abuse of right reason, or whether they are at least such are not the least becoming for one who desires eternal and heavenly good. Such are the love of the world, and worldly things, anxious and perpetual cares and concerns about getting them, possessing and retaining them, etc. For truly there are others which deserve to be called lighter slips rather than crimes,[k] for which, in consequence of the gracious covenant of God and his fatherly kindness,[l] a man is not excluded from the hope of eternal life, although he is not entirely set free from some of them if he does not knowingly and foreseeingly cast this difficulty of freeing himself from them upon himself, or by any other means whatever of continuing in them, but that he falls into them only through thoughtlessness, frailty, lack of attention, or some sudden passion, whether it arises from some natural temperament, or evil practice, or some unexpected chance, etc. Therefore acts here are almost always accurately to be distinguished from habits and, in that respect, manifest imperfections and frailties from those acts committed against the express and ready dictate of natural reason or supernatural revelation, and accompanied with an open transgression of some commandment and injury of our neighbor (especially according to the sense of the New Testament).

a. Luke 12:47, Ja. 4.
b. 2 Cor. 7:1.

f. Luke 12:47, Ps. 19:13.
g. Rom. 6:12.

c. 1 Tim. 1:13, Luke 23:34, Acts 3:17.
d. Gal. 6:1, Mat. 26:70, 1 Sam. 2513, 21.
e. Ps. 19:14, Num. 15:30, etc., Matt. 16:14-15, 2 Sam. 11:15.

h. 1 John 5:16.
i. Mat. 12:31-32, Mark 3:29, Luke 12:10.
k. Num. 15:30, Rom. 1:28 & 2:17, 21-23, & 3:8.
l. John 2:15, Mat. 6:31-32.

7. Pro diversa *quantitate*, & *qualitate* peccatorum, varia[a] quoque *pœna* à Deo contitua est: puta tum damni, tum sensus, tum temporalis, tum æternæ, tum denique corporalis, tum spiritualis. &c.

a. Gen. 3:16, Deut. 27 & 28, Rom. 5:12, 6:23.

7. Various punishments are ordained by God for the diverse quantity and quality of sins,[a] namely, first of condemnation, then of sense, whether temporal or eternal; finally, whether bodily or spiritual, etc.

8. *Duplex* autem illa peccati *vis & efficacia*, cujus supra mentio facta est (nempe *damnatio*, seu *mors æterna*, & *servitus peccati*, seu *capivitas sub peccati consuetudine*) jam olim clarissime apparuit, quandiu Deus salutarem gratiam suam, ante secula destinatam,[a] peccatoribus planè ac plenè nondum revelavit; sed eminus, obscurè & quasi per transennam tantum ostendit: sub generali scilicet gratiæ & favoris sui promisso,[b] sub rerum corporalium typo[c] & umbra. Etsi enim in veteri Testamento non omnino defuerunt, qui gratiæ istius divinæ auxilio adjuti in Deum crediderunt, & per fidem coram ipso integre ac sincere ambulaverunt; vitaque juxta Dei voluntatem composita, dominium peccati excusserunt, & per eandem vivam fidem etiam vere justificati fuerunt, sive à reatu peccatorum absoluti, & æternæ vitæ præmio donati:[d] prout in *Abelis, Enochi, & Abrahami*, patris omnium credentium &c. exemplis liquet: plerique tamen peccati pondere ac miseriæ mole abrepti fuerunt, & velut obruti. Principio enim cum lex nulla scripta adhuc lata esset; sed rationis naturalis dictamen, paternæ traditiones, aliæque quædam divinæ & Angelicæ revelationes, & apparitiones tantum, Deo ita ordine, inter homines vigerent:[e] peccatum non modo in mundo fuit, sed & vim suam adeo exeruit, ut universa caro (paucis[f] exceptis, qui justi fuerunt & sancte coram Deo per fidem ambularunt) viam suam[g] corrumperet, & omne figmentum hominis tantummodo malum esset esset ipsa pueritia. Unde reatus peccati adeo tunc auctus est, ut diluvium universale in mundum[h] impiorum inductum sit.

a. Ja. 1:18, Mark 11:27, Eph. 3:9-11, 2 Tim. 1:9-10, Tit. 2:11.

8. For that twofold power and efficacy of sin of which mention was made above, (indeed damnation or eternal death, and the servitude of sin, or captivity under the practice of sin), most clearly appeared long ago, in that God did not plainly and fully reveal his saving grace,[a] destined before the ages for sinners, but revealed it only from afar, obscurely and almost as if through a Lattice, namely, under a general promise of his grace and favor, under the type[b] and shadow[c] of corporal things. For even if in the Old Testament they were not entirely lacking those who believed in God by the assistance of that divine grace and by faith walked blamelessly and sincerely before him; and by a life ordered according to the will of God, shook off the dominion of sin, and by that living faith also were truly justified or absolved from the guilt of their sins, and granted the reward of eternal life, as is clear in the examples of Abel, Enoch, and Abraham the father of all who believe, etc.[d] Yet most were burdened by sin and overwhelmed with the weight of their misery. For in the beginning, when there was as yet no written law received, still the dictates of natural reason, paternal traditions and some other God-ordained divine and angelic revelations and apparitions did thrive among men.[e] Sin was not only in the world, but also so exerted its power, that all flesh (with few excepted, who were just and by faith walked before God in holiness[f]) corrupted its way, and every imagination of man was only evil from childhood.[g] By this, the guilt of sin was so increased at that time that a universal flood was brought upon the world of the ungodly.[h]

e. Rom. 5:13.
f. Gen. 5:24 & 6:9, Acts 11:3.

b. Gen. 10:1ff, & 17:7.
c. Heb. 11:16 & 10, 1 John 2:17, Col. 2:17.
d. Gen. 4:4, 7, & 5:24, Heb. 11.

g. Gen. 6:5, 11-12 & 8:21.
h. 2 Pet. 2:5.

9. Deinde post diluvium non modo non est delectum peccatum, sed potius, fermenti instar, diffusum ac dilatatum per universum genus humanum: adeo[a] ut integri populi, nationes & regiones idolatria aliisque fœdis & abominandis peccatis passim se polluerent; & in maximis amplissimisque hominem communitatibus vix[b] decem justi aliquando extarent. Tandem cum Deum, præteritis aliis nationibus,[c] certos quosdam homines ex reliqua idololatrarum & peccatorum turba sibi seligeret, eorumque posteris speciali gratia legem scriptam, multis variisque præceptis (moralibus, ceremonialibus, policitis) constantem,[d] veluti jugum ac præsidium onerosum atque insupportabile imoneret,[e] &, quo melius hi à peccando quotidie reprimerentur, & ad officium faciendum compellerentur, etiam severissimis[f] minis promissionibus multiplicibus eandem sanciret: quin & subinde gratiosæ suæ voluntaris conciones, per[g] prophetas, aliosque servos suos, repeti atque inculcari iis curaret ad transgressiones amplius impediendum, nihilominus tamen vicit peccatum, & non modo non est exstinctum ejus dominium per legem istam; reatusque[h] per sanguinem taurorum & hircorum, aliaque id genus sacrificia, non sublatus; sed magis etiam magisque peccatum auctum, & veluti aculeo indito per legem exstimulatum; reatusque mortis & condemnationis usque adeo aggravatus est, ut universus mundus sub peccatum conclusus, & condemnationi factus fuerit obnoxius.

9. Then, after the flood, sin was not only not washed away, but rather like leaven, diffused and spread throughout the whole human race[a] so that all peoples, nations and regions thoroughly polluted themselves with idolatry and other foul and abominable sins. In the greatest and most ample communities there hardly existed ten righteous men.[b] Finally, when God passed by other nations, he chose some certain men to himself from the mob of idolaters and sinners to himself,[c] and out of his special grace established with their posterity a written law of many and various commandments (moral, ceremonial, political) as a burdensome and insupportable yoke and garrison,[d] that they might be better restrained from sinning,[e] and compelled to do their duty, also consecrated it with most severe threats and multiplied promises.[f] In fact, he constantly provided messages of his gracious will and pleasure to be repeated and pressed upon them by the prophets and his other servants[g] for the ample impeding of transgressions. Nevertheless, sin conquered, its dominion was by no means destroyed by that law, the guilt was not removed by the blood of bulls and goats[h] and other sacrifices of that kind. But sin increased more and more, stimulated by the law like an embedded thorn, and the guilt of death and condemnation were so aggravated that the whole world was shut up under sin and liable to condemnation.

a. Josh. 24:1-2, Gen. 12:1-2.
b. Gen. 18:32
c. Acts 14:16, Ps. 147:19-20; Deut. 7:6-7 & 9:4-6.
d. Acts 15:10, Gal. 3:23.

e. Gal. 3:24.
f. Lev. 26:3ff, Deut. 27:15ff & 28.
g. Is. 61:1 & 62:6, 2 Chron 36:15, Acts 7:51-53.
h. Rom. 5:20 & 7:8, Heb. 7:18-19 & 7:20, & 10:4, Rom. 3:19-20 & 11:32.

10. Ex quo tandem summa *gratiæ divinæ,* in Christo Servatore nobis ante secula præparatæ, *necessitas* simul & *utilitas* evidenter apparuit: quippe sine qua nec miserabile peccati jugum excutere,[a] nec quicquam in tota Religione vere bonum operari, nec denique mortem æternam,

10. It was from this that the highest necessity and also advantage of divine grace, prepared for us in Christ the Savior before the ages, clearly appeared. For without it we could neither shake off the miserable yoke of sin, nor do anything truly good in all religion, nor finally ever escape eternal

aut ullam veram peccati pœnam, effugere unquam possimus: nedum ut salutem æternam sine illa per nos ipsos, aut per alias creaturas, consequi aliquando possimus.

a. Rom. 6:14 & 7:1, & 8:1, Gal. 3:24, Acts 4:12, & 13:38-39.

death or any true punishment of sin.[a] Much less could we at any time obtain eternal salvation without it or through ourselves.

• CHAPTER 8 •

CAPUT VIII.
De Opere Redemtionis, deque Persona & Officiis Iesu Christi.

CHAPTER 8
On the work of redemption, and the person and offices of Jesus Christ.

1. Quare visum fuit clementissimo Deo, in[a] fine seculorum, sive in plenitudine temporis, excellentissimum opus illud, quod[b] ante mundi fundamenta præsciverat, sive in se ipso proposuerat, & labentibus seculis sub variis figures,[c] umbris ac typis, (rudi quasi minerva delineatum) mortalibus eminus vivendum, atque obscure cognoscendum dederat, reipsa ordiri & probe exequi: videlicet opus *Redemtionis*[d] sive *Nova creationis*: quo hominem, per peccatum mortis ac condemnationis æternæ reum factum, & sub servitude peccati misere jacentem, ex mera sua gratia & misericorida à reatu illa liberaret, & in spem vitæ æternæ atque immortalis restitueret; viresque sufficientes, imo exuberantes, ad peccati dominium excutiendum, & divinæ voluntati toto corde obsequendum suppeditaret.

a. 1 Cor. 10:11, Gal. 4:4.
b. 1 Pet. 1:20, Eph. 1:9-10.

2. Hoc opus peregit Deus per unicum filium suum unigenitum, D. N. Jesum Christum:[a] quem videlicet propterea in mundum misit, ut clementissiman voluntatem suam, de peccatoribus serio resipiscentibus & vere credentibus æterna salute gratis donandis, non modo nobis apertissime per ipsum declaret,

1. Wherefore it seemed good to the most merciful God, in the end of the age[a] or in the fullness of time, to begin and properly execute that most excellent work which he had foreknown or proposed in himself[b] before the foundation of the world, and [which] in passing ages he had indicated under various figures, shadows and types[c] (almost as in a rude sketch), that it might be seen at a distance and obscurely known by mortals, namely, the work of Redemption or a New Creation,[d] by which he would deliver man, made liable to eternal death and condemnation and lying under the miserable bondage of sin, from that guilt by his mercy and grace alone, restore him to the hope of an eternal and immortal life and supply sufficient, indeed superabundant, powers for shaking off the dominion of sin and obeying the will of God with a whole heart.

c. Heb. 9.
d. 2 Cor. 5:15, Rom. 5:12, 8:3, Eph. 1:1.

2. God accomplished this work through his unique only begotten Son, our Lord Jesus Christ,[a] whom he manifestly sent into the world, not only that he might by him most openly declare to us and in various ways confirm his most merciful will concerning his freely bestowing eternal life upon sinners who seriously repent and truly believe, but

variisque modis confirmaret; sed & reipsa, per sanctissimam ipsius obedientiam, & efficacem Spiritus S. operationem, in nobis ad optatum finem, quantum in se est, gradatim perduceret.

also indeed, that as far as it is in him, he might gradually lead us to that desired end through his most holy obedience and the efficacious operation of his Holy Spirit

a. John 3:16, 8:26, Matt. 11:27, John 1:18, Acts 4:11 & 10:43, Gal. 4:4, Titus 2:11-12.

3. Porro hujus Filii Dei, domini nostri Jesu Christi, universa cognitio, quatenus quidem ad salutem necessaria est, duabus potissimum partibus continetur. Nam partim ad *personam*, partim ad *officium* ipsius pertinet. Respectu *personæ*, Jesus Christus est verus æternusque Deus[a] & simul verus ac perfecte justus homo,[b] in una eademque persona: quippe naturalis, unigenitus, ac proprius Dei filius,[c] in 2 Cor. 5. 21. 1. Petr. 2. 22. &c. 3. 18. Plenitudine temporis, per operationem Spiritus S. verus & integer homo factus, atque ex Maria virgine, sine ulla peccati labe, natus.

3. Furthermore, the entire knowledge about the Son of God, our Lord Jesus Christ, as far indeed as is necessary for salvation, is chiefly contained in two parts. For it pertains partly to the person and partly to the office. In respect of his person, Jesus Christ is true and eternal God,[a] and at the same time, true and perfectly just man,[b] in one and the same person. For as the natural, only begotten, and proper son of God,[c] [seen] in 2 Cor. 5:21, 1 Pet. 2:22 and 3:18, in the fullness of time, through the operation of the Holy Spirit, he was made a man true and complete and born of the Virgin Mary, without any stain of sin.

a. John 1:1, 20:28, Rom. 9:5, 1 John 5:20.
b. 1 Tim. 2:5-6, Matt. 16:16, 1 Cor. 10:21-22, Rom. 1:3.

c. John 1:14, 3:18, Rom. 1:3-4, & 8:32, Gal. 4:4, Luke 2:31ff, Heb. 4:14.

4. Factus autem est homo non modo verus, sive quoad substantiam integer, ac perfectus, corpore scilicet vere humano, anima rationali constans: sed etiam iisdem, quibus non, infirmitatibus,[a] passionis, ærumnis, afflictionibus, angustiis, doloribus, tristitiis, ignominiis, opprobriis, adeoque acerbissimæ morti, vere obnoxius: idque hoc ipso fine, ut fratribus suis per omnia similis effectus (attamen sine peccato) misericors ac fidelis noster Pontifex esset in iis, quæ apud Deum agenda erant, ad expiandum peccata populi &c. Atque hoc sibi vult articulus illa Symboli Apostolici, de Jesu Christo: *Credo in Iesum Christum, Filium Dei inugentium, Dominum nostrum: qui conceptus est ex Spiritu S. natus ex Maria virgine.*

4. And he was made not only a true or complete man with respect to his substance, consisting certainly of a truly human body and rational soul, but also truly subject to the same infirmities,[a] passions, labors, afflictions, straits, pains, griefs, shames, reproaches and even the most bitter, to death, and for the very purpose that being in all things made like to his brothers (yet without sin) he might be a merciful and faithful high priest in things pertaining to God, for expiating the sins of the people, etc. And this is proposed by that Article of the Apostles' Creed concerning Christ Jesus, "I believe in Jesus Christ the only begotten Son of God, our Lord, who was conceived by the Holy Spirit, born of the Virgin Mary."

a. John 1:14, Heb. 2:13 & 4:15, 5:7, Rom. 1:3 & 8:3, Gal. 4:4.

5. *Officium* Jesu Christi *triplex* est: *Propheticum, Sacerdotale, Regium*:[a] quod ille universum, partim jam olim in his terris, sub statu humilitatis & ex minorationis, fideliter, administravit, partim etiam nunc in cælo, sub statu gloriæ & exaltationis, gloriose administrat. Ad priorem statum pertinent articuli sequentes:[b]

5. The office of Jesus Christ is threefold: prophetic, priestly and kingly,[a] which the whole, in part, he faithfully administered now long ago in this world under that state of humiliation and abasement, and now also in part gloriously administers in heaven in a state of glory and exaltation. To the prior state pertain the following

passus sub Pontio Pilato, crucifixus, mortuus & sepultus, descendit ad inferos. Quibus, quasi gradibus quibusdam, universa Jesu Christi humiliatio, qualis scilicet Prophetam & Sacerdotem nostrum decebat; sensim consummata fuit. Ad posteriorem referendi sunt isti:[c] *Tertia die resurrexit à mortuis, ascendit ad cælos, sedet ad dextram Dei Patris omnipotentis: inde venturus est ad judicandum vivos & mortuos.* Quibus rebus, partim præparatio quædam ad regiam simul & pontificiam J. Christi dignitatem, partim hæc ipsa dignitas, ejusque magnifica exsertio, egregie describitur.

a. Luke 1:32-33, Acts 3:22-23, Heb. 5:6-7, Rev. 1:5, 19:16.
b. 1 Tim. 6:13, Acts 2:36, 1 Cor. 1:23 & 2:2, Eph. 4:9,

6. *Propheticum* munus olim totum peregit, cum voluntatem Dei de vera salute seu vita æterna omnibus vere credentibus & obedientibus post mortem communicanda, non modo nobis per[a] Evangelium suum palam exposuit; sed & manifestis, atque omni exceptione majoribus, signis[b] & miraculis, adeoque propriæ obedientiæ[c] exemplo, in vita simul & morte sua, luculenter confirmavit; quin & jam post[d] mortem suam variis argumentis, per quadraginta dies, solidissime, asseruit & comprobavit.

a. John 1:18 & 5:19, 2 Tim. 1:10.
b. John 5:36, 15:24, Acts 2:22, 10:36.

7. *Sacerdotale* munus ex parte olim obiit, cum mandato Patris, cui[a] humiliter morem gerens, maledictam[b] crucis mortem pro nobis subiit, seque ipsum pro peccatis totius generis humani victissimam propitiatoriam Deo Patri obtulit, atque innoxium in ara crucis mactari passus est:[c] partim adhuc assidue obit, dum redivivus hominum causa in cœlo coram facie Dei continenter apparet, proque credentibus efficiter & gloriose intercedit, advocatum scilicet, ac patronum fidelissimum se iis semper & ubique præstans.

a. Phil. 2:3.
b. Eph. 5:2, gal. 3:13, Heb. 1:9-10 & 10:5-6, 1 John 2:2.

articles: "He suffered under Pontius Pilate, was crucified, dead and buried, he descended into hell."[b] By these, as if by certain degrees, the entire humiliation of Jesus Christ, which was gradually consummated, clearly became him as our prophet, and priest. To the latter these are to be referred: "The third day he arose from the dead, ascended to Heaven, sits at the right hand of God the Father Almighty. From there he shall come to judge the quick and the dead."[c] By these things is excellently described, partly a certain preparation to both the regal and priestly dignity of Jesus Christ and partly his very dignity in himself, and of the magnificent display of the same.

Ps. 24, Heb. 2:16.
c. Mark 16:19-20, Rom. 8:34, Heb. 7:25 & 8:1.

6. He has entirely fulfilled his prophetic ministry, not only when he openly explained to us the will of God through sharing the Gospel of true salvation[a] or eternal life after death to all who truly believe and obey, but also brilliantly confirmed by manifest signs and miracles too great to be questioned,[b] and also by the example of his own proper obedience,[c] brilliantly confirmed in both his life and death, and moreover after his death solidly asserted and proved by various arguments for forty days.[d]

c. 1 Pet. 2:21, Phil. 2:3.
d. Acts 1:3, John 20:21.

7. His priestly ministry he partly attended to long ago, when by the Father's command,[a] whose will humbly bearing, he submitted to the cursed death of the cross for us,[b] and offered himself to God the Father as a propitiatory sacrifice for the sins of the entire human race, and though innocent, suffered himself to be sacrificed upon the alter of the cross. In part, he still daily performs the same,[c] while resurrected he continually appears before the face of God in heaven for the sake of men and effectively and gloriously intercedes for believers, exhibiting himself indeed always and everywhere as a most faithful advocate and patron to them.

c. Rom. 8:34, Heb. 7:24-25.

8. *Regium* officium etiam nunc perpetuo exerceret, dum semel ex morte à Patre suscitatus, inque[a] cœlestem summæ majestatis thronum sublatus,[b] & ad dextram Dei in excelsis collocatus, omnemque in cœlo & terra potestatem adeptus, magnifice ubique imperat:[c] & quidem omnia pro arbitrio suo sic administrat, ut inprimis saluti fidelium suorum consulat: dum scilicet non modo ministerium Evangelii nostro bono jam olim instituit; sed & continuo, adversus omnis generis obstacula, potenter conservat, inque eo spiritualem suam efficaciam mirabiliter adhuc exserit: dumque[d] fideles subditos adversus satanæ, tyrannorum, aliorumque omnium inimicorum, artes, fraudes, infidias, vim ac potentiam per Spiritum suum Angelosque administros, potenter in hac vita munit, protegit & defendit: donec in[e] extremo judicio & hos omnes prorsus aboleat, & illos in gloriam suam cœlestem atque immortalem assumat, æternumque felices ac beatos reddat. Et hisce quidem officiis superstruitur, & agnitio, & cultus Jesu Christi proprius, quatenus Mediator est, de quibus postea, suo loco.

a. Heb. 1:3, Rev. 3:21, 1 Thes. 1:10, Ps. 110:1.
b. Mat. 28:19, Acts 2:35.
c. Eph. 1:20-22 & 4:11ff., Ps. 2:8ff. & 110:1ff.

9. Cæterum hinc patet Jesum Christum non una ratione *servatorem* nostrum esse, puta non solo præconio, exemplo, martyrioque suo: sive non ideo tantum, quia æternæ salutis viam nobis annunciavit, ac miraculis, item exemplo vitæ, & morte suâ confirmavit, sibique hac via supremam nos salvando potestatem, ac virtutem acquisivit: sed etiam vero erga Deum *merito & efficacia* hinc orta & immediate nos respiciente. *Merito* quidem,[a] quia salutem æternam nobis obedientia sua promeruit, seu quia hoc mediante, præsertim violentam & cruentam ipsius morte, (veluti $\lambda \acute{v} \tau \rho o v$ seu redemtonis pretio, ac sacrificio propitiatorio) Deus hactenus sibi omnes peccatores reconciliavit, ut per & propter hoc ipsum $\lambda \acute{v} \tau \rho o v$ ac sacrificium in gratiam cum iis redire, & ostium salutis æternæ,

8. His kingly office he already perpetually exercises, since, being once revived from death by the Father and raised to the throne of supreme majesty in heaven,[a] and placed at the right hand of God in the highest,[b] and having gained all power in heaven and earth, he magnificently rules everywhere. Indeed he administrates all things according to his own will, that in the first place he may consider the safety of his believers,[c] namely, since not only has he long ago instituted the ministry of the gospel for our good, but also powerfully preserves it uninterrupted against all types of obstacles and therein still admirably exerts his own spiritual efficacy. And he powerfully guards, protects and defends his faithful subjects in this life by the Spirit and his ministering angels against the schemes, frauds, snares, force and power of Satan, tyrants and all their other enemies,[d] until in the last judgment he utterly destroys the latter, and takes the former up into his heavenly and immortal glory and renders them eternally happy and blessed.[e] And indeed upon these offices is built both the knowledge and worship of Jesus Christ himself, in so far as he is the mediator, about which [we will say] more later, in its place.

d. Rev. chs. 2 & 3, Acts 12:11 & 18:10, Heb. 14.
e. Matt. 25:30ff, 1 Cor. 15:24, 2 Thess. 1:7-9, 4:17, 2 Thess. 1:9-10, Matt. 24:31.

9. But from this it appears that Jesus Christ is not our savior for just one reason, namely, for his office, example and suffering, nor only because he declared to us the way of eternal salvation and confirmed it by miracles, likewise the example of his life and death and in this way acquired for himself supreme power and virtue to save us, but indeed it rises from his virtue of merit and efficacy before God, and immediately provided for us. Indeed by this merit,[a] whether he earned eternal salvation for us because of his obedience, or because of that mediation, especially of his violent and bloody death (just as a $\lambda \acute{v} \tau \rho o v$, or price of redemption, and propitiatory sacrifice), God has thus far reconciled all sinners to himself, in order to restore them by his grace through and because of this ranson and sacrifice, and he willed to open

viam que immortalitatis pandere ipsis voluerit: prout id ipsum multis ante seculis sub variis typis, figuris, & umbris[b] veteris Testamenti, atque imprimis sub typo sacrificii istius solemnis, quod semel quotannis in Sancto sanctorum peragebat Pontifex maximus, præfiguratum fuerat. *Efficacia* vero Servator noster est,[c] quatenus spiritualem meriti illius sui virtutem ac fructum fidelis suis efficaciter applicat, & reipsa fruendum dat, eosque omnium beneficiorum, obedientia sua partorum, reipsa per fidem participes reddit, de quibus statim amplius.

a. Mat. 20:28, Rom. 5:8-9, 19, Phil. 2:5, 1 Tim. 2:5-6.

10. Meriti autem hujus universam vim, atque efficaciæ veritatem enervant, imo funditus evertunt ii, qui & *electionem & reprobationem absolutam* certarum personarum (sive ante lapsum, sive in & sub lapsu tantum, citra fidem in Christum, & contrariam inobedientiam, consideratarum) ordine primo factam esse asserunt, quam Jesus Christus à Patre ipsis destinatus sit Mediator. Neque enim pro illis veram peccatorum expiationem per Christi λύτρον fieri necesse fuit, immo ne possibile quidem (si verum ingenue dicendum est) quorum peremtoria & absoluta, partim ad vitam, partim ad mortem, destinatio jam ante nominatim facta fuit, *Electi* enim, quos vocant, sive ad vitam prædestinati, expiatione & reconciliatone tali opus non habent: quia eo ipso, quod præcise ad salutem electi sunt, in flagranti Dei gratia sunt, jamque à Deo amore summo & immutabili, qualis filiorum & hæredum Dei proprius est, necessario diliguntur. Pro reprobis autemquo isti vocant, expiationem vere factam esse ipsimet negant; & res alioqui per se absurda est; quippe quæ contradictionem implicat. Eo ipso enim, quod existorum hominum sensu *reprobi* sunt, ab expiatione per Christura facta prorsus excluduntur: quia quos Deus immutabili decreto semel à salute reprobavit sive æterno exitio devovit, illis nec serio vult, nec velle potest, ut ullum salutare bonum re ipsa conferatur, nedum ut expiatio jam dicta iisdem cum electis revera communis sit. Atque hæc de præcipuis Dei operibus summatim hactenus.

the door of eternal salvation and the way of immortality to them, even as it was prefigured many ages before under various types, figures and shadows of the Old Testament,[b] and especially under the type of that solemn sacrifice, which the High-Priest performed once every year in the holy of holies. Truly he is our savior by efficacy, in as much as he efficaciously applies the virtue and fruit of his merit to his believers,[c] and really gives them to enjoy of all the benefits gained by his obedience, and makes them partakers of these things by faith, about which [we will say] more later.

b. Rom. 3:24, 14:9, 1 John 2:12, Heb. 4:4, 1 Pet. 1:3.

10. But they enervate, indeed they completely overthrow, the universal power of his merit and the truth of its efficacy, who assert that both the absolute election and reprobation of certain persons (whether considered before the fall, or only in or under the Fall, without regard for faith in Christ, or to the contrary, disobedience) was made first in order, before Jesus Christ was designated by the Father to be a mediator for them. For neither was it necessary that there be any true expiation of sins by the ranson of Christ for them, nor indeed was it even possible (if truth may be frankly spoken) for those who were long before by name peremptorily and absolutely predestined, part to life, part to death. For the Elect, as they call them, or those who are predestinated to life, have no need of any such expiation and reconciliation because they have been absolutely elected to salvation. They are in the flaming grace of God and are already esteemed by God with the highest and immutable love that belongs to sons and heirs of God. But concerning the reprobate, as they call them, they themselves deny any atonement was truly made for them, and besides being something absurd in itself, of course it implies a contradiction. For once they were reprobated, according to the opinion of these men, they are thereupon wholly altogether excluded from the atonement made by Christ. Because those whom God has by an immutable decree once reprobated from salvation or cursed to eternal destruction, he does not seriously will, nor can will, that anything good

should really be conferred for salvation, much less that the atonement should be shared by them with the elect. And this concludes the summation of the special works of God.

CHAPTER 9

CAPUT IX.
De Cognitione voluntatis divina in Fadere Novo patesacta.

I. Porro voluntas Dei,[a] Fœdere gratuito comprehensa, quam nobis in Evangelio suo summus Propheta noster unigenitus Dei Filius clare ac plene revelavit, duo præcipua capita complectitur. Primum, ea quæ Deus à parte sua, per Jesum Christum Filium suum, in nobis, aut circa nos, facere decrevit, ut salutis æternæ, per ipsum oblatæ, participes efficiamur. Secundum, ea, quæ à nobis, mediante gratia sua, omnino fieri vult, si salutem æternam reipsa consequi velimus.

a. Jer. 31:31, Heb. 8:9 & 9:15, 10:15.

2. Quæ Deus à *parte sua* facere ad salutem nostram decrevit, duo potissimum sunt. 1. Decrevit ad honorem Filii sui dilecti[a] omnes & solos vere in nomen ipsius credentes, sive ipsius Evangelio obedientes, & in side atque obedientia ista ad mortem usque perseverantes, per ipsum ad salutem & vitam æternam eligere sibi in fillios, adoptare, justificare, Spiritu S. obsignare & tantem glorificare: contra vero incredulos[b] & impœnitentes à salute & vita reprobare, & perpetuo damnare. 2 Decrevit ejusmodi efficacem gratiam, per eumdem filium suum, omnibus vocatis, quantumvis miseris peccatoribus, conferre:[c] per quam reipsa in Christum Servatorem suum credere, Evangelio ejus obedire, atque à dominio & reatu peccati liberari possint: imo

CHAPTER 9
On the knowledge of God's will, revealed in the new covenant

1. Further, the will of God,[a] comprehended in the gracious covenant which our greatest prophet, the only begotten Son of God, clearly and fully revealed to us in his Gospel, is embraced in two principle heads. First, those things which God for his part decreed to do in us or about us through by his Son Jesus Christ, that we may be made partakers of that eternal salvation offered by him. Second, those things which he wholly wills to be done by us through his own grace, if we really want to obtain eternal salvation.

2. Those things which God decreed to do for his part in order to provide our salvation, are principally two. 1. He decreed for the honor of his beloved Son to choose for himself sons through him to salvation and life eternal, to adopt, justify, seal with his Holy Spirit and finally to glorify all those and only those truly believing in his name, or obeying his gospel, and persevering in faith and obedience until death,[a] and to the contrary, to reprobate unbelievers and the impenitent from life and salvation and to damn them perpetually.[b] 2. He has decreed through his same Son, to confer to all that are called, although miserable sinners, such efficacious grace through which they may really believe in their Christ the Savior, obey his gospel and be freed from the dominion and guilt of sin,

etiam per quam reipsa credant, obediant, & liberentur, nisi nova contumacia & rebellione gratiam Dei oblatam rejiciant.

a. John 3:16, 6:29, Eph. 1:3-4, Rom. 8:28, 2 Tim. 1:9, Heb. 3:6, 14.
b. John 3:18, 36, Matt. 25:41.

3. Primum decretum est decretum *Pradestinationis ad salutem*, sive *electionis ad gloriam*: quo statuitur vera necessitas simul atque utilitas fidei & obedientiæ nostræ ad salutem & gloriam consequendam: ante quod aliud ordine prius decretum, quo certæ quædam singulares personæ nominatim, & quidem peremptorie, ad gloriam electæ cæteræ vero omnes ad æternos cruciatus reprobatæ fuerint, dogmatice statuere, revera est veram decreti hujus naturam abnegare, rectum ordinem invertere, Jesu Christi meritum tollere; divinæ tum bonitatis, tum justitiæ, tum sapientiæ gloriam obscurare; imo S. Ministerii totius, adeoque Religionis omnis veram vim atque efficaciam funditus evertere.

See Calvin and the Canons of the Synod of Dort.

4. Alterum decretum est decretum *vocationis ad fidem*, sive *electionis ad gratiam*: quo statiur necessitas, simul atque utilitas[a] gratiæ divinæ, seu mediorum nobis necessariorum ad fidem & obedientiam Jesu Christo, juxta voluntatem Dei, Evangelio ipsius revelatam, ex parte nostra præstandam. Quia verò de *Voluntate* illa Dei, quam ipse à nobis præstari vult, prius constare nobis debet; quam de *gratia* ad voluntatem illam præstandam necessaria; deque *gloria*, divinam voluntatem præstantibus promissa, & olim verto conferenda: hinc est, quod de ijsdem omnibus eodem, quo hic proposita sunt, ordine deinceps acturi sumus.

a. Rom 10:14, 2 Tim. 1:9-10, Tit. 2:11-12.

indeed also through which they may really believe, obey and be freed, unless by a new defiance and rebellion they reject the grace offered by God.[c]

c. Tit. 2:11-12. Acts 3:26, 5:31 & 26:16, 2 Cor. 5:18-20 & 6:1, 2 Pet. 1:3-4.

3. The first decree is the decree of predestination to salvation or election to glory, by which is established the true necessity and at the same time the usefulness of our faith and obedience for obtaining salvation and glory. But to dogmatically establish some other anterior, prior decree by which certain individual people were peremptorily elected by name to glory and all others were reprobated to eternal torture, is indeed to deny the true nature of this decree, to invert right order, to take away the merit of Jesus Christ, to obscure the glory of divine goodness, righteousness and wisdom, and indeed utterly to subvert the true power and efficacy of the whole sacred ministry, and thus of all religion.

4. The second decree is the decree of calling to faith or election to grace, by which is established the necessity and at the same time the usefulness of divine grace,[a] or of the means necessary for us to yield faith and obedience to Jesus Christ according to the will of God, revealed in his Gospel. Because truly we ought first to be sure about that will of God which he wants us to yield to him, than of the grace necessary for fulfilling that will, of the glory promised to be conferred to those performing the divine will. It is for this that we shall treat them all henceforth in the same order in which they have been proposed.

Chapter 10

CAPUT X
De Praceptis Iesu Christi in genere, deque fide ac pœnitentia, seu conversione ad Deum.

I. Voluntas Dei, quam à nobis præstari vult, æternam salutem per Christum consequamur, plene continetur *praceptis* Jesu Christi: quæ omnia,[a] licet multa ac varia sint, sub uno tamen *pracepto fidei* [b] in Jesum Christum (sed veræ, seu vivæ, & per charitatem operantis) comprehendi possunt, & ut plurium sub eo in Scriptura sacra comprehendi solent: licet ibidem pænitentia[c] quoque, seu *conversionis*, præceptum, ad clariorem rei exegesin sæpe solet adjungi.

a. Matt. 5-7.
b. John 3:16, Rom. 1:16-17 & 3:22.

2. Vivam autem ac veram fidem hanc appellamus,[a] qua necessario sibi conjuncta habet *bona opera*, totiusque vitæ sinceram emendationem, juxta præcepta Jesu Christi institutam. Quia enim *fide* veræ[b] passim à Servatore nostro promissio vitæ æternæ adjuncta est, imo[c] fides ipsa in justitiam credenti imputari dicitur; & nihilominus tamen non etiam[d] ex operibus justificari, ac non ex *fide tantum* Jacobus affirmat:[e] Paulus vero etiam pietatem habere promissuinem præsentis & futuræ vitæ asserit: quinimo fine[f] sanctimonia neminem visurum Dominum author ad Hebræos asseverat, aliaque[g] in eandem setentiam non pauca in Sacris literis expressa leguntur: utique necesse est, ut fidei præscriptum non alio modo hic confideretur, qua quatenus proprietate sua naturali *obedien-*

CHAPTER 10
On the commandments of Jesus Christ in general: faith and repentance, or turning to God.

1. The will of God, which he desires to be performed by us that we might obtain eternal salvation through Christ, is fully contained in the commandments of Jesus Christ, all of which, although they may be many and varied,[a] still may be comprehended under this one commandment of faith in Jesus Christ[b] (but true or living faith, working through charity) and usually are comprehended under it in the Sacred Scripture. At the same time, it must be granted that often the commandment of repentance[c] or conversion ought to be closely connected, in order to clarify the exegesis of the matter.

c. Matt. 3:2, Acts 3:19.

2. But we call living and true faith that which necessarily has joined to itself good works[a] and a sincere correction of the whole life, structured upon the commandments of Jesus Christ. For because the promise of eternal life is everywhere joined by our Savior to true faith,[b] indeed faith itself is said to be imputed for righteousness to the one who believes,[c] yet nevertheless James affirms[e] that we are justified by works also and not by faith alone.[d] For Paul also asserts that godliness has promise for the present and the future life. Indeed further, the author to the Hebrews peremptorily declares that without holiness none will see the Lord[f] and not a few others of the same opinion are expressly read in the Holy Scriptures.[g] It is certainly necessary that the prescription of faith is not to be considered in any other way than as to

tiam fidei includit, & tanquam fœcunda bonorum operum mater[h] est, totiusque Christianæ pietatis ac sanctimoniæ fons ac scaturigo. Tantum abest, ut huic obedientiæ ad pietati & ipsa opponi debeat aut jure possit.

a. Gal. 5:6 & 6:15, 1 Cor. 7:19, Ja. 1:15.
b. John 3.36 & 6:40.
c. Rom. 4:5.
d. Ja. 2:24.

3. Hac igitur ratione considerate *fides*, totam hominis conversionem, Evangelio præscriptam, ambitu suo continet: quæ ipsa non tantum *pœnitentiam*, vulgo sic dictam, sive contritionem, ac dolorem serium de peccatis præteritis: sed[a] *resipiscentiam* etiam plane ac propriè acceptam; sive sinceram mentis, animi, & totius vitæ mutationem in melius juxta Scripturam complecitur: quamvis etiam interdum,[b] ad utranque plenius explicandam, hæc ibidem ab illa distinguatur.

a. Matt. 3:3, Acts 3:15, Luke 3:3, 5, Acts 26:18, 1 Thess. 1:9, John 3:5, Gal. 6:15, Eph. 2:1, 5:15.

4. De hac autem illud Christiano cuilibet in genere tenedum est: Ut resipiscentia, seu conversion ad salutem Deo grata sit, ordinarie tria ad eam necessaria esse. I. Ut[a] *efficax* sit, ad proinde non velleitate sola, meroque affectu, aut nudo pietatis studio adsolvatur: sed per actus etiam virtutum, quoties occasio est, & fieri potest, semper sese foris exserat; ita nimirum, ut quis[b] nec ipse negligat, quod præceptum est, nec deditâ operâ faciat, quod malum ac vetitum esse novit;[c] aut de quo, an gratum Deo sit, dubitat; nec etiam ad peccata aliorum facile[d] conniveat, eaque consesu suo, silentio, dissimulatione, aliaveratione approbet. II. Ut sincera sit,[e] ac proinde non tantum ex certa solidaque divinæ voluntatis notitiâ proficiscantur: sed etiam veram animi probitatem supponat: hoc est, talem, quæ non ex diviso, simulato, aut ficto; sed ex toto atque integro corde oriatur. III. Ut continua sit,[f] ac proinde non semel tantum, aut certis temporibus, quasi per intervalla, præstetur: nec aliquamdiu tantum duret, sed ad finem usque vitæ nostræ perseveret, id est, usque dum

include the obedience of faith in its own natural property, and is like a fruitful mother of all good works[h] and the fountain or spring of all Christian godliness and holiness. There is no reason why it ought or rightly may be opposed to obedience and godliness.

e. 1 Tim. 4:8.
f. Heb. 12:14.
g. Matt. 7:21, Heb. 10:36, Ja. 1:15.
h. 1 John 5:1, 2 Pet. 1:5-7, Eph. 3:17.

3. Therefore, for this reason faith encompasses the whole conversion of man as prescribed by the gospel, which not only contains what is vulgarly called penitence or contrition and serious sorrow for past sins, but also repentance plainly and properly taken,[a] or a sincere change for the better of the mind, soul and the whole life according to the Scriptures. Sometimes, however, in order to fuller explain them both, they are distinguished from one another.[b]

b. Acts 16:18.

4. For concerning this, every Christian in general must hold that for repentance or conversion to be pleasing to God for salvation, three things are ordinarily necessary. 1. That it be effectual[a] and therefore is not completed by willing alone and mere emotion, or bare zeal for godliness. But it must always outwardly exert itself through acts of virtue, as often as there is occasion and can be done, clearly so that one does not neglect what is commanded,[b] nor willfully does works which he knows are evil or forbidden[c] or which he doubts is pleasing to God, neither easily overlooks the sins of others[d] and approves them by his consent, silence, disregard or by other means. 2. That it be sincere[e] and therefore not only proceed from a certain and solid knowledge of the divine will, but it also supposes a true and honest soul, that is, which does not arise from a divided, dissembling, feigned heart, but from one which is complete and whole. 3. That it be continual[f] and therefore that it not be performed only once, or for certain times, almost at intervals, nor endure only for a time, but that it persists to the end of our life, that is, until

Deus ipse terminum obedientiæ nostræ ponat. Sed operæpretium est, ut utrumque hoc caput tum *fidem*, tum *bona opera*, speciatim etiam consideremus.

a. Ja. 1:22, 2:26 & 4:15, 2 Pet. 1:8-9, chapter 2, Rom. 8:1.
b. John 8:34, 1 John 3:7-9.
c. Rom. 14:32.

God himself puts an end to our obedience. But it is a rewarding work that we give special consideration to these heads of faith and good works.

d. Eph. 5:11, 2 Pet. 2:8, Rev. 2:2.
e. Matt. 6:1, 19:8, 22:11-12, 1 Tim. 1:5.
f. Matt. 10:24 & 24:13, Heb. 3:6, 14 & 10:38-39, Rev. 2:7, 10, 16 & 3:21.

• CHAPTER 11 •

CAPUT XI.
De fide in Iesum Christum.

Fides in Jesum Christum, est[a] deliberatus & firmus animi assensus, verbo Dei adhibitus, & cum vera in Christum fiducia conjuctus; quo non tantum doctrinæ Jesu Christj, tamquam veræ ac divinæ, firmiter assentimur, ac fidenter inhæremus: sed in ipsum etiam[b] Jesum Christum, ut Prophetam, Sacerdotem ac Regem nostrum unicum, ad salutem à Deo nobis, ex pura gratia, datum, toti recumbimus: ita ut ab eo solo,[c] tanquam unico Redemptore nostro, salutem & vitam æternam, at non nisi ea ratione via obtinendam, quam ipse nobis in verbo suo revelavit, exspectare non dubitemus.

a. Heb. 11;1, Rom. 4:18.
b. John 14:1, Heb. 4:16, Eph. 3:12, 17.

2. Itaque ad fidem veram & salvificam non sufficit sola[a] *notitia* divinæ voluntatis: seu sensuum omnium ad salutem scitu necessarium, qui scilicet Evangelio continentur. Hæc enim & sine *assensu*, & sine fiducia esse potest. imo & in[b] dæmonibus, atque impiis multis & infidelibus reipsa inest. Neque assensus etiam quilibet,[c] puta subitus, perfunctorius, implicitus, brutus aut cœcus; nulla ratione nixus, nullo judiocio adhibitus: hic enim per se, seorsim acceptus,

CHAPTER 11
On faith in Jesus Christ

1. Faith in Jesus Christ is a deliberate and firm assent of the mind placed in the Word of God,[a] joined with true trust in Christ by which we not only firmly assent to the doctrine of Jesus Christ as true and divine, but whereby we totally rest in Jesus Christ himself as our only prophet, priest, and king,[b] given to us by God for salvation purely by grace, so that we do not doubt to expect from him alone, as our only redeemer,[c] salvation and eternal life, but unobtainable except by reason of that way which he himself has revealed in his Word.

c. Heb. 5:9 & 10:15, Acts 4:12 & 13:39.

2. Therefore knowledge alone of the divine will does not suffice for true and saving faith,[a] or understanding of all the concepts are contained in the gospel. For this is possible without assent and trust. Indeed, it really is in the demons,[b] and in many of the ungodly and unbelieving. Nor indeed is it any assent whatever,[c] namely sudden, perfunctory, implicit, brutish or blind, ungrounded in reason and yielded without judgment. For this by itself, taken alone, is not saving, nor can it ever

salutaris non est, nec voluntatem sufficienter ad rationale & liberum obsequium movere unquam potest: & propterea non raro etiam in iis reperitur, qui parum Christiane vivunt: sed requiritur omnino *firmus & solidus*, voluntatiaque deliberatæ imperio roboratus:[d] denique *fiducialis & obsequisus assensus*: qui & *fiducia* dicitur: non quidem absoluta fiducia specialis misericordiæ, quasi reipsa jam perceptæ: qua scilicet credo, mihi jam remissa esse peccata mea:[e] (hæc enim non est essentialis forma fidem justificantem constituens: sed quoddam tantum consequens adjunctum: imo ipsam salvificam fidem necessario, tanquam prærequisitam sui conditionem, præsupponit:) sed qua firmiter statuo,[f] fieri non posse, ut aliter, quam se Jesum Christum, & alia quam per ipsum præscripta ratione, æternam mortem evadam, & contra vitam sempiternam consequar: ac proinde quæ novam obedientiam ipsi Jesu Christo à nobis debitam, id est, non sterile aliquod obediendi propositum, aut affectum sine affectu, sed ipsum verum & actuale obsequium ex sese continuo parit, & sibi conjunctum semper habet.

a. John 13:3
b. Ja. 2:14, Luke 13:47, Tit. 1:16.
c. Matt. 13:22, Heb. 4:1, Rom. 12:1, Eph. 5:17.

3. Ex quibus porro concludimus, se fides est talis assensus, qualem diximus, à Deo sub promisso vitæ æternæ & comminatione contrariæ mortis serio imperatus, & ab homine ex mandato Dei præstitus: non posse igitur eum esse quippiam, in nobis, sine nobis,[a] effectum: nedum per irresistibilem vim, aut omnipotentem Dei operationem, cui reluctari non possimus, in voluntate nostra productum, quocunque tandem nomine, aut titulo id vocetur. Quæ enim pure pute à Deo patimur, quæque in nobis per invictam Dei omnipotentiam sine nobis producuntur; ea sub præceptum proprie dictum non cadunt, nec veræ obedietiæ nomine venire jure possunt: proinde nec præmio aliquo aut remuneratione justa affici, aut laude ac præconio ullo digna judicari queunt.

sufficiently move the will to any rational and free obedience. And therefore [assent] is not rarely found in those who live little like Christians, but it must be entirely firm and solid, strengthened by the command of a deliberate will. Finally, assent which is faithful and obedient is called faith,[d] not just an absolute confidence of special mercy, almost as if already secured, namely, by which I believe that my sins are already forgiven me[e] (for this is not the essential form which constitutes justifying faith, but only a certain additional consequent, indeed it necessarily presupposes saving faith itself, as its prerequisite condition), but by which I firmly establish that it is impossible that I should escape eternal death and to the contrary obtain eternal life by any other means than Jesus Christ,[f] and in any other way than by that prescribed by him. And hence this has always had joined to it our debt of new obedience to Jesus Christ, that is, not some sterile purpose of obeying or feelings without effect, but which continually brings forth of itself true and actual obedience itself.

d. Eph. 1:17, 3:17-18, Matt. 9:2, Heb. 11:1.
e. Rom. 1:17 3:25, 4:4, 5:1 & 10:9, Acts 4:12 & 13:38.
f. Heb. 5:9, Acts 5:32, John 3:36, Rom. 10:16.

3. From these things we conclude, if faith is such assent as we have said, namely, that which was seriously commanded by God under the promise of eternal life and the contrary threat of death and performed by man according to the commandment of God, then it cannot therefore be effected in us without us, neither is it produced through an irresistible power or omnipotent operation of God (by whatever name or title it is called) in our wills, which we cannot oppose. For what we merely, purely suffer from God and whatever are produced in us by God's invincible omnipotence without us, these do not fall under any commandment properly called, nor can they justly come under the name of obedience. Hence, they cannot be justly bestowed reward or recompense or judged worthy of any praise or consideration.

See the Canons of the Synod of Dort, ch. 3 & 4, Article 11:14, 17., Reject. Art. 8.

4. Ut autem commode assensus hic à nobis eliciatur, duo imprimis necessaria sunt. I. Argumenta talia ex parte Dei, quibus verisimiliter nihil opponi potest, cur credibilia non sunt & fidem non mereantur ea, quæ credenda nobis proponuntur. II. Pia docilitas, vel animi probitas in eo, à quo fides ista postulatur. *Fides enim non*[a] *est omnium.* Et *qui voluntatem Dei facere vult,*[b] *is cognoscet* (vel *intelliget*) *utrum doctrina Christi à Deo sit, necne. Qui autem, quæ mala sunt, facit,*[c] *is odit lucem, nec venit ad lucem, ne redarguantur opera ipsius: at qui faciat veritatem, is venit ad lucem, ut manifestafiant opera ipsius, eo quod in Deo facta sint.* Item, *qui ex Deo*[d] *est, is audit verba Dei; propterea vos* (improbi) *non auditus, quia ex Deo non estis.* Item *vos non creditis, quia non est is ex ovibus meis.*

a. 2 Thess. 3:2.
b. John 7:17.

5. Ad sensus igitur ejusmodi fiducialis, vel obsequiosa hæc fiducia, demum est vera ac viva fides, quæ secum necessario trahit observationem mandatorum Jesu Christi,[a] sive bona opera. Qui enim vere credit, & certo persuasus est, Jesum Christum à Deo constitutum esse auctorem salutis omnibus & solis ipsi obedientibus; & pie sancteque viventibus: neque fieri posse, ut talia ratione[b] ad salutem eternam perveniatur, aut mors sempiterna evadatur, quam per viam veræ obedientiæ, seu bonorum operum: ille procul dubio, bona spe plenus, & libenter & alacriter, viam istam ingredietur: & per veram resipiscentiam, sive mutationem mentis, voluntatis, actionunque omnium in melius, ad æternam gloriam contendet: si modo, quid tum salus, tum mors æterna sit, rite secum perpenderit.

a. John 5:3-5, Gal. 5:6 & 6:15, Matt. ?.17 & 12:34-35.

6. Quia tamen ij, qui ad finem recenter convertuntur, ut plurimum consuetudine quadam peccandi laborare solent: hinc plerumque fit, adsensus hic, licet deliberatus & firmus, non statim omnino excutiat[a] habitum illum peccato-

4. And that this assent may be commodiously drawn from us, two things are necessary. 1. Such arguments proposed to by God which cannot be opposed as incredible or unworthy of being believed. 2. Godly teachableness or honesty of mind in the one of whom this faith is demanded. "For all do not have faith.[a] And he who wants to do the will of God will recognize" (or understand) "whether a doctrine of Christ is from God or not.[b] But he who does what is evil, he hates the light, neither comes to the light, lest his deeds be reproved.[c] But he who does the truth, he comes to the light, that his deeds may be manifested, that they are done by God." Likewise, "He who is of God, hears the Word of God.[d] For this reason you" (the wicked) "do not hear, because you are not from God." Likewise, "You do not believe, because you are not of my sheep."

c. John 3:19-21.
d. John 8:47 & 10:26-27, Acts 2:41 & 13:46.

5. Therefore, this understanding of this type of confident assent or obedient trust is precisely true and living faith, which necessarily draws with it the observation of the commandments of Jesus Christ or good works.[a] For he who truly trusts and is certainly persuaded that Jesus Christ is ordained by God to be the author of salvation for all and only those who obey him, live godly and holy lives, and that it is impossible that men should arrive at eternal salvation or escape eternal death[b] but through the way of true obedience or good works, he, far from doubt and filled with good hope, will both willingly and cheerfully enter this way. And by true repentance, or a change of mind, will and all his actions for the better, he will contend for eternal glory, if he rightly and duly has considered within himself what is eternal salvation and eternal death.

b. Heb. 5:9, 11:6 & 12:1, 5, 16.

6. Nevertheless, because those who are recently converted to the faith for the most part usually labor under the practice of sinning, from this it happens that this assent, although deliberate and strong, does not immediately, entirely shake

rum, præsertim profunde jam & alte per consuetudinem diuturnam radicatum; sed pedetentim ac gradatim vires majores acquirat. Unde gradus quidam hujus fidei distingui solent, pro quibus porro ipsorum credentium ac resipiscentium, seu renatorum, hoc est, eorum qui per fidem bona opera faciunt, tres diversæ classes vel ordines oriuntur. Primus ordo est *Incipientium*,[b] qui Evangelio quidem vere assentiuntur: sed propter consuetudinem peccati inveteratam, & habitum quemdam inolitum, cum magno labore, molestia & lucta carnis, subinde adhuc ebullientis, & contra spiritum (seu mentem Spiritu Dei per Evangelium illustratam) recalcitrantis, impetus ac motus domant ac subigunt. II. *Proficientium*,[c] qui beneficio fidei jam aliquandiu severiori & castigatiori vitæ assuefacti, & in studio pietatis plusculum exercitati, facilius & minore cum resistentia à peccandi consuetudine se continent: etiamsi aliquando non levem adhuc luctam intra se sentiant. III. *Adultorum*,[d] sive aliquatenus perfectorum, hoc est eorum, qui jam in pietate confirmati, auxilio fidei suæ, cum voluptate, gaudio & delectatione quadam, sanctimoniæ operam dant; & justitiam ac veritatem toto corde, tota anima & omnibus virinus suis diligunt: adeo ut Scriptura de ijs potissimum afferat,[e] *quod non peccent*, imo, *quod non possint peccare* &c. non quod nunquam, ne quidem per errorem, aut subitam aliquam passionem, vel aliam similem infirmitatem (imprimis in gravi aliqua tentatione) delictum ullum, vel minimum, committere possint; aut nunquam reipsa committant (*non enim est homo in terra, qui non peccet*[f]) sed quod vitiosos habitus jam prorsus exuerint,[g] à consuetudine peccandi abstineant: & proinde, si forte in peccatum aliquod incidant (quod tamen non nisi perraro accidit, quamdiu quidem ipsi sunt, & permanent vere regeniti) id tantum per errorem, vel obreptionem, vel aliquam mentis obnubilationem contingat. De his igitur omnibus, & singulis, statuimus, quod per gratiam & Spiritum Dei vere renati, seu vere credentes & resipiscentes sint: dummodo quam diligentissimè

off that habit of sin, especially having now been deeply rooted by long practice.[a] But he acquires greater strength by steps and degrees. From this, faith is usually distinguished into certain degrees, and there arise from this three classes or orders for those who believe and repent, or are regenerate, that is, of those who by faith do good works. The first order are the beginners,[b] which indeed truly assent to the gospel but because of the long practice of sin, and the ingrown habit of it, with great labor, trouble and wrestling with the flesh, ever boiling up and resisting against the Spirit (or their mind illuminated by the Spirit of God through the gospel) dominate and subjugate their come and subdue their assaults and motions. 2. The second are the proficient,[c] who, by the benefit of faith have for some time accustomed themselves to some more strict and confined life and exercised themselves somewhat more in godliness, more easily and with less resistance restrain themselves from the practice of sinning, even if sometimes they feel no light struggle about it within themselves. 3. The third are adults,[d] or those who are in some respects mature, that is, those who work at holiness with pleasure, joy and a certain delight, and love justice and truth with all their heart, all their soul and with all their strength, so that the Scripture affirms principally about them, that they do not sin, indeed, that they cannot sin, etc.[e] Not that they never could commit or never really do commit some failure, however small, through some error or some sudden passion, or other similar infirmity (especially in some grave temptation) any offence or miscarriage, ("for there is no man on Earth who does not sin"[f]) but that they have now entirely put off all vicious habits,[g] and abstain from the practice of sinning. And therefore, if by chance they fall into some sin (which still does not happen except very rarely, and they truly remain regenerate), it happens only through error or surprise, or some clouding of the mind. Therefore, we think concerning each and every one, that they are truly born again through the grace and Spirit of God, or they are truly believers and repenters, provided that they diligently labor in order that they may be entirely

operam dent, ut à vitiosa illa peccandi *consuetudine* prorsus immunes fiant; & infirmitates illas, quibus plerumque omnes, pro diversa ratione ætatis, temperamenti, locorum, status, conditionis, aliarumque circumstantiarum, plus minusve obnoxii sunt, magis magisque corrigere semper student. Quod[h] quidem utrumque per gratiam Dei fieri posse, imo necessarium esse, ut fiat, religiose credimus.

a. John 2:1-3, 2 Cor. 3:1, Heb. 5:13 & 6:1.
b. Heb. 5:13-14 ^ 6:1-2, Col. 3:5, Gal. 6:1, Ja. 4:1, Rev. 3:1.
c. Gal. 5:16-17, Eph. 4:14.
d. Rom. 12:1 & 9, Rom. 15:1, Phil. 3:17.

7. Etsi vero,[a] qui jam habitum ipsum fidei, & sanctimoniæ sunt adepti, difficulter admodum ad pristinam vitæ profanitatem & dissolutionem relabi queunt: fieri tamen omnino posse,[b] imo non raro factum esse credimus, ut paulatim huc relabantur, & tandem etiam à priore fide ac charitate sua plane deficiant; desertaque via justitiæ, ad pristina, quæ vere reliquerant, mundi inquinamenta, veluti sues ad volutabrum cæni, & canes ad vomitum suum, revertantur; iisque, quas antea vere effugerant, carnis cupiditatibus iterum implicentur; & sic totaliter, tandemque etiam finaliter, nisi serio in tempore resipiscant, divina gratia excidant. Neque interim tamen absolute negamus,[c] fieri posse, ut ii, qui semel vere crediderunt, quando ad pristinam vitæ profanitatem relabuntur, divinæ gratiæ beneficio denuo renoventur, & ad frugem redant: etamsi id raro fieri solere, ac difficulter[d] admodum fieri posse credamus. Atque hos etiam tales, quoties per Dei gratiam id fit, in ordine vere piorum, ac resipiscentium certoque salvandorum, siquidem in iterata ista conversione perseverent, omnino collocandos esse arbitramur.

a. Heb. 6.
b. Heb. 6:4, Rev. 2 & 3, 2 Pet. 2:18, Ez. 18:24, Heb. 4:1-2 & 10:28-29, 38-39, 1 Tim. 1:19-20, Rom. 11:18.

free from the vicious practice of sinning, and continually strive more and more to correct those infirmities which for the most part all are more or less liable, depending on their age, temperament, place, state, condition and of other circumstances. Both indeed we religiously believe are possible to do through entirely necessary grace of God.[h]

e. 1 John 3:9 & 5:18.
f. 1 Ki. 8:47.
g. Eph. 4:23, Col. 2:23, Rom. 6:4.
h. Rom. 6:14, Eph. 6:13, Phil. 4:13, 1 John 4:4, Jude v. 24.

7. Even if it is true that those who are adept in the habit of faith and holiness can only with difficulty fall back to their former profaneness and dissoluteness of life,[a] yet we believe that it is entirely possible, if not rarely done,[b] that they fall back little by little and until they completely lack their prior faith and charity. And having abandoned the way of righteousness, they revert to their worldly impurity which they had truly left, returning like pigs to wallowing in the mud and dogs to their vomit, and are again entangled in lusts of the flesh which they had formerly, truly fled. And thus totally and at length also they are finally torn from the grace of God unless they seriously repent in time. And yet in the meantime we do not absolutely deny it is possible that those who have once truly believed,[c] when they fall back to their former profanity of life, may be renewed again by benefit divine grace, become good men, even if we believe that it usually rarely happens and with great difficult.[d] But as often as it happens by the grace of God with such as these, we judge that they are placed entirely among the number of the truly godly, repentant and truly saved, if indeed they persevere in this renewed conversion.

c. Contrary to the Canons of the Synod of Dort, ch. 5; Ps. 51, 2 Cor. 2, Is. 1, Deut. 30.
d. Luke 11:24, Heb. 6:4, 2. Pet. 2:2.

Chapter 12

CAPUT XII.
De bonis operibus in specie,
deque decalogi expositione

CHAPTER 12
Types of good works,
and an exposition of the Decalogue.

Bonorum operum alia Christianis omnibus[a] *communia*, alia certarum vocationum[b] *propria* sunt. Horum vero, quæ Christianis omnibus ex æquo sine discrimine præscripta sunt, summa *tribus* hisce capitibus comprehendi potest. I. Dilectione Dei & proximi, quæ lege morali, quatenus à Jesu Christo exposita est, tota continetur. II. Directione, sive abnegatione nostri ipsorum. III. Assidua ad Deum precatione, & pro acceptis beneficiis gratiarum actione.

1. Some good works are common to all Christians in general;[a] others are proper to certain vocations.[b] The sum of those which are common to all Christians alike without distinction may be comprised under these three heads. 1. In our loving of God and our neighbor, which is wholly contained in the moral law as it was expounded by Jesus Christ. 2. In the directing or denying ourselves. 3. In daily praying to God, and giving him thanks for his benefits received.

a. Matt. 5-7.

b. Eph. 5:12 & 6:1.

2. Epitone legis moralis est *Decalogus*, qui continetur *duabus talibus*: quarum *prima* quatuor; at secunda sex præcepta continet.[a] Illa immediate ac primo ad dilectionem Dei; ista ad amorem proximi tota refertur. Utraque habet fere præcepta generalia & prorsus negativa, quæ ubique, semper, & absolute obligant: sed sub quibus etiam affirmativa, & specialia præcepta non pauca passim in Scripturis comprehensa sunt: ad quæ utraque Christianus animus sedulo semper attendat, necesse est.

2. The Decalogue is the epitome of the moral law, which is contained in two tablets, of which the first contains four commandments and the second six.[a] The one immediately and firstly refers to loving God, the other entirely to the love of our neighbor. For the most part, both of them have general and entirely negative commandments, which are absolutely binding everywhere and always, but under which are also comprehended affirmative and not a few special commandments everywhere in the Scriptures, to both of which it is necessary that a Christian soul always carefully attend.

a. Ex. 20, Deut. 5 & 6, Matt. 22:37-40, Mark 12:30-31.

3. *Primum* prioris tabulæ præceptum jubet, *ne Deum alium* (nedum *alios Deos*) *coram uno illo vero Deo, aut præter illum habeamus*: id est,[a] ne vel ipsi pro arbitrio nostro comminiscamur, aut per traditionem aliorum, citra expres-

3. The first commandment of the former tablet commands that we have no another god (much less other gods) before him the one true God, or beyond him,[a] that is, neither do we devise one according to our will, or by tradition from others, without the

sum Dei mandatum, admittamus quippiam, (sive verum, sive fictum, sive creatum, sive fabrafactum, sive vivum, sive mortuum, sive rationale, sive brutum) cui vel naturam ac vim divinam, vel proprietates, vel actiones, vel auctoritatem & imperium in nos divinum, aut directe aut indirecte tribuamus: neve ilud actibus hujusmodi, sive internis, sive externis honoremus, qui divinitatis illi tributæ opinionem certam arguant: quales sunt actus[b] religiosi cultus, puta fidei Deo & Christo debitæ, simulque spei, fiduciæ, amoris, timoris, adorationis, invocationis, & hinc ortæ analoge laudis & gratiarum actionis; item externi sacrificii, juramenti, voti, aut similis alicujus sacræ devotionis. Quicunque enim, sive rei,[c] sive personæ alicui, hunc talem honorem exhibet, vel circa eam hos aut similes actus præstat, is rem aut personam illam pro Deo suo habere in Scriptura dicitur. Itaque mens præcepti est, ut omnem *idolatriam*, internam simul, & externam, sedulo vitemus: contraque unum[d] illum verum Deum, qui se nobis in verbo suo patefecit, religioso cultu semper adficiamus: id est, recte agnoscamus, sancte amemus ac timeamus, suppliciter adoremus, humiliter invocemus, grata mente laudemus ac celebremus, omnem que spem & fiduciam ipso solo, veluti unico bonorum omnium auctore & fonte, perpetuo collocemus.

express command of God, admit anything (whether true or feigned or fabricated, whether alive or dead, whether rational or irrational) to which we would either directly or indirectly attribute either natural or divine power or properties or actions or divine authority or rule over us. Nor that we honor it with any actions, either internal or external, which may show a certain opinion of divinity attributed to it. Such are acts of religious worship, namely, of due faith in God and Christ, together with hope, trust, love, fear, adoration, invocation and from this arise proportional praise and thanksgiving, likewise external sacrifice, oaths, vows, or other similar acts of holy devotion.[b] For whoever gives such an honor to any thing or person, or performs such acts as these, he is said in Scripture to hold that thing or person for his god.[c] Therefore the meaning of the commandment is that we must carefully avoid all idolatry, both internal and external, and on the contrary, that we must make religious worship to the one true God[d] who revealed himself to us in his Word, that is, that we correctly know, love and fear with holiness, submissively adore, humbly invoke, praise and celebrate him with a grateful mind, and perpetually place all our hope and trust in him alone as the only author and fountain of all good.

a. Deut. 6:11-12, 32:16-17, 1 Ki. 11:4, 12:28, Jer. 2:11-13, Matt. 4:10, 1 Thess. 1:9, Acts 14;15, Gal. 4:8.
b. Deut. 6:13 & 10:20.

c. Eph. 5:5, Phil. 3:19, Is. 44:16-17, Jer. 2:17.
d. Matt. 4:10, Jer. 17:13, Ps. 50:14-15 & 116:5-6, Rev. 14:7 & 15:4 & 19

4. Secundum præceptum est, *ne imagines aut simulacra ullius generis colamus ac veneremur*: id est, ne coram statuis, picturis, aut imaginibus ullis (sive verum, sive fictum numen, sive rem, quæ revera est, sive figmentum, quod non est, sive hominem, sive bestiam, sive Angelum, sive quidvis aliud, in cœlo aut in terra representatibus) venerabundi[a] procidamus: vel ad illas aut circa illas ejusmodi externa opera faciamus, quæ religiosi, & Deo soli debiti cultus indicia esse, sacra Scriptura clare asserit:[b] etiam cum quis eas, coram ista facit, imagines, vel simulacra pro Deo se non

4. The second commandment is that "we neither worship nor reverence images, or likenesses of any type." That is, that we do not fall prostrate before statues, pictures or any other images (whether true or imagined, whether something which really is or a figment which is not, whether man, beast, angel or anything else, in heaven or on earth),[a] or perform for them or concerning them any manner of external works which the Sacred Scripture clearly affirms to be signs of religious worship due only to God,[b] indeed, even when a man professes and openly declares that he does not hold as a god those

habere profitetur & palam declarat. In ejusmodi enim cultu vetito non judicat Deus actiones ex animo colentis, sed animum potius ex actionibus: adeo ut idolum id facere, & reipsa *Deum ac Patrem suum appellare* homines dicantur, quod ista ratione venerantur, etiamsi nil nisi saxum, aut lignum id esse norint, imo etiam pro eo se habere protestentur:[c] sed contra ut totum hoc externæ idolatriæ genus studiose vitemus, & sicut Apostolus Johannes monet,[d] *ab idolis fugiamus*: nimirum certi ex Apostolo Paulo,[e] quod *nulla sit communio templi Dei cum idolis*. Denique ut ipsum verum Deum, acerrimum gloriæ suæ zelotem,[f] in spiritu & veritate, ubi ubi simus, juxta verbi ipsius præscriptum, externæ etiam ratione semper colamus, adoremus ac veneremur.

images or likenesses before whom he does those things. For in this manner of forbidden worship, God does not judge actions according to the mind of the worshipper, but rather judges the mind by the actions, so that men are said to make that an idol, and really call it their god and father, which they venerate in this manner, even if they know it is nothing but stone or wood, and indeed also protest that they hold it such.[c] But to the contrary, we are warned again every kind of external idolatry, just as the Apostle John warns us,[d] and that we "flee from idols," namely, being assured by the Apostle Paul[e] that "the temple of God has no communion with idols." Finally, that in spirit and truth, wherever we may be, we always worship, adore and venerate the one true God, who is most severely zealous of his glory,[f] according to what was prescribed in his Word, even in an outward manner.

a. Lev. 16:1, Deut. 4:15, Ps. 97:8 & 115:4, Is. 42:18-19 & 54:9, Acts 17:29, Rom. 1:23, 25, 1 Cor. 12:2.
b. Is. 44:16-17, Jer. 2:27-28, Matt. 6:24, Eph. 5:5, Phil. 3:19.
c. 1 Cor. 10:14-15.
d. 1 John 5:21.
e. 2 Cor. 6:16.
f. Is. 42:8 & 48:11, John 4:23.

5. *Tertium* præceptum est, *ne nomen Dei in vanum aut temere usurpemus*: hoc est, ne in verbis & oratione nostra,[a] (sive asserere, aut negare, sive promittere, aut comminari aliquid velimus) magnificum Dei nomen[b] irreverenter, aut leviter unquam usurpemus: præsertim vero, ne ipsum unquam[c] blasphememus; aut[d] temere, inconsiderate, vel falso, per ipsum juremus: denique ne falsa nominis divini jactione (prout falsi[e] Prophetæ sæpe olim fecerunt) alios fallamus aut seducamus: sed contra, ut de Deo, rebusque divinis loquentes, iis verbis, eaque oratione utamur, quæ tum sanctimoniæ, ac piæ gravitatis plenissima sint, tum Dei ac S. Scripturæ reverentissima: sintque sermones nostri ex Domini Jesu Christi instituto, *est & non:* aut quando religiose nobis jurandum sit. (quod quidem Christianis etiam nunc, in casu veræ necessitatis, omnino[f] licitum est; cum videlicet de gloria Dei, aut hominum salute agitur) non modo non mendaciter temere, aut sine vera nec necessitate: sed neque absque summa reverentia, pia animi submissione, decoro gestu, & sinceris,

5. The third commandment is that "we do not use the name of God in vain or rashly," that is, that in our words or speech[a] (whether we want to either affirm or deny, promise or threaten anything) we do not use the magnificent name of God irreverently or lightly.[b] But especially, that we never blaspheme it,[c] or swear rashly, inconsiderately or falsely by it.[d] And finally, that we do not deceive or seduce other by boasting in the divine name (as the false prophets of old often did).[e] But on the contrary, that when speaking of God and divine things, we use those words and that speech which are fullest both of holiness and godly dignity, and also most reverential of God and the sacred Scripture. And that our speech, as instituted by our Lord Jesus Christ, be yes and no, or if at any time it is necessary to take an oath (which indeed even now is entirely permitted for Christians in case of true necessity, namely, when the glory of God and the salvation of men is concerned[f]), that by no means we falsely, rashly or without truth or necessity invoke that most holy and tremendous majesty as witness and avenger of

candidisque verbis, sanctissimam illam ac tremendam Majestatem, testem ac vindicem veritatis in animas nostra invocemus.

a. Lev. 19:12, Deut. 5:11.
b. Lev. 5:4.
c. Lev. 24:10.

6. *Quartum* præceptum, *de sanctificando die septimo, sive Sabbatho,* quod attinet, in V. quidem T. rigide observandum id erat:[a] sed quia à Domino Jesu Christo sub Novi Testamenti tempore,[b] discrimen dierum prorsus sublatum est, ad ejus observationem præcise nemo Christianus obligatur. Interim tamen, quia primum hebdomadæ diem, qui *Dominicus* dici solet,[c] conventibus & exercitiis sacris ab Ecclesia primitiva destinatum fuisse legimus; & maximè, quia spiritualibus, sanctisque operibus, atque externis etiam pietatis exercitiis vacare, res per se laudabilis ac pia est: omnino arbitramur, Christianos recte pieque facere, quod ad exemplum Ecclesiæ primitivæ, piam istam consuetudinem (nisi gravior necessitas aliter intendum facere cogat) servare non negligunt; & primum hebdomandæ diem, procul tamen omni superstitione Iudaica, quasi sanctum, à reliquis segregant: eoque fine ab operibus non necessitatis se continent, quo attentius divinis & cælestibus meditationibus, aliisque piis officis, absque ulla distractione vacare, animumque totum possint intendere: contraque eos, qui secus faciunt, tanquam publici ordinis decori violatores,[d] justa reprehensione dignos esse censemus. Atque hæc de *primæ* tabulæ præceptis: Sequitur altera.

a. Deut. 5:12.
b. Rom. 14:5-6, Gal. 4:10, Col. 2:16.
c. Acts. 20:7, 1 Cor. 16. 2, Rev. 1. 10.

7. *Primum* secunda tabulæ præceptum, sive ordine *quintum,* est ut *Parentes honorem,* id est,[a] ut debitam illis reverentiam, sive honorem & amorem, non tantum externis verbis & gestibus, sed animo etiam submisso, sinceroque affectu exhibeamus: imo prompta obedientia, & obsequio spontaneo atque hilari non ipsis commendemus: veruntamen semper *in Domino,* id est, non nisi in iis, quæ cum præceptis supremi omnium Domini,

truth against our souls, but also not without the highest reverence, godly submission of mind, decorous gesture and sincere and candid words.

d. Lev. 5:4, Mat. 5:33, Ja. 5:12.
e. Deut. 10:20, 22.
f. Rom. 1:9 & 9:1, 2 Cor. 1:23 & 11:31, Heb. 6:16, Phil. 1:8, Rev. 10:6.

6. As for what pertains to the fourth commandment concerning sanctifying the seventh day or the Sabbath,[a] it was indeed strictly to be observed in the Old Testament, but because the difference of days was entirely removed by Jesus Christ in the times of the New Testament,[b] no Christian is absolutely bound to its observation. But in the interim, because we read that the first day of the week, which is usually called the Lord's,[c] was dedicated by the primitive church for sacred assemblies and exercises, and mostly because to be unoccupied for external and godly exercises is a thing worthy of praise in itself, we judge that Christians do rightly and piously following the example of the primitive church not to neglect to preserve this pious practice (unless some more grave necessity force them to do otherwise), and set apart the first day of the week, yet far from all Jewish superstition, as almost holy from the rest, and to that end refrain from all unnecessary works in order that they may be able to attend attentively to divine and celestial meditations and other godly duties without any distraction. And to the contrary, those who do otherwise we consider as violators of the public order and decency.[d] And this concludes the commandments of the first tablet. The second follows.

d. Tertul. Apol. c. 18. & De Corona Militis, likewise Historiae Tripart. Lib. 1. c. 10.

7. The first commandment of the second tablet, or fifth in order, is honor to parents,[a] that is, that we furnish to them due reverence or honor and love, not only with external words and gestures, but also a submissive mind and sincere affection. Indeed, that we commend ourselves to them by prompt obedience and free and cheerful compliance. However, always in the Lord, that is, in nothing but those things which rightly agree

Jesu Christi, probe consentiunt, aut certe iis non repugnant.[b] (Hac enim pugnâ existente, parentes etiam odisse, ac relinquere jubentur:) Denique ut vicem iis rependamus, porroque acceptis beneficiis omnem[c] gratidunem ex animo ipsis præstemus: necessitatibus scilicet ipsorum succurrendo, ad infirmitates eorundem connivendo, vitia etiam verecunde obtegendo, seu benignè excusando, & leniter interpretando: & speciatim duritiem & morositatem eorum patienter & longanimiter tolerando, & quantum fieri potest, blandis atque humanis modis emendando.

a. Ex. 21:15, Lev. 20:9, Prov. 20:10, Eph. 6:1, Col. 3:20.
b. Matt. 10:37, Luke 14:26.

8. *Parentum* autem nomine comprehendi possunt ac solent, non tantum parentes proprie dicti; sed & alii[a] superiores omnes, puta Domini, seu heri, Tutores, Præceptores, Pastores, Seniores; & inprimis boni piique Magistratus, qui scilicet parentum loco vere se gerunt: id est, qui subditos suos[b] justis legibus & æquis judiciis regunt: & probos quidem innoxiosque adversus improborum injurias defendunt; Nefarios autem & flagitiosos terrore justo coêrcent: imo ex amore publici boni & zelo veræ justitiæ (ratione tamen semper habita clementiæ, moderationis & lenitatis Christianæ) impunitos non dimittunt: atque ita bonis præmia, malis pænas, & unicuique quod suum est juste tribuunt: subditos denique suos fideles, cum plane sic necesse est, & post, omnia leniora remedia frustra tentata, aliter fieri nequit, gladio etiam adversus omnem injustam vim (ut quidem salva pietate & charitate Christiana possunt) tuentur ac defendunt. Quibus vicissim subditi[c] non honorem tantum, & reverentiam exhibere, sed & tributa & vectigalia solvere, aliaque id genus obedientiæ officia præstare tenentur. Quod usque adeo verum est, ut ne quidem duris & iniquis Magistratibus, quatenus salva conscientiæ integritate fieri potest, ista deneganda sint.

a. Eph. 6:5, Ex. 22:28, Acts 23:5, 1 Tim. 5:1.
b. Deut. 17:14ff, Ps. 82 & 101, Acts 25:10ff, Rom. 13:1ff.

with the commandments of the Supreme Lord of all, Jesus Christ, or at least not repugnant to them.[b] (For when there is a conflict, we are even commanded to hate and forsake our parents.) Finally, that we repay them in turn and render all gratitude from the heart for the benefits which we have formerly received,[c] namely, by helping their necessities, living with their infirmities, modestly hiding or kindly excusing and leniently interpreting their faults, tolerating especially their harshness and fussiness with patience and forbearance and, as far as possible, gently and humanely correcting them.

c. 1 Tim. 5:4, Matt. 15:4.

8. But under the name of "parents" are customarily included not only parents properly called, but also all other superiors,[a] namely, lords or owners, tutors or guardians, schoolmasters, pastors, elders, especially good and godly magistrates, who indeed bear the place of parents, that is, who rule their subjects by just laws and fair judgments[b] and indeed defend the good and innocent against the injuries of the wicked, but repress restrain criminals and profligates with just terror. Indeed, out of love for the public good and zeal of true justice (yet always having regard for Christian clemency, moderation and lenience) they do not let them go unpunished. And so they bestow rewards on the good, punishments to the evil and to each whatever is just. And finally, they protect and defend their faithful subjects when necessity plainly so requires it, and when after all calm remedies are tried in vain and it cannot be otherwise, even by the sword against all unjust power (as far as they can preserve Christian godliness and charity). To whom in return their subjects are held to render not just honor and respect, but also to pay tribute, and taxes, and other duties of obedience in kind.[c] This is so very true that they ought not to deny this even with hard and unjust magistrates, as long as they can do so with the preservation of a clear conscience.

c. Matt. 22:21, 1 Pet. 2:13-14, Tit. 3:1-2, 1 Tim. 2:1ff, Rom. 15:1ff.

9. *Sextum* præceptum est, *Ne occidamus:*ᵃ hoc est, ne vitam aut valetudinem proximi nostri destinato unquam lædamus; neque si forte inimicus sit, à quo læsi vel injuria affecti simus,ᵇ ex affectu ultionis vicissim ipsi noceamusᶜ aut malum ullum imprecemur, nedum inferamus: sed ab omniᵈ injusta ira, odio & vindictæ studio alieni semper simus:ᵉ idque verbis, gestibus & factis ubique declaremus: contraque non animo tantum & factis ubique bene velimus, sed ore etiam ac lingua benedicamus; omniaque tum animæ, tum corpori salutaria ipsi optemus, voveamus, precemur. Quin & reipsa eidem,ᶠ pro viribus & facultatibus nostris, benefaciamus & opere ipso subveniamus: si esuriat;ᵍ cibando; si sitiat potando; si nudus sit, vestiendo; si peregrimus sit, hospitio excipiendo; si æger sit, visitando; si captivus sit; consolando; si nos offenderit, condonando: denique si male velit, optet, faciat nobis, ut ei contraria omnia faciamus, atque ita malum bono vinciamus.

a. Gen. 9:5, Ex. 20:13.
b. Prov. 29:22 & 17:13ff, Lev. 19:16-18.
c. Rom. 12:14.
d. Eph. 4:6, Rom. 12:10.

10. *Septimum* præceptum est, *ne adulterium committamus:* id est, neᵃ thorum proximi nostri ulla ratione, sive soluti, sive ligati simus, libidinose conspurcemus, aut pudicitiam violemus. Acᵇ speciatim ut polygamiam, & voluntaria omnia divortia (extra casum adulterij) sedulo vitemus:ᶜ eoque desertam ob aliam causam, quam ob adulterium, ducere caveamus:ᵈ fornicationem, vagam venerem, &ᵉ impuritatem omnem, ejusque occasiones & irritamenta, tum in conjugio, tum vitæ cœlibe, procul habeamus:ᶠ contraque continentiæ, castitati, pudicitiæ & simili honestati, semper & ubique, etiam in verbis & gestibulis, sollicite operam demus.

a. Lev. 19 & 20:10ff, Matt. 19:1-12.
b. 1 Cor. 65, 10ff, 7:2ff,

11. *Octavum* præceptum est, *ne furemur:*ᵃ id est, ne proximi nostri bona (sive publica, sive

9. The sixth commandment is that "we do not kill," that is,ᵃ that we never by design prejudice the life or health of our neighbor. And if perhaps he is our enemy by whom we have been wounded or injured,ᵇ that we do not harm him from a feeling of revenge,ᶜ nor pray for any evil, much less inflict it. But we must be always be averse to all unjust wrath, hatred and spirit of revenge,ᵈ and everywhere declare the same by our words, gestures and deeds.ᵉ And to the contrary, not only do we wish him well with the mind, but also that we bless him with our mouth and tongue, and wish, vow and pray for all things healthful to him in both body and soul, and furthermore, that we really do good to him by our strengths and faculties and come to his need.ᶠ If he hungers, by feeding him. If he thirsts, by giving him drink. If he is naked, by clothing him. If he is sick, by visiting him.ᵍ If he is a captive, by consoling him. If he offended us, by forgiving him. And finally, if he wills, wishes and does evil to us, that we do all the contrary to him and so conquer evil with good.

e. Matt. 5:22-23.
f. Deut. 15:7-8ff, 12:1-2, Luke 6:35.
g. Rom. 12:20, Matt. 25:35, 1 Thess. 5:15, 1 Pet. 3:9.

10. The seventh commandment is that "we do not commit adultery," that is, that we do not for any reason, whether we are free or bound, lustfully defile our neighbor's bed or violate his purity.ᵃ And in particular that we carefully avoid polygamy and all voluntary divorces (except in case of adultery),ᵇ and we take precautions against marrying a person deserted for any other cause than adultery.ᶜ That we keep far from fornication, wandering lust and all impurity,ᵈ and their occasions and provocations,ᵉ whether in marriage or a life of celibacy.ᶠ And to the contrary, that we always and everywhere anxiously exercise continence, chastity, modesty and honesty, even in words and gestures.

c. Matt. 5:32.
d. 1 Thess. 4:3-5.

11. The eight commandment that "we do not steal,"ᵃ that is, that we do not strive to take or

privata, sive sacra sive profana) ulla illegitima ratione, seu vi, seu fraude & dolo, ad nos transferre aut nobis retinere studeamus: sed potius damna ipsius omnia, quantum id nobis est, avertamus ac præveniamus,[b] proprie fi forte simplex sit, eum ne fallamus; si imprudens, ne circum veniamus; si infirmus, ne obruamus: nec terrore, aut minis allisve modis iniquis, ad dandum nobis, aut mutuandum constringamus: si inops & egenus, usura & fœnore ne gravemus: sed potius eleemosynis, omnique consilio, auxilio & studio nostro eum juvemus: & de iis, quæ naturæ nostræ præcise necessaria non sunt, libenter & liberaliter ei suppeditemus: ne forte quæ ipsi, inprimis in summa ejus necessitate, tum naturali, tum divino jure debentur, nobis retinentes, obliquum aliquod vel occultum furtum coram Deo committamus.

retain for ourselves the goods of our neighbor (whether public or private, whether sacred or profane) by any illegitimate means, whether by force, fraud or deceit. Instead, we avert and prevent all damage to him, as far as it lies with us.[b] Therefore, if he happen to be simple, we will not cheat him. If he is imprudent, we will not circumvent him. If he is weak, we will not crush him. We will not compel him to give to us, or compel him to lend to us by terror, threats or other unjust methods. If he is destitute and needy, we will not oppress him with usury and interest. Rather, we will assist him with our alms, abundant counsel and enthusiasm, and we will freely and liberally make available those things which are not precisely necessary for our own needs, lest perhaps while retaining something for ourselves which are justly owed to him, especially in his greatest necessity, first by the law of nature, and then the law of God, we commit some indirect or hidden theft before God.

a. Ex. 11:1ff., Deut. 25:13ff., Is. 5:8, Amos 8:4-7, Mich. 6:11-12, Ja. 5:1ff.

b. Ps. 15, Eph. 4:28, Luke 30:31ff. & 23:33, 1 Tim. 6:17-19, Ez. 18:7-8, 12ff., 1 Thess. 4:6, 1 John 3:17.

12. *Nonum* præceptum est, *ne dicamus contra proximum nostrum falsum testimonium*:[a] id est, ut non solum mendacia, calumnias, obtrectationes, & temeraria de aliis judicia (imprimis si ea damnum aliquod inferre ipsis possint) prorsus omittamus: sed & aliorum mendaciis, calumniis, falsisque testimoniis, aurem ne præbeamus: neque silentio nostro, veluti muto testimonio, vel tacito assensu gravari proximum patiamur: sed contra[b] honorem, faman & existimationem ipsius, qua publice, qua privatim, pro virili tueamur: Denique ut candorem, veritatem, ac sinceram fidem, in verbis, contractibus, factis, ac testimoniis ubique, sive in judiciis, sive extra ea, studiose sectemur.

12. The ninth commandment is that "we do not speak false testimony against our neighbor,"[a] that is, that we not only lay aside lies, slanders, disparagements and rash judgments of others (especially if they may bring any harm to them) but also that we do not give ears to the lies, slanders and false testimonies of others, nor do we allow our neighbor to be oppressed through our silence, as a mute testimony or tacit agreement. But on the contrary, we should protect his honor, reputation and esteem both in public and in private.[b] And finally, that we must everywhere earnestly pursue candor, truth, and sincere faithfulness in words, contracts, deeds, and testimonies, whether in court or out.

a. Deut. 19:15ff., Prov. 19:5, 9, 18, Job 31:16ff., Ps. 15:2-3.

b. Matt. 7:1, Luke 6:37, Eph. 4:15, Ja. 4:11.

13. *Decimum* præceptum est, *ne vel uxorem, vel domum, aliasve res proximi nostri, concupiscamus:* id est, non tantum nullam externam injuriam proximo inferamus; sed nulla etiam ipsius bona,[a] quæ ipsi necessaria, aut utilia, aut jucunda sunt, cum damno & injuria illius

13. The tenth commandment is that "we do not covet either our neighbor's wife, or home, or any of his things," that is, that we not only do not inflict eternal injury to our neighbor, but also that we do not long for any of his goods,[a] whether necessary, useful or delightful to him, to his harm

appetamus: aut quacunque tandem iniqua rationem quantumvis occulta, nobis ea usurpate aut nostra facere cupiamus: sed animum,[b] cogitationes, desideria, & cupiditates nostras, ab ijs omnibus deflectamus, quæ alterius juri, aut usui obnoxia esse voluit optimus ac sapientissimus Deus: sique affectus nostros intra justitiæ concellos ac præscriptos à Deo limites pie semper contineamus: subinde *duo* illa cogitantes. I. *officij nostri esse, ut[c] proximum diligamus, sicut nosmet ipsos.* 2. *ne[d] alteri faciamus quod nobis ipsis fieri non vellemus.* Quibus omnibus, quasi colophon, accedere debet ultimus ille charitatis actus, quem Christus ipse per Apostolum suum Johannem[e] inculcat, ut pro fratribus etiam nostris vitam ponere non dubitemus.

a. Rom. 7:7-8, Ja. 1:14 & 4:1-2.
b. Job 31:1ff., Matt. 5:28.
c. Lev. 19:18.

and injury, or at least by any unjust way, however hidden, desire to seize or make them our own. Rather, that we turn away our minds, thoughts, desires and lusts from all those things which the most good and most wise God would have subject to the right or use of another.[b] And so we must always piously contain our affections within those limits of justice prescribed by God, thinking constantly of these two: 1. that it is our duty to love our neighbor as ourselves;[c] 2. that we not do to another what we do not want done to ourselves.[d] To all of which ought to be added, as a colophon, end or complement, that ultimate act of charity which Christ himself teaches through his Apostle John,[e] that we do not hesitate to lay down our lives for our brothers.

d. Matt. 7:12.
e. John 15:12-13, 1 John 3:10, 16.

• CHAPTER 13 •

CAPUT XIII.
De directione & abnegatione nostri ipsorum, deque tolerantia crucis Christi.

I. Præter hæc, quæ diximus, præcepta etiam ilud requiritur, ut[a] nos ipsos dirigamus, seu studiose ad regulam & præscriptum divinæ voluntatis componamus. Quod quidem fieri potest duobus præcipue modis.[b] I. Si nos ipsos & omnia nostra prorsus abnegemus. 2. Si mundum hunc præsentem ejusque cupiditates[c] minime diligamus; sed sponte potius, propter Deum, omnia, etiam charissima, deseramus: eoque crucem Jesu Christi, continuo vestigiis ipsius insistentes, portare non renuamus.

a. Rom. 6:12-13, 16 & 12:1, 2 Cor. 7:1.
b. Luke 9:23ff., chs. 14, 16ff.

CHAPTER 13
On governing and denying ourselves, and bearing the cross of Christ.

1. Beside the commandments about which we have already, still it is required that we direct ourselves, or studiously compose ourselves according to the rule and order of the divine will.[a] This indeed may chiefly be done in two ways. 1. If we utterly deny ourselves and everything that is ours.[b] 2. If we do in the least love this present world and its lusts,[c] but instead voluntarily give up everything most dear for God, and so to not refuse to bear the cross of Jesus Christ, continually following in his steps.

c. 1 John 2:15, 16, Matt. 10:38 & 16:24.

2. Nos ipsos rite hoc modo abnegamus: *Primo*, cum in cultu divino carnalem nostram rationem, ac mundanam prudentiam in consilium minime adhibemus:[a] sed ductum atque imperium ejus solius per omnia sequimur, (idque libenter ac sine ullo scrupulo,) qui solius errare non potest, fallare non vult. *Deinde*, cum affectus nostros vitiosos, &[b] imprimis affectum illum peculiarem, quo in certa quædam vitia (aut interdum in vitium aliquod unum) proclives ferimur, omnino subjicimus divinæ voluntati, & contrariis vitutibus, atque operibus illis spiritus, quæ Apostolus recenset ad *Gal*: 5. veluti crucifigimus, atque in ordinem redigimus: puta iracundiam, lenitate & mansuetudine; morositatem, comitate; pigritiam, zelo ac fervore; tristitiam, gaudio; litigiositatem, facilitate, & pacis studio, &c. *Denique* maxime; & quidem proprissime, nos ipsos abnegamus, cum primum & naturalissimum illum amorem,[c] quo in vitam & vitæ nostræ felicitatem, seu commoditatem, toti propendemus, propter Christum exuere parati sumus: & vitam potius ipsam deserere, immo cum summo dolore cruciatu violento amittere, non detrectamus, quam indignum quippiam nostra professione & gloriosa Christi religione committere sustineamus.

a. Matt. 11:25ff., 1 Cor. 1:19ff., 3:18-19, Is. 5:21, Prov. 3:7.
b. Rom. 8:6-7, 12ff., Gal. 5:17, Tit. 2:12, Eph. 4:12, Col. 3:8, 11.

3. Mundum hunc ejusque cupidiates tum abnegamus sive non diligimus:[a] cum non tantum crassis & fœdis illis,[b] atque ab ipsa meliore gentilitate damnatis vitiis, quæ scilicet cum civili honestate ac justitia pugnant, cumque aperta Dei & proximi injuria fere conjuncta sunt, ex animo valedicimus: quæque respectu animalis vitæ in hoc mundo bona sunt,[c] carnique nostræ grata & jucunda, non ita concupiscimus, ut, quacumque demum ratione fieri poterit (etiam cum incommodo & detrimento nostræ valetudinis, cumque injuria ac læsione proximi) ea consectari ac possidere, iisve frui, in animum inducamus: sed[d] cum nulla etiam ejusmodi bona immoderatius aut amplius, quam oportet, amamus aut appetimus: cum dispendio scilicet

2. We correctly deny ourselves in this manner. First, when in divine worship we do not consult our own carnal reason and worldly prudence,[a] but follow only his leadership and command in all things (and that willingly and without any scruple) he who alone cannot err nor wills to deceive. Then, when we wholly subject our corrupt affections to the will of God and especially that particular affection by which we are struck down to some certain vices[b] (or sometimes to some one), and by those opposite virtues and the works of the Spirit, which the Apostle lists in Gal. 5, we crucify them and reduce them in turns, namely, anger by gentleness and meekness, fussiness by courtesy, laziness by zeal and fervor, sadness by joy, contentiousness by cooperation and a peaceable spirit. And finally, the greatest and most personal, we deny ourselves when we are ready for Christ to lay aside that first and most natural love by which we are totally inclined to favor our lives and our happiness in life or its accommodation,[c] that we do not refuse to forsake life itself, indeed to lose it with greatest pain and violent torment, rather than endure to commit anything unworthy of our profession and the glorious religion of Christ.

c. Matt. 16:24, Luke 14:26, John 12:15, Acts 20:24 & 21:13.

3. We then deny or not love this world and its lusts, not only when we say goodbye to gross and foul vices,[a] together with those that have been condemned by the better Gentiles themselves,[b] namely, which fight against civil honesty and justice and which are closely joined with injury to God and neighbor, and we do not lust for things which are good with respect to our physical life in this world and gratifying and pleasing to our flesh,[c] that we be mentally induced in any way (to the disadvantage and detriment of our health, and the injury and wounding of our neighbor) to pursue, possess or enjoy them, but also we must not love and long immoderately or more than is proper for things of that kind which are not good,[d] namely, to the hindrance of our duty imposed on us by the

officii divinitus nobis injuncti, & meliorum ac celestium curarum damno atque detrimento. Quod tunc quidem fieri solet,[e] cum vera, cælestia, & æterna bona, vel prorsus negligimus; vel saltem frigide aut tepide, aut perfunctorie, ac non nisi per occasionem alicunde oblatam, vel per subitam aliquam ὅρμημα seu præcipitem impetum, obiter curamus: sive cum in continua rerum mundanarum sollicitudine, & animalis vitæ cura ita impliciti & implexi hæremus, quasi aut totam, aut præcipuam felicitatem nostram in iis poneremus: & tanquam si cælestium amor & cura vix, ac ne vix quidem, animum nostrum tangeret atque afficeret.

divinity or to the loss and detriment of heavenly concerns. Then it usually happens when we either utterly neglect true, heavenly and eternal goods,[e] or at leastwise coldly, lukewarmly, perfunctorily and only when convenient, or we are worried in passing by some sudden ὅρμημα or violent assault, or when we are stuck, entangled and entwined in continual care of worldly things and the cares of this life, as if we placed either our whole or principle happiness in them, and as if the love and care of heaven hardly or not even hardly, touched or affected our souls.

a. 1 John 2:15-15.
b. 1 Cor. 3:1ff., Eph. 4:17-19.
c. Matt. 6:31ff., Luke 21:34, Ja. 5:1ff.,

    2 Pet. 2:10, 13.
d. Matt. 6:19-20, Tit. 2:12, Col. 3:1ff.
e. Rom. 12:11ff., Phil. 3:20, Rev. 3:15ff.

4. Immoderatius vero bona mundi hujus tunc non amamus, cum nec mundo ipso[a] nec bonis illis, quæ in mundo sunt, ita frui desideramus, tanquam si in iis bonum aliquod verum ac solidum, aut stabile ac perenne positum esset: sed contra uti iis tantum cupimus idque duntaxat quantum ad necesitatem explendum, & vitam Christiano homine dignam vivensdum satis est: (sine ulla scilicet alterius læsione aut gravitione, ac mandatorum Jesu Christi transgressione). Denique cum victu & amictu[b] necessario contenti sumus, quidquam ultra sollicite quærimus, aut appetimus.

4. And indeed we do not immoderately love the goods of this world when we neither desire to enjoy the world itself nor its goods,[a] as if something good, true and solid, or stable and lasting were placed in them. But on the contrary, we only desire to use them no further than is sufficient to satisfy necessity and living a life worthy of a Christian (that is, without the wounding or burdening of another, and transgressing of the commands of Jesus Christ). And finally, when we are content with necessary food and clothing and do not anxiously seek or desire anything further.[b]

a. 1 Cor. 7:29-32, Heb. 13:5-6, 1 Tim. 6:6ff.

5. Mundana hujusmodi bona, juxta Apostolum Johannem,[a] *tria* sunt; ad quæ omnia alia sat commode revocari possunt: nempe, *divitia honores, & voluptates*: quorum immodica appetitio, sive nimius amor, dicitur *cupiditas oculorum, fastus vitæ, & cupiditas carnis*. Quæ & ipsa, quia contra solidam pietatem animæque salutem militant, homini vere pio serio abneganda sunt.

5. There are three kinds of worldly goods, according to the Apostle John,[a] to which all other may easily enough be reduced, namely, riches, honors and pleasures. The immoderate desire or excessive love for them is called the lust of the eyes, the pride of life and the lust of the flesh. These very things are seriously to be rejected by the truly godly man because they war against solid godliness and the salvation of the soul.

a. 1 John 2:16ff., 1 Pet. 2:11, Ja. 4:1.

6. Immoderatus divitiarum amor, est[a] *avaritia*, sive πλεονεξία. Hoc est, cupiditas plus habendi, aut φιλαργυρία hoc est, pecuniæ amor.

6. The immoderate love of riches is avarice, or πλεονεξία.[a] This is the desire of having more, or φιλαργυρία, the love of money. He truly denies this

Eum vero abnegat, is, qui pecunias, opes, aut possessiones plures, quam necesse sibi suisque sit, nec sollicite atque impense sediderat, cum forte non habet, videlicet contentus semper solis alimentis, & quibus tegatur vestimentis: nec[b] cum beneficio divino ipsi affluunt, ita mordicus tenet, ac cupide possidet, ut non libenter de ijs, quæ supra sui suorumque necessariam sustentationem redundant, erogare aliis, ac distribuere velit (siquidem ita necesse sit,) & quidem[c] omnibus, qui opus habent; imprimis autem fratribus ac fidei domesticis: nec, cum divina voluntate, sive permissione ipsi eripiuntur, aut casu aliquo adverso effluunt, ita dolet ac tristatur, tanquam si verum ac præcipuum aliquod bonum amisisset Deo ejusque paterna benignitate nixus,[d] sive adsint, sive desint opes istæ, perpetuam & sedulam officij sui rationem habet; denique qui bona hujus vitæ sic acquirit, possidet, & amittit, tanquam[e] si non acquireret, possideret ac amitteret.

who does not anxiously and eagerly want more monies, wealth or possessions, if perhaps he does not have them, than is necessary for him, that is, always being content only with food and covering. Nor, when they flow upon him through the blessing of God,[b] does he secure them with his teeth and greedily possess them, but whatever abounds to him over and above what is necessary for the support of himself and his, he willingly pays out and distributes (if indeed it is necessary) to all who have need,[c] especially to brothers, and those who are of the household of faith. Nor, when they are snatched away by God's will or permission, or flow away by some adverse misfortune, he is so grieved and saddened as if be had lost any true and principle good.[d] But relying on God and his fatherly kindness, whether he has or lack this wealth, he has a continual and careful for his duty. And finally, he who gets, possesses and loses the goods of this life, [lives] as if he had not gotten, possessed and lost them.[e]

a. Matt. 6:25ff., Luke 12:15ff., 16:11ff., 1 Tim. 6:10, Heb. 13:5.
b. Ps. 62:10, Mark 10:13-14, 2 Cor. 9:7-9.

c. Ps. 37:21, 26 & 112:5, 9, Matt. 25:40, Gal. 6:10.
d. Phil. 4:11-12.
e. 1 Cor. 7:39ff., Luke 10:1ff.

7. Immoderatus honorum amor, sive fastus vitæ, est *ambitio*,[a] & superbia. Eam vero abnegat is, qui honoribus, supereminentiis, dignitatibus, atque applausibus populi nullo modo studet; nec, si forte contingant, ita iis delectatur, tanquam si vera illis & solida aliqua felicitas consisteret;[b] proinde qui nec ipse supra alios (quacunque demum de causa) sermone, vultu, gestu, incessu, habitu &c. se ipsum essert atque attollit; nec, si efferatur ab aliis, ea re, tanquam vero aliquo ac stabili bono, delectatur; sed[c] divinæ semper gratiæ suæque coram Deo vilitatis, at que indignitatis & Christianæ humilitatis, in omni vita & statu, recordatur; ita ut modestum, comem,[d] affabilem, & humanum, imo demissum, ubique se, erga omnes (nisi quod interdum Magistratibus etiam publicæ majestatis, & authoritatis suæ justa ratio habenda est) haud gravate præstet; eoque in gestibus & verbis, inque[e] vestitu, victu, ædibus, & suppellectile, modestiam cum decoro servet, ita scilicet, ut nec temere contemtibilem se

7. An immoderate love of honors or pride of life is ambition and arrogance.[a] He truly denies this who by no means seeks honors, high places, dignities and the applauses of the people, nor, if perhaps they happen, he does so delight in them as if some true and solid happiness depended upon them.[b] Hence, he does not raise and exalt himself above others (for whatever reason) by word, expression, gesture, manner of walking, habit, etc. And if he is praised by other, he does not delight in them as some true and stable good, but in every condition of life he always reminds himself of divine grace and his own unworthiness before God, and indignity and Christian humility.[c] So then he must keep himself modest, courteous, friendly and kind, indeed lowly,[d] in all places and towards all (except sometimes magistrates must have their due grandeur and authorities their rights), and therefore he must preserve modesty in his gestures and words, in clothes, food, house and furniture,[e] so that clearly he does not rashly render himself contemptible though aspirations of filth,

reddat ex affectatis sordibus; nec inanem gloriam captet ex immodico & fastuoso splendore; denique ut in omnibus habitum talem præ se serat, qui veram & seriam sanctimoniam decet, &[f] affectum eum semper induat, qui Jesum Christum, pedes discipulorum suorum lavantem, sequi non erubescat.

a. Matt. 7:22, Acts 12:21, Ja. 4:2, 1 Pet. 5:6.
b. Mat. 6:1ff, & 23:5-7, Luke 16:15, John 5:44 & 12:43.
c. Rom. 12:16, Phil. 2:3.

8. Immoderatus amor voluptarum est *cupiditas carnis*.[a] Eam abnegat is, qui exteriorum sensuum suorum, per quos caro voluptatibus suis fruitur, delectationi nullam dat operam; ac proinde[b] qui nec oculos suos pascit aspectu rerum vanarum seu piis illicitarum, ac prorsus inutilium; nec aures demulcet obscænis, illiberalibus & futilibus jocis, lascivaque dicteria, vel scurrilia &[c] proterva carmina nec ipse profert, nec nisi gravate[d] audit; item qui sobrietati ac temperantiæ studet, nec gulæ aut ventris curam operosam agit; sive in cibo & potu[e] superflua, sumtuosa & splendida non quærit; nec iis cor suum degravat, ut ineptus reddatur ad vocationem suam recte & rite obeundam; ad hæc, qui[f] vas suum possidere studet in honore, & veram castitatem, qualis à Christo præscripta est, acte semper & ubique servat, occasionesque & irritamenta omnia libidinis[g] (nempe crapulam, luxum, comessationes,[h] otium, omnemque vanitatem in verbis & gestibus) studiose vitat; & contra, continentiæ ac castitati vivendæ idoneis adjumentis (puta[i] vigiliis, studiis,[k] piis colloquiis,[l] ac conversationibus sanctis ac honestis) serio incumbit ac delectatus; denique qui singulariter commendatum sibi habet[m] jejunium, ad carmen melius subigendum, & spiritum magis excitandum, imprimis tempore crucis, seu publicæ privatiæve calamitatis, nec proinde quietem, nec commoditatem, nec suavitatem rerum ularum, quæ in sensus externos incurrere possunt, tanti facit, ut non malit omnibus istis carere ac destitui, quam à præceptis Jesu Christi, vel latum unguem discedere.

nor try for vain glory from immoderate and proud splendor, and finally, so that in all things he shows such demeanor as is fitting for true and serious holiness and always clothes himself with that disposition which is not ashamed to follow Jesus Christ, who washed his disciples' feet.[f]

d. Eph. 4:2, Col. 3:12, 1 Thess. 2:6-7, 1 Pet. 3:8.
e. Luke 16:19, Acts 12:21 & 25:23, Ja. 2:1ff., & 5:1ff, 1 Pet. 3:3ff., 1 Tim. 2:9.
f. John chs. 13-15, 1 Tim. 5:10.

8. An immoderate love of pleasures is the lust of the flesh.[a] He denies it who does not at all take advantage of delighting his external senses, through which the flesh enjoys pleasures, and accordingly does not feed his eyes with a sight vain or forbidden for the godly, and utterly useless,[b] nor strokes his ears with obscene, demeaning and futile jokes and lascivious stories,[c] nor offers scurrilous and shameless songs.[d] Likewise, he pursues sobriety and temperance, does not act with painstaking care for his gullet and stomach, and does not seek food or drink which are in excess, sumptuous or splendid,[e] nor so burden his heart with them that he renders himself inept to attend his calling rightly and correctly. Moreover, he seeks to possess his vessel in honor[f] and always and everywhere protect that true chastity such as prescribed by Christ, and earnestly avoids occasions and stimulating of desire[g] (namely, drunkenness, luxury, carousing, leisure and all vanity in words and gestures[h]), and to the contrary, he seriously presses and desires all suitable aids of self-control and chastity (such as in vigilance,[i] studies,[k] pious conferences[g] and in holy and honest conversation). And finally, he gives himself exceptionally to fasting for the better subjugating of the flesh and greater exciting of the spirit,[m] especially in time of persecution or public or private calamity, and accordingly does not make much of the quiet nor convenience nor sweetness of any of these things which may enter the external senses, that he would prefer to lack and be destitute of all those things than depart even a fingernail's breadth from the commands of Jesus Christ.

a. Rom. 13:12-14, 2 Pet. 2:10, 13-14, Jude vv. 8, 12, 16.
b. Job 31:1, Ps. 119:37, 2 Pet. 2:14.
c. Eph. 2:29 & 5:4.
d. 2 Pet. 2:8.
e. Luke 16:19 & 21:34, 1 Pet. 4:3-4, 2 Pet. 2:13.
f. 1 Thess. 4:4-5, 1 Cor. 6:15ff.
g. Luke 16:19 & 21:34, Eph. 5:18-19.
h. Eph. 4:28, 1 Thess. 4:11-12, 2 Thess. 3:8ff.
i. Matt. 26:41, 1 Pet. 5:8, 2 Cor. 6:5.
k. Rom. 12:11.
l. 1 Cor. 15:33, 1 Pet. 2:12.
m. Dan. 9:3, Joel 1:14 & 2:15, Jonah 3:7, 1 Esdras 8:21, Matt. 4:2, Luke 2:37, 1 Cor. 7:5, Acts 132-3 & 14:23.

9. Quisquis hoc pacto animatus est, is demum rite Christum imitabitur; eique speciatim grave non erit[a] *crucem Iesu Christi æquo portare*: hoc est, per[b] ignominiam, infamiam,[c] spoliationem bonorum, egestatem, famem, nuditatem; imo per carceres,[d] ignes, rotas, cruces, ac gladios, &c. ad exemplum[e] ducis ac Domini sui, (quoties necesse erit, &[f] Deo ita videbitur) ad æternam gloriam & immortalem ac stabilem tum quietem, tum felicitatem hac via grassari. Hujus enim rei pia meditatio tantos animos, tamque ingentes spiritus, olim[g] Apostolis, ac Prophetis, sanctisque aliis Dei viris (& nostro etiam seculo non paucis fidelibus Jesu Christi martyribus) addidit, ut etiam gaudentes & hilares ad tormenta, licet crudelissima, sæpius inverint: inque mediis ignibus & flammis Deo, & Christo Filio ipsius, cum cantu & hymnis benedixerint:[h] quin & in ipsis afflictionibus gloriati suerint (idque sub spe gloriæ filiorum Dei) quod digni haberentur, qui pro Jesu Christo Domino suo mala ista paterentur, & sanguine suo veritatem ejus obsignarent ac gloriam illustrarent.[i]

9. Whosoever is motivated in this manner will in the end rightly imitate Christ. And it will not be especially grievous for him to patiently bear the cross of Christ,[a] that is, through shame,[b] reproach,[c] spoiling of goods, poverty, famine, nakedness, indeed through prisons,[d] fires, wheels, crosses and swords, etc., after the example of his commander and Lord[e] (as often as is necessary and seems good to God), and proceed in this way to eternal and immortal glory and to a stable rest and happiness. For the pious meditation of this matter has added such courage and such enormous spirit to the ancient apostles and prophets, and other holy men of God,[g] (and to not a few faithful martyrs of Jesus Christ in our own age), that they often went rejoicing and cheerful to torments, be they ever so cruel. And in the midst of fires and flames have blessed God, and Jesus Christ his Son, with songs and hymns.[h] In fact, they went into these afflictions to be honored (and that under the hope of the glory of the Sons of God) that they were considered worthy to suffer those evils for the sake of their Lord Jesus Christ, and by their blood to seal his truth and illuminate his glory.[i]

a. Mark 16:14, Luke 9:24.
b. 2 Cor. 6:8.
c. 2 Cor. 6:8.
d. Heb. 10:34 & 11:36.
e. Rom. 8:25ff.
f. Heb. 12:2.
g. 1 Pet. 3:17-18.
h. Acts 5:41, 7:60, 16:25, 20:24 & 21:13, Heb. 11:3ff., Rev. 6:9 & 7:14.
i. Rom. 5:3 & 8:21ff.

• Chapter 14 •

CAPUT XIV.
*De Precatione & gratiarum actione,
& speciatim de Oratione Dominica*

I. Cæterum quia universa hominum fidelium vita (uti apud ante diximus) & præsertim ipsa fidei obedientia, quam Jesu Christo assidue præstant, variis periculis, tentationibus, & assaultibus Satanæ, carnis, ac mundi, quotidie exposita, & necessitatibus non paucis obnoxia est: ne in tam difficili certamine sucumberent aut desperarent, voluit[a] Jesus Christus, ut omnes & singuli fideles perpetuam Dei opem ac gratiam,[b] in suo unius nomine, indefessa[c] & indivisa, idque semper[d] & indesinenter (imprimis autem in gravibus tentationibus & adversitatibus) implorarent; proque acceptis beneficijs ei gratias[e] perpetuo agerent: Testantes hac ratione, se Deo, tanquam summo & primo authori, universam felicitatem suam debere: & ipsius unius auxilio, & gratuito beneficio, præstare posse, imo reipsa præstare, quæcunque ad eam obtinendam factu aut præstitu necessaria sunt. Unde duæ quædam præcipuæ cultus divini partes, seu species existunt: tum *precatio*, stricte ac proprie dicta, seu divinæ opis imploratio, pro bonis consequendis, aut malis averruncandis: tum pro acceptis beneficijs *gratiarum actio*, & divini nominis celebratio.

a. Matt. 7:7ff., 26:4, Luke 18:1.
b. John 14:13 & 16:23.
c. Matt. 11:24, Ja. 1:5-6.

2. Utramque partem seu speciem passim in verbo suo nobis commendat Deus:[a] potissimum autem in N. Testamento[b] Jesus Christus: dum ubique locorum, sive publice[a] Psal. 50. 14. 15. & 91. 14. 15. & 145. 18. 19.[b] iTim. 2. 18. Joan.

CHAPTER 14
On prayer and thanksgiving,
and especially the Lord's prayer

1. But because the whole life of believers (just as we said before) and especially their obedience of faith which they constantly render to Jesus Christ, is daily exposed to various dangers, temptations and assaults of Satan, the flesh, and the world, and liable to not a few necessities, Jesus Christ has willed,[a] lest in such difficult conflict they should faint or despair, that each and every believer should appeal to his perpetual grace and power, in his name alone,[b] with untiringly and undivided [faith],[c] and that always and without ceasing[d] (especially in grave temptations and adversities). And they should continually give thanks for the benefits received,[e] testifying in this manner that they owe to God, as the greatest and first author, their whole happiness, and that by his aid alone and free benefit, they are able to perform, indeed really do perform, whatever are necessary to be done or performed for obtaining it. From this appear the two principal parts or kinds of divine worship. First, prayer, strictly and properly called, or the imploring of divine power for good consequences or the averting of evil ones, then thanksgiving for benefits received and celebration of the divine name.

d. Rom. 12:12, 1 Thess. 5.17.
e. Phil. 4:6, Ps. 116:12-13, Pss. 102, 103 & 104. 1 Tim. 2:1, Col. 3:17 & 4:2.

2. God commends both parts or kinds to us everywhere in his Word,[a] but especially Jesus Christ in the New Testament,[b] while anywhere, whether in public or private, as the matter or occasion offers, he commands both be exercised in

4. 24. sive privatim prout res aut occasio dederit, utramque in spiritu & veritate exerci præcipit. Et *precationem* quidem, sive *invocationem*, quod attinet, eam non tantum verbis[c] mandavit Jesus Christus, sed &[d] exemplo suo commendavit: ejusque etiam exercendæ[e] modum, ac formulam certam præscripsit, ad quam preces nostræ (sive pro nobis ipsis, sive pro alijs concipiantur) veluti ad infallibilem & indubitatam normam, perpetuo conformandæ sint: addito etiam promisso, preces nostras, si modo fiant[f] secundum voluntatem Dei (adeo ut accedat etiam debita precantium dispositio, secundum interiorem simul & exteriorem hominem: puta[g] pænitentia vera de peccatis ante commisis, fiducia firma[h] de gratia Dei per Christum parta,[i] sincerum sanctimoniæ, &[k] fraternæ imprimis charitatis studium: item[l] attentio seria,[m] submissio devota, & indefessa denique precandi assiduitas) certo certius à Deo exaudiendas esse.

a. Ps. 50:14-15 & 91:14-15 & 145:18-19.
b. 1 Tim. 2:18, Job 4:24.
c. Matt. 7:7ff., Luke 11:9.
d. Mat. 14:13 & 16:39, Luke 21:41ff., Job 17.
e. Mat. 6:9ff., Luke 18:2ff.
f. 1 John 3:22 & 5:14.

3. Formula hæc Precationis vocatur, ab authore suo D. N. I. Christo *Oratio dominica*: cujus tres sunt præcipuæ partes, *Proœmium, Narratio, & Epilogus*: licet iste totus apud Lucam[a] desit, nec ad substantiam rei per se necessario pertineat.

a. Matt. 6:9ff., Luke 11:2-4.

4. In *proœmio* docetur, quis nobis perpetuo invocandus sit, & quo animo ac modo: nempe *Pater noster cœlestis*, sive *qui in cœlis est*: hoc est, qui affectu humili simul ac filiali nobis compellandus, quippe qui non modo per naturam altissimus, & potentissimus est, sive Optimus Maximus (jamque non ut olim, in tabernaculo Mosis,[a] aut in templo[b] Salomonis, sub Cherubinis; sed in ipsis duntaxat altissimis[c] cælis, æternitatis atque immortalitatis verissima sede, & quasi arce,[d] unde omnia bona ad nos defluunt, gloriose habitans) sed qui etiam[e]

spirit and truth. And indeed what touches prayer or invocation, Jesus Christ has not just commanded it in words,[c] but also has commended it by his own example.[d] And so he also has prescribed the manner and correct form of exercising it,[e] according to which our petitions (whether they be uttered for ourselves or for others) ought to be perpetually conformed as to infallible and indubitable rules, if done in a manner according to the will of God,[f] (exactly as accompanied with a due disposition of those who pray, according to both our inward and outer man, namely, both in respect of our inward and outward man, namely, with true repentance for sins formerly committed,[g] firm trust[h] in the grace of God acquired by Christ,[i] a sincere zeal for holiness and especially for brotherly love;[k] likewise, serious attention,[l] devout submission,[m] and finally, with an untiring attention in prayer) shall most certainly be clearly heard by God.

g. 1 John 1:5, Ps. 32:2ff. & 51.
h. Heb. 4:16 & 10:22, Eph. 1:18 & 2:12.
i. 1 John 3:21-22, 1 Pet. 3:12.
k. Mark 11:25, Matt. 5:23-24 & 6:14.
l. Luke 18:1ff., 18:10.
m. Luke 18:1ff., Rom. 12:12, 1 Thess. 5:17.

3. This formula of prayer is called the Lord's Prayer from its author, our Lord Jesus Christ. It has three principle parts: the preface, the narration, and the conclusion, although the latter is completely lacking in Luke,[a] although this by itself does not pertain to the substance of it.

4. In the preface is taught who ought to be perpetually invoked by us and with what heart and manner, namely, "our Heavenly Father," or "who is in heaven," that is, to whom we are compelled to speak with a humble yet son-like affection, who is obviously not only by nature most high and powerful or the greatest good (and now not dwelling as in the past, in the tabernacle of Moses[a] or in the temple of Solomon beneath the cherubim,[b] but gloriously dwelling only in the highest heavens themselves,[c] in the truest seat of eternity and immortality, and almost a citadel,[d]

clementem ac benignum sese omnibus offert: & reipsa[f] paterne semper erga fideles suos affectus est; quippe quos in Christo gratiose semper diligit: ita ut eos omnes ac solos pro[g] filijs, & hæredibus cælestis suæ gloriæ & immortalitatis, scripturus sit: & proinde qui[h] largiri nobis omnia salutaria & facile possit & libenter velit: cuique propterea vicissim nos, & quidem unanimiter conjuncti, seu[i] fraternæ charitatis vinculo colligati, per[k] eundem Jesum Christum, unicum patronum ac Meditatorem nostrum, cum summa reverentia & filiali adfectu confidere & tuto possimus, jure debeamus.

a. Ex. 40:34.
b. 1 Ki. 8:12.
c. Acts 7:43, 49.
d. Ja. 1:17.
e. 1 Tim. 2:4 & 4:10.

5. *Narratio seu* petitiones habet: quarum[a] *tres* priores immediate, ac proprie, ad Dei gloriam; tres autem sequentes ad utilitatem & salutem nostram maxime spectant: Quanquam utraæque per mutuam relationem ac certam consequentiam, ad utrumque illum scopum simul collineant,[b] quum nec gloria Dei à salute se jungi possit, & hæc vicissim tota ad illam referri debeat.

a. John 14:13, 1 Cor. 10:31, Col. 3;17, 1 Pet. 4:11.

6. *Prima* itaque pertitione orare jubemur, ut *Sanctificetur nomen Dei*: id est, ut divinæ bonitatis,[a] sapientiæ ac potentiæ gloria, Evangelio præcipue patefecta, passim recte cognoscatur, ac digne celebretur: ac proinde ut Deus auxilio suo nos aliosque juvet, quo tum ipsi,[b] tum alij omnes mortales, exemplo & hortatu etiam nostro incitati, desertis omnibus idolis seu profanis numinibus & deastris, unicum illum verum Deum, Patrem Domini nostri Jesu Christi, super omnia verbis, factis, hymnis, precibus, scriptis, idque uno quasi ore, laudemus & prædicemus: subinde & corde & voce illud canentes: *Sanctus, Sanctus, Sanctus Deus ille & Pater Domini nostri Jesu Christi: illi sit laus, honor, benedictio in omnia secula*

from where all good things flow to us) but who presents himself as merciful and kind to all,[e] and really has fatherly affections toward all his believing ones,[f] as those whom he always graciously loves in Christ. For thus they all and only they were written down for sons and heirs of his celestial glory and immortality.[g] Thus he is easily can and freely wills to grant us everything necessary for salvation.[h] Therefore, in return, we safely can and ought to trust in him with highest reverence and brotherly affection,[i] and that indeed as we have been joined together as one by the chain of brotherly love by the same Jesus Christ,[k] our only patron and mediator.

f. Ps. 103:1-2, Job 14:13ff., Rom. 8:15.
g. Gal. 4:6, Rom. 8:17.
h. Luke 11:10ff., Ja. 1:5.
i. Rom. 12:10, 2 Pet. 1:7.
k. Eph. 2:18 & 3:11.

5. The narration contains six petitions, of which the three former immediately and properly consider the glory of God,[a] and the three following greatly consider our advantage and salvation. Although both aim at the same mark by mutual relation and certain consequence, since the glory of God cannot be disjoined from salvation,[b] and the latter ought totally be referred to the former.

b. Ps. 50:14-15 & 34:16ff., & ch. 91.

6. And so in the first petition we are commanded to pray, that "the name of God may be sanctified," that is, that the glory of the divine goodness, wisdom and power,[a] especially as revealed in the gospel, might every where be correctly rightly known and worthily celebrated, and therefore that God would assist us and others with his aid by which both they and all other mortals,[b] incited by our example and encouragement, abandon all idols or profane deities and goddesses, and above all, that as if with one mouth, we may praise and extol the one true God, the Father of our Lord Jesus Christ, in words, deeds, hymns, prayers, writings, constantly singing with heart and voice, "Holy, Holy, Holy is the God and Father of our Lord Jesus Christ; to him be

seculorum, Amen.

a. Is. 6:3, 42:8 & 48:11, Ez. 20:41 & 28: 21 & 25, Ps. 96, 97 & 99.

7. *Secunda* petitio est, *ut regnum ipsius adveniat*: id est,[a] ut ipse per veram & plenam Christianæ Religionis notitiam, quæ tunc temporis adhuc tenuis & parca erat, ac velut eminus adventabat, magis magisque corda nostra dirigat in solidam nominis sui divini sanctificationem: utque aliis etiam compluribus eandem gratiam largiri velit,[b] quo totos ipsi regendos tradant, seu legibus ac mandatis ejus sese ultro subjiciant: utque ita utrique ad regnum[c] cælorum, olim in beata immortalitate plene possidendum, indies magis magisque apti hic atque idonei efficiamur.

a. Matt. 1:2ff, Col. 1:6ff, John 1:17-18 & 3:16-17.
b. Is. 2:3ff., Mich. 4:1ff., Ps. 122:1ff.

8. *Tertia* est, ut *voluntas Dei in terra fiat, sicut in cælo*: id est, ut eam nobis, aliisque mortalibus, gratiam faciat Deus,[a] quo voluntatem ipsius, jam ante in præceptis expositam, tam prompte tamque alacriter quisque faciamus, quam[b] sancti Angeli eam in cælis præstare solent. Deinde, ut ea, quæ nobis evenire mala[c] Deus aut sinit, aut interdum vult, ac curat, patienter feramus; & sine obmurmuratione ulla ad utilitatem nostram spiritualem, sive ad fidei & obedientiæ, ac porro ad salutis nostræ profectum, sedulo convertamus.

a. Phil. 2:13-14, 1 Thess. 5:23-24, 2 Thess. 1:11.
b. Dan. 7:10, Mat. 18:10, Heb. 1:14.

9. *Quarta* est, ut *panem nostrum quotidianum nobis det hodie*: id est, ut largiri nobis semper omnia dignetur,[a] quæ ad vitam hanc sine vera egestate, ac corporis debilitate transigendum; contraque in pace ac tranquilitate degendum; & sanctissimis curis (cum seria animi, spirituumque alacritate) vacandum, atque incumbendum, necessaria nobis sunt: ijsque quæ jam dedit & benigne contulit, porro semper benedicat, ut eorum adminiculo, veluti[b] baculo sustentati, divino ipsius nomine sanctificando, regno propagando, & voluntate exequenda, melius occupari, & sine ulla distractione pietati

praise, honor and blessing forever and ever, Amen."

b. Rom. 10:6, 9, Eph. 3:10 & 5:19-20, Col. 3:16-17, 2 Thess. 1:11-12, Rev. 48:9 & 9:12-13.

7. The second petition is that "his kingdom may come," that is, that through a true and full knowledge of the Christian religion,[a] which as yet was then tenuous and sparing and coming from afar, more and more would direct our hearts to a solid sanctifying of his divine name, and that he would be willing to grant to many others his grace by which they may deliver themselves to be ruled by him,[b] or voluntarily subject themselves to his laws and commandments, so that more and more each day we may be both fit and suitable for the kingdom of heaven,[c] most fully possessed by blessed immortality.

c. 1 Cor. 15:24ff.

8. The third is that "the will of God be done in earth as in heaven," that is, that God would grant his grace to us and to other mortals,[a] that we might every one do his will, now already expressed in his commandments, as promptly and cheerfully as the holy angels in heaven are accustomed to perform it.[b] Then, that we may patiently bear those evils that come to us which God either allows, suffers, wills, or arranges,[c] and without any murmuring we turn them to our spiritual advantage or proficiency in faith and obedience, and further on to our salvation.

c. Heb. 10:36 & 12:7ff, 1 Pet. 3:17 & 4:12ff.

9. The fourth is that "he would give us this day our daily bread," that is, that he would deign to grant us all things which are necessary for us to pass this life without any true want or weakness of body,[a] and to the contrary, that it be passed in peace and tranquility, and to attend upon, and (with a serious cheerfulness of mind and spirits) diligently to apply ourselves, and to mind those things, that are most sacred and holy. And those things which he has already given and kindly conveyed, he would always bless further, that being sustained by their support as by a staff[b] we may be better occupied with sanctifying his divine

vacare possimus.

a. Matt. 5:25, 31ff., 1 Tim. 6:8, Heb. 13:5, Phil. 4:11-13.
b. Lev. 26:26.

10. *Quinta* est, ut *debita nobis remittas, sicut & nos remittimus debitoribus nostris*: id est, ut peccata nostra[a] universa, sive per errorem, aut infirmitatem, sive imprimis per improbitatem aut malitiam unquam commissa, gratiose in Christo nobis condonet: sicut nos quoque[b] injurias, & offensas omnes (idque ideo tantum, quia ipse ita vult & jubet) omnibus iis, qui nos unquam læserunt, ex animo condonamus, & condonare semper parati sumus.

a. Matt. 6:14-14 & 18:21, 35, Luke 7:47 & 18:13, Rom. 4:7ff.

11. *Sexta* est, *ne nos inducat in tentationem, sed liberet nos à malo*: id est, ne nimium[a] gravibus ac diuturnis tentationibus nos opprimi, nedum vinci,[b] aut supra vires nostras periclitari, unquam sinat: sed[c] semper, pro singulari sua potentia, simul & charitate paterna, sancto suo Spiritu nos roboret, ac sustentet: imprimis in gravibus afflictionibus, arduis periculis, ac calamitatibus, aliisque id genus mali, per quæ omnino perdere nos, atque à Deo avertere tentat diabolus: ne forte, quâ sumus fragilitate, iis nimium pressi, aliquid designemus, quod divinæ ipsius voluntati contrarium, & saluti nostræ, seu bonæ conscientiæ, noxium esse possit. Denique,[d] ut semper una cum tentatione lætum eventum præstare velit, quo eam sufferre possimus, atque ita ab omnibus tandem insidiis, & illecebris, omnique fraude ac vi satanæ gloriose liberari, imo ab universo æternæ perditionis periculo immunes reddi queamus.

a. Mark 6:41, 2 Pet. 2:9, Rev. 3:10.
b. 1 Cor. 10:13.

12. *Epilogus* habet fundamentum, vel rationem triplicem, cur ea, quæ jam dicta sunt, petere à Deo atque orare audeamus, adeoque cur ea petere nos deceat. Quia videlicet *Ipsius est Regnum*: id est, quia[a] ipse solus absolutus, nullique obnoxius, omnium Rex ac dominus est, cui imperium ac jus est in omnia; ac proinde in

name,[c] propagating his kingdom and executing his will, and without any distraction from godliness.

c. Luke 10:41-42.

10. The fifth is that "he would forgive us our debts, as we also forgive our debtors," that is, that in Christ he would graciously pardon us all our sins,[a] committed either through error or infirmity, or principally through wickedness and malice, just as we also pardon from the heart and are always ready to pardon all injuries and offences[b] (and that for this reason alone, because he so wills commands it) all those who at any time wound us.

b. Col. 3:12-13, 1 Pet. 4:8, 1 John 1:7, 9 & 2:7, 9.

11. The sixth is that "he would not lead us into temptation, but deliver us from evil," that is, that he would never permit us to be oppressed too much by grave and lasting temptations,[a] much less defeated, or to be tested beyond our strength,[b] but that he would always strengthen and sustain us by his Holy Spirit[c] according to his singular power and also fatherly love, especially in grave afflictions, arduous dangers and calamities, and other evils of that kind, through which Satan tries to utterly destroy us, and turn us from God, lest perhaps being too pressed by them, we choose something contrary to his divine will and harmful to our salvation or a good conscience. And finally, that always together with the temptation he would will to grant a happy outcome,[d] that we would be able to suffer it and so finally be gloriously freed from all the snares and enticements and all the fraud and power of Satan, indeed that we may be rendered immune from all danger of eternal perdition.

c. Eph. 3:16-18 & 6:11ff., 1 Thess. 3:2ff, 1 Pet. 5:10, Heb. 13:20-21, Rom. 5:2ff.
d. 1 Cor. 10:13, 1 Pet. 5:8-10, 1 John 5:18.

12. The conclusion has a threefold foundation or reason, why we should dare to ask or pray to God about those thing which we have already spoken. Because indeed his is the kingdom, that is, because he only is absolute king and lord of all,[a] and liable to no one, and who has command and right in all, and therefore even over Satan himself,

ipsum etiam satanam, licet mundi hujus Deum ac principem, Quia item *ipsius est potentia*:[b] id est, quia ipse solus facere potest, (hoc est dare, auferre, immittere, avertere, permittere, impedire) quicquid vult, idque pro suo unius arbitrio ac beneplacito: & proinde contra quem satanas, cum toto mundo, nihil in perniciem nostram valet. Quia denique *ipsius est gloria*: id est,[c] quia ipse solus & unus est, cui acceptum ferri debet, quicquid boni, vel optamus ac petimus, vel jam habemus & possidemus: & in cujus solius gloriam, ut ultimum finem, universum bonum nostrum semper redundaturum est.

a. Ps. 145:11-13 & 146:10, Rev. 12:10, 2 Pet. 3:4.
b. Ps. 115:3, Mark 14:36, Rev. 12:7-8.

13. Quia vero pii Dei cultores de exauditione precum suarum, quas juxta Dei voluntate, fundunt, certo persuasi sunt,[a] & perpetuam divini nominis gloriam, suamque ipsorum salutem, magis magisque per easdem promoveri optant & summopere desiderant, id circo subjicitur vocula, *Amen*: quæ partim certam rei propositæ adseverationem, partim etiam piam fidelis animæ optationem, ac religiosum votum complectitur.

a. 1 John 3:22 & 5:14-15, 1 Cor. 14:16, Ps. 89:52.

14. Altera pars seu species *præcationis* late acceptæ, est *gratiarum actio*,[a] qua Deo pro beneficiis jam acceptis, sive ad hanc, sive ad futuram vitam pertinentibus, gratias agimus per Jesum Christum: idque qua privatim, qua publice, præsertim in Ecclesia ipsius: animumque[b] gratum ac memorem, tum singulari sanctimoniæ studio, tum laudibus, psalmis, hymnis, eleemosynis, aliisque piis, & ad Dei gloriam ac proximi nostri utilitatem facientibus officiis, pro qualitate ac quantitate, tum virium nostrarum, tum acceptorum beneficiorum, testamur ac declaramus.

a. Eph. 5:10, 19-20, Phil. 4:6, 1 Thess. 5:15, 18, 2 Thess. 1:3 & 2:13, 1 Tim. 2:1.

although god and prince of this world. Likewise, because his is the power,[b] that is, because he alone is able to do (namely, give, take away, send, avert, permit or impede) whatever he wills, and that according to his own will and good pleasure, and therefore is he one against whom Satan, with the entire world, cannot prevail in order to destroy us. And finally, because "his is the glory," that is, because he is the only one to whom we ought to ascribe whatever good we either wish and desire[c] or already have and possess and to whose alone glory, as to its final purpose, our whole good is always to overflow.

c. 1 Cor. 6:20 & 10:30-31, Col. 3:17, 1 Pet. 4:11, Rev. 10:5-6.

13. But because pious worshippers of God are certainly persuaded of the hearing of their prayers which they pour out according to the will of God,[a] and because they wish and very much desire that the everlasting glory of the divine name and their own salvation may promoted more and more by the same, for this [purpose] is subjoined the word "Amen," which in part contains a certain affirmation of the things proposed and in part a pious wish and religious vow of the believing soul.

14. The other part or kind of prayer widely accepted is thanksgiving,[a] by which we give thanks to God for benefits already received through Jesus Christ, whether pertaining to this or the future life, and whether in public or private, [but] especially in his church. And we testify and declare a thankful and mindful soul,[b] first by a singular zeal and exercise of holiness, then by praises, psalms, hymns, love and other godly deeds, doing our duty to the glory of God and the advantage of our neighbor, in quality and quantity, first of our own abilities and then of the benefits received.

b. Ps. 116:1ff, 2 Cor. 9:11, ch. 11ff., Col. 1:12-13 & 3:16-17.

Chapter 15

CAPUT XV.
De specialibus vocationibus, deque præceptis ac træditionibus humanis

1. Et hæc quidem summa est illorum mandatorum, quæ à Jesu Christo communiter nobis præcepta, seu Christianis omnibus ex æquo, ad æternam salutem conseuquendam, observatu necessaria sunt. Præter quæ tamen unicuique fidelium sua *peculiaris vocatio*, quæ unicuique sedulo spectanda est: Qualis, verbi gratia, est[a] magistratuum,[b] subditorum; parentum, liberorum; dominorum,[c] servorum; item[d] conjugum,[e] cœlibum,[f] virginum,[g] viduarum;[h] divitum, pauperum &c. de quibus jam ante, in expositione Decalogi, aliqua ex parte actum fuit: de reliquis vero specialia passim monita (sed jam dictis analoga, & singulorum statui congrua) in S. literis obvia sunt.

a. Rom. 13:1ff.
b. 1 Pet. 2:13-14.
c. Eph. 6:1ff.
d. Eph. 5:22, 1 Pet. 3:1ff.

2. De his generatim tenenda illa Apostoli regula: *Unusquisque maneat*[a] *in ea vocatione, in qua vocatus est.* Quam tamen, si meliorem, salva pietate, facere possumus, id nobis liberum est. Omnes enim hæ conditiones per se adiaphoræ sunt:[b] eoque nec Christo nos commendant, nec invisos ei, minusve gratos efficiunt. Quare nec (verbi gratia) virginitati,[c] aut cœlibatui, major quam conjugio, nec paupertati major, quam opulentiæ &c. sanctitas adscribenda est: nec temeraria de his rebus vota Deo nuncupanda, quibus scilicet in perpetuum huc, illucve, nos astringamus: imo per quæ Deum tentemus, & laqueum ipsi nobis ac libertati nostræ

CHAPTER 15
Special callings, and the commandments and traditions of men.

1. And this indeed is the sum of those commandments which are taught to us by Jesus Christ, or which are necessary for all Christians to observe equally in order to gain eternal salvation. Nevertheless, aside from these every believer has his particular calling, which is to be carefully observed by everyone. Of such are magistrates,[a] subjects,[b] parents, children, masters and servants;[c] likewise of the married,[d] bachelors, virgins[e] and widows; of rich,[f] poor,[g] etc. Some of them were already treated in the exposition of the Decalogue, and for the rest special instructions or admonitions (but proportionable to those already spoken and suitable to every individual's state) are obvious throughout the Holy Scriptures.

e. 1 Cor. 7 & 8.
f. 1 Tim. 6:3ff.
g. 1 Tim. 6:17ff., Ja. 2:1ff & 5:1ff.

2. Of these in general we must hold to the rule of the Apostle: let every one remain in that calling in which he was called.[a] Yet as much as possible, if we can do better, it is permitted for us to do so, preserving piety. For all these conditions in themselves are indifferent and therefore neither commend us to Christ[b] nor make us hostile or less pleasing to him. Wherefore (for instance) more holiness is not to be ascribed to virginity or celibacy than to a married estate,[c] neither more to poverty than to wealth, etc. Neither are rash vows to be made to God concerning these things by which we perpetually bind ourselves to this or that, indeed through which we test God and cast a snare

injiciamus.

a. 1 Cor. 7:20ff.
b. Col. 3:11.

3. Alia vero omnia opera, præsertim mere externa, quæ religiosa putantur, quæque præter & extra Dei verbum,ᵃ ab humano spiritu excogitantur (sive ea cum aliorum auctoritate, præsertim Ecclesiasticâ, sub Traditionum prætextu, conscientijs hominum imponantur: sive ultro & voluntarie, cum opinione tamen cultus, si non omnino necessarij, ai saltem meritorij, vel satisfactorij, à nobis præstentur) ad salutem certe necessaria non sunt: immo etiam vere bonorum operum, vel cultus divini (nedum supererogationis, vel eximiæ Religionis) specioso titulo digna nomine censenda: quippe quæ nec veræᵇ obedientiæ Deo & Christo, unico legislatori nostro, per se gratæ & jure debitæ (ideoque cum vitæ æternæ promissione nobis imperatæ) augusto nomine venire possunt. Imo etiam, quæ raroᶜ principiali cultui divino (dilectioni, puta, Dei & proximi) magno impedimanto sunt, ac veræ pietati noxiæ; præsertim si divinis præceptis, ut sæpe fit, non modo æquiparentur, sed etiam præferantur.

a. Mat. 15:2ff, Gal. 4:9ff, 5:1ff, Col. 2:8ff.
b. 1 John 2:17, Matt. 7:21ff., 15:16 & 23:23.

to ourselves and our liberty.

c. 1 Cor. 7:25ff.

3. Truly all other works, especially the merely external, which are considered religious, and which are invented by the human spirit above and beyond the Word of Godᵃ (as when some opinion regarding worship, if not utterly necessary, then at least meritorious or satisfactory, is imposed on men's consciences by the authority of others, especially the church, under the pretence of traditions, or whether they be freely and voluntarily performed by us), they certainly are not necessary for salvation. Indeed besides, they cannot be considered worthy of the respectable title of truly good works or of divine worship (much less of supererogation or any excellent religion) because they cannot come under the solemn name of true obedience, which is of itself acceptable and of right due to God and Christ,ᵇ our only lawgiverᶜ (and therefore is commanded under the promise of eternal life). For indeed not rarely they are a great impediment to the principal part of divine worship (namely loving God and neighbor) and hurtful to true godliness, especially if, as often happens, they are not only made equal to divine commandments but even preferred.

c. 1 Tim. 4:8ff., 6:3ff., Titus 3:8-9.

• CHAPTER 16 •

CAPUT XVI.
De cultu venerationeque Iesu Christi,
unici Mediatoris,
deque invocationis Sanctorum.

1. Et hactenus quidem præcipue de agnitione & cultu solius Dei actum est. Hanc autem

CHAPTER 16
On the worship and veneration of Jesus Christ, the only mediator, and the invocation of the saints.

1. Thus far we have principally deliberated the knowledge and worship of God alone. Now

partem excipit agnitio & cultus Iesu Christi proprius, qua quidem is Mediator est. In ea enim agnitione, quique hinc sequitur, cultu, expresse etiam vita æterna posita esse dicitur, Joh. 17. 3. Quippe Jesu Christo, ut unico N. T. Mediatori,[a] *data est omnis potestas in cœlo & terra, & omne judicium,*[b] *seu regimen universale, a Patre ipsi traditum, ut omnes eum honorent, sicut honorant & Patrem: &*[c] *auctoritas ei data est judicium faciendi, quia filius hominis est. Ideo etiam coronavit*[d] *eum Deus gloria & honore, & subjecit omnia pedibus ejus:*[e] *constituitque eum caput Ecclesiæ suæ super omnia &c. Quin & nomen dabit supra*[f] *omne nomen, ut in nomine Iesu se flectat omne genu, cœlestium, ac terrestrium, & subterraneorum; omnisque lingua confiteatur, Iesum Christum esse Dominum, ad gloriam Dei Patris &c.* Quæ sane ipsius propria Majestas,[g] ad nostrum imprimis solatium ipsi à Deo Patre collata, & religiosis & gratis animis agnoscenda, & perpetuo nobis ad Dei Christique ipsius gloriam, prædicanda est.

a. Matt. 28:18.
b. John 5:22-23, 3:35 & 17:2.
c. John 5:17.
d. Heb. 2:7-8.

2. Itaque qui Jesum Christum, quatenus[a] Mediator noster apud Deum est (præsertim ex quo tempore[b] ad summan illam sublimitatem evectus,[c] inque Patris sui throno, ad dextram ipsius collocatus est) sancte ac religiose colit, id est,[d] adorat, invocat,[e] spem & fiduciam suam in eo collocat,[f] eique suppliciter gratias,[g] pro parta nobis salute, agit, ac beneficit, rectè omnino & secundum certissiman Dei voluntatem agit. Qui autem prædictam ejus Majestatem ac gloriam non agnoscit, ac proinde hunc cultum ac venerationem ipsi præstare recusat, Deo simul & Christo non levem injuriam facit: maxime si idololatriæ etiam, aut falsi cultus, ac superstitionis nomine id ipsum accuset, vel potius infamet.

a. 1 Tim. 2:5, 1 John 2:1-2.
b. Phil. 2:9ff.

follows this part the knowledge and worship of Jesus Christ proper, in that he is mediator. For eternal life itself is expressly said to consist in the knowledge and from the worship that follows (John 17:3). For to Jesus Christ, as the only mediator of the New Testament, "is given all power in heaven and earth, and all judgment,[a] or universal control, given by the Father himself,[b] that all men honor him, just as they also honor the Father. And authority was given him to execute judgment, because he is the Son of man.[c] Therefore also God crowned him with glory and honor,[d] and put all things under his feet, and made him the head of his church over all etc."[e] In truth, "he gave him a name above every name, that at the name of Jesus every knee should bow, of those in heaven, on earth, and under the earth, and every tongue confess that Jesus Christ is Lord, to the glory of God the Father," etc.[f] This majesty was reasonably and properly conferred on him by God the Father, especially for our consolation, and is to be acknowledged with religious and thankful souls and continually announced by us to the glory of God and Christ himself.[g]

e. Eph. 1:221-22.
f. Phil. 2:9-11.
g. 1 Pet. 1:21 & 3:22, 1 Cor. 15:27, Acts 2:36, 5:32 & 10:36, 42, Rev. 1:5ff., 3:11.

2. Therefore he who religiously worships Jesus Christ in a holy manner, in as much as he is our mediator with God[a] (especially from the time he was exalted[b] and placed on the throne at the right hand of his Father[c]), that is, he that adores,[d] invokes, places his hope and trust in him,[e] and humbly gives thanks and blesses him[f] for the salvation purchased on his part for us,[g] acts according to the most certain will of God. For he who does not acknowledge his prescribed majesty and glory and so refuses to render to him this worship and veneration he makes no light injury to God and Christ, especially if he reproaches it, or rather, defames it, under the name of idolatry or false worship and superstition.

e. Acts 7:59 & 9.13-14, 1 Cor. 1:2.
f. John 14:1ff, 1 Thess 3:5.

c. Heb. 1:3, 7:26 & 8:1, Rev. 3:21.
d. Heb. 1:6, John 5:23, Phil. 2:10-11.

g. Rev. 5:8-9, 12-13.

3. Præter hunc vero unicum[a] Mediatorem Dei & hominum, alios ullos, vel[b] Angelos, vel homines: sive vivos, sive mortuos (sive hi revera, sive opinione tantum nostra, sancti fuerint) religiose colere: id est, plus quam civiliter adorare, vel invocare, tanquam scilicet patronos & advocatos nostros apud Deum: aut templa, altaria, festa iis consecrare, sacrificia offere, vota nuncupare, vel eorum meritis, ac potestate, gratiaque, apud Deum confidere &c. prorsus illicitum, Deoque ingratum esse statuimus: præsertim quum de mortuis, quantumvis sanctis, agitur: quippe de quibus S. Scriptura[c] passim affirmat, quod res nostras ignorent, & ea, quæ sub sole fiunt, minime curent &c. Memoriam tamen & horum & illorum sancte colendam, & virtutes cum præconio digne celebrandas, & ad imitationem nobis aliisque proponendas esse, jure censemus. Tantum abest, ut fidelium[d] adhuc viventium, mutuam pro sese apud Deum intercessionem, aut damnemus, aut ulla ratione vituperemus.

a. 1 Tim. 2:5.
b. Col. 2:18, Rev. 19:10 & 22:9.
c. Heb. 4:10, Rev. 14:13, Job 3:11-13, 41:21,

3. Truly we think it utterly illicit and ungrateful to God to worship religiously any others apart from this one mediator between God and man,[a] whether angels or men,[b] whether living or dead, especially concerning the dead however holy (whether they were really holy or only so in our opinion), that is, to adore them more than is civil or invocate them as our patrons and advocates with God, or consecrate temples, altars, feasts to them, offer sacrifices, utter vows to them, or trust in either their merits and power or their grace and favor with God, etc. For the Holy Scriptures everywhere affirm that [the dead] do not know our concerns[c] or have the least interest in those things that occur under the sun. Yet we rightly think that their memory is to be kept in a holy manner, their virtues celebrate with deserved praise and put forth to us and others to imitate. Yet far be it from us that we should condemn or reproach in any way the mutual intercession of believers who are still alive for one another before God.[d]

Eccles. 9:5, 2 Ki. 22:20, Is. 38:19 & 63:16.
d. Rom. 15:30, 2 Cor. 1:11, Eph. 6:18-19, Col. 4:3, 2 Thess. 3:2, Heb. 13:18.

• CHAPTER 17 •

CAPUT XVII.
De beneficiis & promisis divinis;
ac primo de Electione ad gratiam,
seu Vocatione ad fidem.

I. Cæterum ut præcepta hæc divina, hactenus exposita, non tantum præstare posset homo; sed & libenter, atque ex animo, præstare vellet; voluit Deus etiam à parte sua facere omnia, quæ ad utrumque efficiendum in homine[a] necessaria

CHAPTER 17
On the benefits and promises of God,
and principally of election to grace,
or calling to faith.

1. But that man may not just perform the commandments of God thus far explained, but also willingly want to perform them from the mind, God willed for his part to do everything necessary for effecting both in man,[a] that is, he determined to

erant: id est, statui ejusmodi conferre gratiam homini peccatori, per quam idoneus & aptus reddetur ad præstandum id omne, quod ab eo in Evangelio postulatur: & porro ejusmodi bona ipsi promittere, quorum excellentia & pulchritudo longe excederet capacitatem intellectus humani, & quorum desiderium, ac certa spes voluntatem hominis ab obsequium actu præstandum accendere posset, atque inflammare. Quæ quidem beneficia omnia Deus, ex se ipso clementissimus, & erga nos in Christo paterne affectus, per^b Spiritum suum S. (de quo supra pluribus actum fuit) tum patefacere, tum reipsa etiam largiri nobis solet.

a. Jer. 31:32-34, Heb. 8:8ff, Ez. 11:19 & 36:22, 2 Cor. 7:1, 2 Pet. 1:3-4, 1 John 3, Col. 1:4-5, 1 Pet. 1:3-4.

2. *Primo* itaque^a gratiam, ad fidem & obedientiam præstandum, non modo necessariam, sed & sufficientem, largitur Deus peccatoribus, cum eos per Evangelium ad se vocat: ipsisque sub promisso æternæ vitæ, & contraria mortis sempiternæ commitatione, fidem & obedientim serio præscribit. Hæc *vocatio* appellatur interdum in Scriptura^b *Electio*, ad gratiam scilicet, & ad media salutis: multum differens ab Electione ad gloriam, sive ad ipsam salutem, de qua infra. Efficitur autem & perficitur ista vocatio per^c prædicationem Evangelij, eique adjunctam virtutem Spiritus: & quidem ex gratiosa & seria intentione salvandi, eoque ad fidem adducendi, eos^d omnes, qui vocantur: sive reipsa credant, ac salventur, sive non, adeoque credere ac proinde salvari pertinaciter nolint.

a. Matt. 11:20, John 5:34, 40 & 6:44-45, 2 Pet. 1:2-3.
b. 1 Cor. 1:26, 2 Tim. 1:9, 1 Pet. 2:9.

3. Et enim alia vocatio^a *efficax*, ab eventu potius, quam à sola intentione Dei sic dicta, quæ scilicet effectum suum salutarem reipsa sortitur: non quidem idcirco, quod ex præcisa salvandi intentione, per singularem & arcanam quandam Dei sapientiam sic administretur, ut fructuose congruat voluntati ejus, qui vocatur: neque^b quod in ea efficaciter, per potentiam irresistibilem, aut vim quandam omnipotentem (quæ nec creatione, nec suscitatione è mortuis minor sit)

confer such grace to sinful man by which he might be suitable and apt to render everything which is required of him in the gospel, and even more, to promise such good things to him, whose excellence and beauty might far exceed the capacity of human understanding, and that the desire and certain hope of this might kindle and inflame the will of man to render obedience in acts to him. Indeed, God habitually both makes known and bestows all these benefits to us by his Holy Spirit^b (about which we have declared more fully above).

b. 1 Cor. 2:10, 12:3ff, 1 John 2:20, 27, Rom. 5:5, 8-9.

2. Therefore, in the first place, when God calls sinners to himself through the gospel and seriously commands faith and obedience either under the promise of eternal life, or to the contrary, under the threat of eternal death, he not only bestows necessary but also sufficient grace for sinners to render faith and obedience.^{a} This calling is sometimes called election in Scriptures, namely, to grace as the means of salvation, very different from election to glory or to salvation itself;^{b} more on this below. This calling, however, is effected and executed by the preaching of the gospel,^{c} together with the power of the Spirit, and that certainly with a gracious and serious intention to save and so to bring to faith all those who are called,^{d} whether they really believe and are saved or not, and so obstinately refuse to believe and be saved.

c. Mat. 28:18, John 5:34, Rom. 10:14-15, 2 Cor. 3:5-6.
d. 1 Tim. 2:4ff., Tit. 2:11, 1 Pet. 1:23, 25.

3. For there is one calling that is effective,^{a} so called because it attains its saving effect from the event rather than from the sole intention of God. Indeed, it not administered by some special and hidden wisdom of God from an absolute intention of saving, so as to fruitfully unite with the will of the one who is called, nor so that by it the will of the one who is called is so efficaciously determined to believe through an irresistible power or some omnipotent force^b (which is nothing less than

voluntas ejus, qui vocatur, ad credendum ita determinetur, ut non possit non credere atque obedire: sed quia vocanti Deo ab homine, jam vocato, & sufficienter præparato, non resistitur, neque gratiæ divinæ obex ponitur, qui alioqui poni ab ipso potuisset. Alia^c *sufficiens* quidem est, sed tamen *inefficax*, quæ videlicet, ex parte hominis, effectu salutari caret: perque solam hominis voluntariam, ac vincibilem culpam, infructuosa est, sive eventum optatum ac debitum non sortitur.

a. Rom. *:28-29, 1 Cor. 1:24, 26.
b. Acts 2:4, 13, 48, Rom. 6:17, 1 Thess. 2:13.
c. Prov. 1:24-25, Ez. 12:1, Is. 5:1ff., Matt.

4. Prior illa, cum effectu suo salutari conjuncta, sive jam in actu exercito constituta, interdum appellatur in Scripturis, *conversio*,^{a} *regeneratio*,^{b} *spiritualis ex mortuis*^{c} *exitatio*, & *nova creatio*:^{d} quia videlicet per eam à pravo vivendi genere, ad juste,^{e} sobrie, ac pie vivendum efficaciter convertimur: &^{f} à morte peccati, sive mortifera peccandi consuetudine, ad vitam spiritualem, sive sanctam vivendi rationem divinitus excitamur: denique ad^g imaginem tum doctrinæ, tum vitæ Jesu Christi, per spiritualem verbi efficaciam reformari, denuo veluti gignimur; sique^h novæ creaturæ per resipiscentiam & veram fidem, in ipso efficimur.

a. Acts 3:19, 26, 1 Thess. 1:9.
b. John 3:5ff, Ja. 1:18.
c. Eph. 2:6.
d. Gal. 4:19, 2 Cor. 5:17, Eph. 2:10.

5. Homo itaque salvificam fidem non habet^a ex seipso; neque ex arbitrij sui liberi viribus regeneratur, aut convertitur: quandoquidem^b in statu peccati nihil boni, quod quidem salutare bonum sit, (cujusmodi imprimis est conversio & fides salvifica) ex seipso, vel à seipso, vel cogitare potest, nedum velle, aut facere: sed necesse est,^{c} ut à Deo, in Christo, per verbum Evangelij, eique adjunctam Spiritus S. virtutem regeneretur, atque totus renovetur; puta intellectu, affectibus, voluntate, omnibusque viribus; ut salutaria bona recte possit intelligere, meditari, velle, ac perficere.

creation, or raising from the dead) that he could not but believe and obey, but because it is not resisted by the one who is now called and sufficiently prepared by God, nor is a barrier placed against divine grace which otherwise was able to be placed by him. Indeed there is another which is sufficient, but nevertheless ineffective,^{c} namely, which on man's part is without saving effect and through the will and avoidable fault of man alone it is unfruitful, or does not attain its desired and due effect.

23:37, Luke 7:30, John 5:40, Acts 7:5 & 13:46, 2 Thess. 3:1-2, contrary to the Canons of the Synod of Dort, chs. 3 & 4.

4. The former, when either joined with its saving effect or already constituted by its exercised act, is sometimes called in Scripture conversion,^{a} regeneration,^{b} a spiritual rising from the dead^c and a new creation,^{d} clearly because by it we are efficaciously turned from a corrupt style of living^e to live justly, soberly and godly,^{f} and are raised on a heavenly account from a death of sin or a deadly custom of sinning to a spiritual life or holy way of living. And finally, being reformed by the spiritual effectiveness of the Word according to the image first of the teaching and then of the life of Christ, it is as if we were born again^g and made new creatures through repentance and true faith.^{h}

e. Tit. 2:11-12.
f. Rom. 6:2ff.
g. Rom. 6:17.
h. Eph. 2:24, Col. 3:10.

5. Man therefore does not have saving faith from himself,^{a} nor is he regenerated or converted by the powers of his own free will, seeing that in the state of sin he cannot of himself or by himself either think or will or do anything that is good enough to be saved^b (of which first of all is conversion and saving faith), but it is necessary that he be regenerated and totally renewed by God, in Christ, through the word of the gospel joined with the power of the Holy Spirit,^{c} namely, in his understanding, affections, will and all his strengths, that he may be able to understand, meditate on, will and finish correctly these things

a. Matt. 11:17, 13:11, &16:17ff.
b. Matt. 7:17 & 12:34; John 6:44-45, 65 & 3:5ff.

6. Gratiam itaque Dei statuimus esse[a] principium,[b] progressium, &[c] complementum omnis boni: adeo ut ne ipse quidem regenitu absque præcedente ista, sive præveniente, excitante, prosequente, & cooperante gratia, bonum ullum salutare cogitare, velle, aut peragere possit;[d] nedum ullis, ad malum trahentibus, tentationibus resistere. Ita ut fides, conversio, & bona opera omnia, omnesque actiones piæ & salutares, quas quis cogitando potest assequi, gratiæ Dei in Christo, tanquam caussæ suæ principiali & primariæ, in solidum sint adscribendæ.

a. Eph. 2:5, 18, Titus 2:11-13 & 3:4-5, Phil. 1:6.
b. John 15:5, 1 Cor. 1:4ff.

7. Gratiam tamen divinam[a] aspernari & respuere, ejusque operationi resistere homo potest: ita ut seipsum, cum divinitus ad fidem & obedientiam vocatur, inidoneum reddere queat ad credendum, & divinæ voluntati obediendum; idque culpa sua propria, eaque vera & vincibili; sive per[b] securam inadvertentiam, sive per[c] cœcum præjudicium; sive per[d] inconsiderandum zelum, sive per[e] mundi, aut[f] sui ipsius inordinatum amorem; sive per alias id genus caussas irritatrices. Irresistibilis enim gratia, sive vis ejusmodi, quæ nec creatione, nec proprie dicta generatione, nec suscitatione è mortuis, quoad efficaciam, minor sit (quæque actum ipsum fidei atque obedientiæ eo modo efficiat, ut ea posita homo non possit non credere, atque obedire) illic certe adhiberi non potest, nisi prorsus inepte atque insipienter, ubi obedientiæ libera serio mandatur; idque sub ingentis præmij promissione, si præstetur; & pœnæ gravissimæ comminatione, si negligantur. Frustra enim hanc obedientiam is mandat, & ab alio postulat, obedientique prœmium sive sine caussa promittit; qui ipse solus, ea vi, cui resisti non potest, ipsum obedientiæ actum efficere & debet, & vult; & inepte præterque rationem præmium consertur illi, tanquam vere obedienti,

that are savingly good.

c. Phil. 1:5-6 & 2:13, Eph. 2:1ff., Ja. 1:17-18, 1 Pet. 1:23.

6. We think therefore that the grace of God is the beginning,[a] progress[b] and completion of all good,[c] so that not even a regenerate man himself can, without this preceding or preventing, exciting, following and cooperating grace, think, will, or finish any good thing to be saved,[d] much less resist any attractions and temptations to evil. Thus faith, conversion, and all good works, and all godly and saving actions which are able to be thought, are to be ascribed solidly to the grace of God in Christ as their principal and primary cause.

c. 1 Thess. 5:23-24, Eph. 6:13.
d. Matt. 26:41, 1 Cor. 10:13, Eph. 2:4ff.

7. Yet a man may despise and reject the grace of God[a] and resist its operation, so that when he is divinely called to faith and obedience, he is able to render himself unfit to believe and obey the divine will, and that by his own true and conquerable fault, either by secure carelessness,[b] or blind prejudice,[c] or thoughtless zeal,[d] or an inordinate love of the world[e] or of himself,[f] or other inciting causes of that kind. For such an irresistible grace or force, which, as to its effectiveness, is no less than creation, nor generation properly called, nor raising from the dead (and causes the very act of faith and obedience in such a way that, being granted, a man cannot not believe or obey) certainly cannot be but ineptly and foolishly applied where free obedience is seriously commanded, and that under the promise of vast reward if performed and the threat of the gravest punishment if neglected. For in vain he commands this obedience and requires it of another, and without cause promises to reward the obedience, who himself alone both ought and wills to cause the very act of obedience by such a force as cannot be resisted. And it is silly and irrational to reward someone as truly obedient in whom this very obedience was caused through such an alien power. And finally, punishment, especially eternal,

in quo ipsa obedientia, per ejusmodi alienam vim effecta est: denique inique & crudeliter infertur ei pœna, maxime æterna, à quo obedientia solo gratiæ illius irresistibilis, utpote necessariæ, defectu præstita non est, tanquam inobedienti, qui revera inobediens non sit. Ut jam non dicamus, passim in Scripturis affirmari de quibusdam, quod restiterint[g] Spiritu S. Quod *indignos*[h] *se judicaverint,* vel potius, *efficerent, vitâ*; quod[i] *consilium Dei contra seipsos irritum reddiderint*: quod[k] *audire,*[l] *venire,*[m] *obedire noluerint*: quod[n] *aures suas occluserint, corda*[o] *sua obduraverint* &c. De aliis certo, quod *prompe*[p] *aut libenter crediderint*: quod *obedierint veritatis ac fidei,* quod *attentos dociles se præbuerint,* quod[q] *assensi fuerint doctrinæ evangelicæ,* quod *sermonem Dei cum alacritate receperint*; quodque *in eo generosiores fuerint ijs, qui illum ipsum rejiciebant*; quod denique *ex animo auscultaverint veritati, sive Evangelio &c*. Quæ quidem omnia tribuere ijs, qui, vel nullo modo possunt credere, aut obedire, vel non possunt non credere & obedire, cum vocantur, nimis profecto ineptum est, & plane ridiculum.

a. Ez. 12:2, Prov. 1:24-25, Mat. 13:19 & 23:27, Acts 7:51 & 13:46.
b. Matt. 13:19.
c. John 7:3-5, 51.
d. 2 Cor. 3:13, Rom. 10:2-3.
e. Luke 14:18.
f. John 5:44.
g. 2 Cor. 4:4, 2 Thess. 3:2, 2 Tim. 3:2ff, 1 John 5:4ff.

8. Etsi vero maxima est[a] gratiæ disparitas, pro liberrima scilicet voluntatis divinæ dispensatione: tamen Spiritus S. omnibus & singulis, quibus verbum fidei ordinarie prædicatur, tantum[b] gratiæ confert, aut saltem conferre paratus est, quantum ad fidem ingenerandum, & ad promovendum suis gradibus salutarem ipsorum conversionem sufficit. Itaque gratia sufficiens ad fidem & conversionem non tantum ijs obtingit, qui actu credunt & convertuntur: sed etiam iis,[c] qui actu ipso non credunt, nec ipsa reipsa convertuntur. Quoscunque enim Deus vocat ad fidem & salutem,

is unjustly and cruelly inflicted on him as disobedient by whom this obedience was not performed solely through the absence of that irresistible and truly necessary grace, who really is not disobedient. We cannot here state how everywhere in the Scriptures it is affirmed of some, that they resisted the Holy Spirit,[g] that they judged, or rather made, themselves unworthy of eternal life,[h] that they made void the counsel of God concerning themselves;[i] that they would not hear,[k] come,[l] obey,[m] that they closed their ears[n] and hardened their hearts,[o] etc. And of others, that they promptly and freely believed,[p] that they obeyed the truth and the faith, that they showed themselves attentive and teachable, that were attentive to the evangelical doctrine,[q] that received the Word of God with cheerfulness, and that they were more generous in this than those who rejected the same, and finally, lastly, that obeyed the truth, or the Gospel, from the heart, etc. To attribute all this to those who in no way can either believe or obey, or cannot not believe and obey when they are called, is very certainly foolish, and plainly ridiculous.

h. Acts 7:51.
i. Acts 13:46.
k. Luke 7:30.
l. Prov. 1:24-25.
m. John 5:40.
n. Acts 7:39.
o. Zech. 7:11-13, Jer. 5:3.
p Acts 28:24, Heb. 3:12-13 & 4:2, Ps. 95:7-8.
q. Acts 2:41, 13:47, 6:7 & 17:11, Rom. 6:17, 1 Pet. 1:22.

8. And even if there truly is the greatest disparity of grace,[a] clearly according to the most free dispensation of the divine will, still the Holy Spirit confers such grace to all,[b] both in general and in particular, to whom the Word of faith is ordinarily preached, as is sufficient for begetting faith in them, and for gradually carrying on their saving conversion. And therefore sufficient grace for faith and conversion not only comes to those who actually believe and are converted, but also to those who do not believe and are not really converted.[c] For whoever God calls to faith and salvation, he calls them seriously,[d] that is, not only

eos^d serio vocat: id est, non externa tantum specie, aut verbo duntaxat vocali (quatenus scilicet in eo seria ipsius præcepta, & promissa vocatis generatim declarantur) sed cum sincera etiam, ac minime simulata salvandi intentione, ac convertendi voluntate: ita ut nullum absolutæ reprobationis, aut improveritæ excæcationis, vel indurationis, decretum de iisdem præcedere unquam voluerit.

a. Rom. 12:6ff, 1 Pet. 4:10.
b. Matt. 11:21, Tit. 3:4ff, 1 Pet. 1:23 & 2:9, Ja. 1:18, 2 Cor. 3:6, Heb. 4:12.

by an external show, or in words alone (that is, when his serious commandments and promises are declared to those that are called in general) but also with a sincere and unfeigned intention of saving them and the will of converting them. Thus he never willed any prior decree of absolute reprobation or undeserved blinding or hardening concerning them.

c. Is. 62:2, Ez. 18:11, Prov. 1:24ff., Matt. 23:37, Luke 8:12.
d. Tit. 2:11-12, 2 Tim. 1:9, 2 Cor. 5:20 & 6:1ff., Is. 5:2ff., Ps. 85:13-14, John 5:34 & 10:10.

• CHAPTER 18 •

CAPUT XVIII.
De promissis divinis, quæ jam conversis ac fidelibus in hac vita præstantur: hoc est, de Electione ad gloriam, Adoptione, Iustificatione, Sanctificatione & Obsignatione

1. Circa homines peccatores, sed qui jam per divinam gratiam efficaciter vocati & ad fidem Jesu Christi conversi sunt, ejusdemque gratiæ auxilio, ex vera fide vitam suam juxta mandata Jesu Christi instituunt, occupari vult & solet Deus^a salutaribus actibus, sed duum generum: quippe quorum alij ad hanc vitam, alij ad futuram pertinent.

a. Rom. 8:28ff., Eph. 1:3ff.

2. Actus ad hanc vitam pertinentes quinque sunt: quorum duo priores sunt, *Electio* ad gloriam, & *Adoptio*, sive υἱοθεσία, hoc est divina filiatio: Quorum illa^a qui jam conversi sunt, & vere credunt, è profana pereuntium turba segregantur, & ex ordine damnadorum (quoad statum præsentem) exempi, velut in

CHAPTER 18
On the promises of God that are performed in this life to those that are already converted and are believers, that is, election to glory, adoption, justification, sanctification, and sealing.

1. Concerning men who are sinners but already efficaciously called by divine grace and converted to faith in Jesus Christ, and who by the aid of the same grace through true faith order their life according to the commandments of Jesus Christ, God^a is wills and wants [them] to be occupied with two kinds of saving acts, those which indeed pertain to this life, and the others [which pertain] to the future.

2. Five acts pertain to this life, two of which are prior, election to glory, and adoption, or υἱοθεσία. By the first they are already converted, and truly believe,^a separated from the multitude of those who perish and exempted from the damned (as their present estate), separated just as God's own flock. By the other they are taken into the

family of God[b] and hence into the right of heavenly inheritance into which they will enter in due time. Thus they are placed among those who will be saved, or among those whom God will in no way punish, but will forgive their sins by grace through Christ. Nevertheless, adoption throughout Scripture usually denotes the very redemption itself of our bodies or the blessed resurrection,[c] because the fulfillment and consummation of it will certainly appear [then].

c. Rom. 8:23, Luke 6:36, 1 John 3:1ff.

3. These are directly connected with three other acts, justification, sanctification, and finally, the unique act of sealing by the Holy Spirit. Justification is a merciful, gracious and indeed full remission of all guilt before God to truly repenting and believing sinners, through and because of Jesus Christ,[a] apprehended by true faith,[b] indeed, even more, the liberal and bountiful imputation of faith for righteousness. For indeed in the judgment of God we cannot obtain to it except by the pure grace of God and only by faith in Jesus Christ[c] (but nevertheless a living one, operating through love) without any merit of our own works. And this is the meaning of that article of the creed, when we say, "I believe in the remission of sins."

b. Rom. 4:3ff & 5:1ff.
c. Gal. 2:16, Eph. 2:4ff., Tit. 3:4.

4. Sanctification specifically called (for in some places in the Holy Scriptures it is sometimes accepted for regeneration or conversion, or effectual calling (about which, see above), or finally for any spiritual cleansing, even if only external[a], is a certain, more complete, continually increasing separation of the sons of God from this impure world, being partly a richer and fuller enlightening of true believers in the knowledge of divine truth and the careful performance of their duty by faith[b] (which even God often effects in many and admirable manners), in part through stimulation to a sharper and deeper abiding hatred

peccatorum, & studium sanctimoniæ, ac veræ pietatis exstimulatio, inque hoc zelo confirmatio: ita ut voluntas hominis vere fidelis pronior atque inclinatior, imo alacrior ad virtutem quotidie reddatur; & ea obstacula, quæ alioquin in studio pietatis ac virtutis occurrere ipsi solent, aut objici sibi non patiatur, aut objecta diligenter removeat, & animose alacriterque superet.

a. 1 Cor. 1:2 & 6:11, Heb. 2:1, 2 Thess. 2:13, 1 Pet. 1:2, Acts 20:32 & 26:18.

5. *Obsignatio* per Spiritum S. est solidor & robubustior in vera fiducia, & cælestis gloriæ spe, gratiæque divinæ certitudine,[a] confirmatio: qua fit, ut fideles, veluti arrhabone, aut pignore quodam accepto, de sui adoptione, justificatione & secutura tandem glorificatione, magis magisque certi reddantur, & nisi per ipsos steterit,[b] ad finem usque, in sensu gratiæ Dei, veraque fide, adversus omne genus tentationum conserventur, seu perseverantia totali finali donentur.

a. Rom. 5:5 & 8:15-16, 2 Cor. 1:21-22, & 5:5.
b. Eph. 1:13-14 & 4:30, 1 Cor. 1:8-9, Phil. 1:6-7.

6. Et hujusmodi quidem actibus gratiosis occupatur Deus circa omnes & solos vere (licet inæqualiter & dispari mensura) credentes & resipiscentes: quorum proinde tria genera seu ordines in Scripturis reperiuntur. I. Eorum[a], qui novitij dici possunt, quique recens ad fidem convertuntur, & una cum sincero adsensu adferunt quidem serium ac deliberatum obediendi voluntati divinæ propositum: sed quod ortâ deinde cruce, & afflictionibus, aliisve periculosis tentationibus, quibus obsistere nondum potest, statim iterum languescit, aut interdum etiam evanescit, & prorfus emoritur. II. Eorum,[b] qui in vera fide & proposito isto sancto aliquanto tempore constantes quidem manent, veritatemque fidei suæ, bonis & sanctis operibus aliquandiu demonstrant: sed tandem tamen, sive mundi, sive carnis, sive satanæ illecebris, aut violentia tyrannide, victi fractique, à fide deficiunt ac desciscunt. III. Eorum, qui vel sine ulla defectione, aut interruptionem in pio illo proposito,[c] sanctique operibus, ad finem

of sin and zeal for holiness and true godliness[c] and their establishment in this zeal, so that the will of the truly believing man is rendered more prone and inclined, indeed more cheerful to daily virtue, and these obstacles or hindrances which otherwise he usually meets with in his zeal for piety and virtue, he either does not permit them to be thrown before him or he diligently removes the object and courageously and cheerfully overcomes them.

b. John 7:17-18, John 2:20, 27, Heb. 6:4 & 10:10, 14.
c. 1 Thess. 5:23, 2 Tim. 2:21.

5. Sealing by the Holy Spirit is a more solid and strong confirmation in a true confidence and hope of the heavenly glory and the certainty of divine grace[a] by which believers are rendered more and more certain of their adoption, justification and glorification, as if by a deposit or pledge, and if they keep themselves in it, they may be preserved even to the end in a sense of the grace of God[b] and in true faith against all kinds of temptations, being granted total, final perseverance.

6. And God is occupied with these kinds of gracious acts towards all those, and only those (although unequally and in different measure) who truly believe and repent. We find three kinds or orders of these in the Scriptures: 1 Those who can be called novices,[a] and who are recently converted to the faith, who together with a sincere assent bring indeed a serious and deliberate will to obey the divine will. But when persecution, afflictions and other dangerous temptations arise which [this kind] is not able to resist, it immediately grows weak once again, and utterly dies. 2. Those who remain constant for some time in the true faith[b] and in a certain holy purpose and demonstrate for a while the truth of their faith by good and holy works, but finally, whether by the enticements of the world, the flesh or Satan, or conquered and broken by some violent tyranny, they defect and desert from the faith. 3. Those who either without any defection or interruption continually persevere to the end in that godly purpose and in holy works,[c] or who have fallen again or even often

usque continuo perseverant: vel semel iterum vel lapsi, autd sæpius etiam deficientes, seria iterum pœnitentia ducuntur: sicque per divinam gratiam restitui, finaliter tandem per sistunt. Itaque duo priores credentium ordines eliguntur, adoptantur & justificantur quidem vere, at non prorsus absolute, nec nisi ad tempus: puta, quatenus & quandiu tales sunt & manent: sed tertius ac postremus solus etiam finaliter, ac peremptorie: nempe juxta is, quod in Evangelio legitur: Qui perseveraverit ad finem usque, salvus erit.

a. Matt. 13:20, Luke 8:12-13, 24, 1 Cor. 3:1ff, Gal. 1:6ff, Rev. 2 & 3.
b. Matt. 10:17ff. & 24:9ff, 1 Thess. 3:3ff., 1 Tim. 1:19 & 4:1ff., Heb. 6:4ff., & 10:31,

7. Actus enim ii divini sunt actus, modo continui, modo interrupti: qui scilicet tantisper hic durantm quamdiu durat conditionis requisitæ (hoc est, pactæ fidei ac sanctimoniæ) in nobis præsentia. Interrumpuntur vero, quando nos pactis amplius non stamus; sive, cum à nobis actus ejusmodi committuntur, qui cum vera fide, & conscientia bona, consistere nullo modo possunt: juxta id quod est apud Ezechielem:[a] Si aversus fuerit justus à justitia sua, & fœcerit iniquitatem, secundum omnes iniquitates, quas fecerit impius, an fecerit, & viveret? Omnes justitiæ ejus, quas fecit, non commemorabantur: propter prævaricationem suam, qua prævariatus est, & propter peccatum suum, quo peccavit, propter ipsa, inquam, morietur. Cui consonant complura alia id genus sacra testimonia simul & exempla.

departed, having once again lapsed or fallen, again are led to serious repentance and so being restored by the grace of God they finally persevere. Therefore the two former orders of believers are indeed truly elected, adopted, and justified, but not absolutely, but only for a time, namely, as far and as long as they are and remain such. But the third and last sort alone are finally and thoroughly such, that is, according to that which we read in the gospel: he who perseveres to the end will be saved.

2 Pet. 2:10ff., & 3:17-18.
c. Luke 22:32, 2 Cor. 1:7-8 & 7:10, 2 Tim. 2:25-26, Matt. 10:22 & 24:13.

7. For these are divine acts, sometimes continous, sometimes interrupted, that is, for as long and as often as the requisite conditions (that is, the faith and holiness of the covenant) continue to be present within us. But they are interrupted when we no longer stand in our covenant, or when such acts are committed by us which can in no way be consistent with true faith and a good conscience, according to Ezekiel, "If the righteous turns away from his righteousness, and does iniquity, according to all the iniquities which the wicked do, will he do it and live? All the righteousness which he has done will not be remembered because of his transgressions by which he has transgressed. And because of his sins which he sinned, I say, he shall die."[a] This is in keeping with many other sacred testimonies and examples of the same kind.

a. Ez. 18:24, Rom. 11:12ff., 1 Cor. 9:17 & 10:10ff, Col. 1:21, 23, Heb. 3:6, 14 & 10:25-36, Rev. 2:10 & 3:11-12.

Chapter 19

CAPUT XIX.
De promissis divinis ad futuram vitam pertinentibus, Sive de mortuorum resuscitatione & vita æterna.

1. Actus divini ad futuram vitam pertinentes, sunt *Resuscitatio* ex[a] morte, (vel hujus loco subita mortalis naturæ transmutatio) & *Glorificatio*,[b] sive gloriæ cœlestis, & vitæ æternæ collatio: juxta ultimos illos duos symboli Apostolici articulos: *Credo carnis resurrectionem, & vitam æternam.*

a. 1 Cor. 15.

2. *Resuscitatio* illa fiet in[a] adventu Jesu Christi secundo ac glorioso, ad judicium universale: cum videlicet mortuos[b] omnes, justos[c] patienter & injustos, in vitam revocaturus, ipsosque pariter, & vivos tunc superstites,[d] de tribunali Patris sui judicaturus; iisque omnibus[e] pro qualitate ac quantitate operum suorum, quæ in corpore suo gesserint, sive bonorum, sive malorum, præmia justa, pœnasve condignas, assignaturus est. Tunc enim fideles & sanctos suos, qui quidem[f] mortui fuerint, ex pulvere terræ in vitam æternam & beatam suscitaturus, eosque solos glorioso & incorruptibili corpore donaturus est. Quos autem[g] vivos tunc & superstites ex ijsdem offendet, eos subito & quasi in momento immutaturus atque beata cum aliis immortalitate adfecturus est.

a. Matt. 16:27 & 25:31ff.
b. Rev. 20:12-13.
c. Acts 24:15.
d. Rom. 14:9-12.

3. Ejusmodi vero suscitationem & partim immutationem, excipiet statim illa, quæ cæto-

CHAPTER 19
On the promises of God pertaining to the life to come, or the resurrection of the dead, and eternal life.

1. The divine acts pertaining to the future life are the resurrection from death[a] (instead a sudden change of our mortal nature) and glorification, or the granting of heavenly glory and life eternal,[b] according to the two last articles of the Apostles' Creed: "I believe the resurrection of the flesh, and eternal life."

b. Mark 25:31.

2. This resurrection will happen at the second and glorious coming of Jesus Christ for the judgment of all,[a] that is, when he will call all the dead to life,[b] first both the just and the unjust,[c] and then those who remain alive,[d] at the judgment seat of his Father. There the just reward or appropriate penalty will be assigned according to the quality and quantity of their works which they have done in the body,[e] whether good or bad. For at that time, he will awaken out of the dust of the earth his faithful and holy ones who were indeed dead[f] to an eternal and blessed life, and give to them alone a glorious and incorruptible body. But those whom he finds alive and surviving will be changed suddenly and almost in a moment, and with the others blessed with immortality.[g]

e. 2 Cor. 5:10, 2 Thess. 1:7ff, Matt. 25:1ff.
f. 1 Thess. 4:16, 2 Cor. 5:4ff., Phil. 3:21.
g. 1 Thess. 4:16, 1 Cor. 15:51-52.

3. This manner of awakening and partial alteration will be immediately followed by that blessed

rum omnium actuum complementum est, beata glorificatio:[a] qua Dominus Jesus (postquam cum hortationis clamore, cum voce Archangeli, & cum tuba ad judicium jam dictum Dei de cœlo descenderit) suscitatos illos per Angelos potentiæ suæ aêra secum assumet: & ex[b] universali totius mundi (tunc omnino conflagraturi) corruptione, seu totali perditione, in æternas & gloriosas[c] cœlorum sedes (quæ in Scripturis novi cœli, nova terra, & futurus orbis vocantur) potentissime tranferet: gloriaque[d] gaudio ineffabili secum, & cum Deo, sanctisque Angelis ipsius, perpetuo iisdem frui dabit.

glorification which is the completion of all the other acts, in which the Lord Jesus[a] (after he descends from heaven with a shout of encouragement, with the voice of the archangel, and with the trumpet of God to the aforementioned judgment) receives those who have awakened by the angels through his power to be with him in the air, and most powerfully transfers them from the universal corruption and total destruction of the whole world[b] (being then entirely in flames) into the eternal and glorious habitations of heaven[c] (which in Scripture are called the new heavens, the new earth and the future world) and will perpetually give them unspeakable glory and joy to enjoy together with himself, with God, and with his holy angels.[d]

a. 1 Thess. 4:16-17, Matt. 24:30-13 & 35:31, 1 John 1:3ff.
b. 2 Thess. 1:8ff, 2 Pet. 3:10-11.
c. Heb. 2:5, 2 Pet. 3:15, Rev. 21:1.
d. John 12:26, Mat. 25:21, 23, Luke 22:29-30, Rev. 3:12:21, 14:13, 21:23 & 22:5.

• CHAPTER 20 •

CAPUT XX.
De divinis comminationibus, ac impiorum pœnis, tum ad hanc, tum ad futuram vitam pertinentibus: puta Reprobatione, Induratione, Excæcatione, deque æterna morte & damnatione.

CHAPTER 20
On the divine threats and punishments of the wicked pertaining both to this life and the life to come: reprobation, hardening, blinding, and eternal death and damnation.

1. Circa impios & incredulos,[a] sive qui præfracte credere ac resipiscere nolunt, & licet diu multumque vocati, moniti, reprehensi, castigati &c. nihilominus tamen Evangelio inobedientes esse pergunt, occupari vult Deus contrarijs plane, nec minus severism, quam justis & sanctis actibus, quod in verbo suo illis comminatus est, partim ad hanc vitam, partim ad futuram pertinentibus.

1. Concerning the wicked and unbelievers, or those who are unwilling to believe and repent,[a] and who, although they have been long and much called, warned, reproved, chastised, etc., nevertheless still continue to disobey the gospel, God wills to employ the action completely to the contrary, and no less severe than just and holy, with which he threatened them in his Word, pertaining in part to this life and in part to the future.

a. Matt. 10:14-15 & 11:20, Luke 19:41, Rom. 2:2ff, 1 Thess. 2:15-16.

2. Actus ad hanc vitam pertinentes sunt Reprobatio, vel Desertio, Item Excæcatio & Induratio, aliæque id genus punitionis temporales: quarum prima est justa improborum hominum abjectio:[a] cum videlicet eos amplius pro populo suo habere non vult Deus: eoque[b] gratiam Spiritus S. ab ipsis sæpe spretam, jure iisdem subtrahit; imo externa etiam media illa interdum iis conferre dedignatur, quibus ordinarie ad salutem populi sui solet: relinquendo scilicet illos in tenebris suis & peccatis, sine veris Pastoribus, piisque Doctoribus, sive monitoribus, & veritatis studiosis indagatoribus.

a. Matt. 8:12 & 11:2, 20.

3. Excæcatio deinde sequitur[a] & Induratio: cum videlicet peccatores isti, luce veritatis cælestis jam destituri, Dei permissione & justo judicio, crassis[b] ignorantiis & erroribus profunde implicantur, & miris variisque modis seducuntur: cumque[c] cupiditatibus suis impuris traduntur, sive fœdis affectibus permittuntur; aut[d] Satanæ tentationibus, præstigiis & insidiis, hinc inde exponuntur: item, cum consilia, studia, factaque[e] ipsorum improba, felici aliquo sucessu ad tempus fluere, ipsique aliquandiu impuni peccare sinuntur; denique cum[f] occasiones errandi & peccandi multiplices ipsis objiciuntur: neque[g] conscientiæ ipsorum interim exstimulantur remorsu aliquo tristi, seu serio dolore, ob admissa peccata &c. Quæ quidem omnia, aliaque id genus compluram, in exitium suum convertere solent homines profani. Unde mira mentis cæcitas, pertinax animi duricies, ac fœdum peccandi studium, magis magisque crescunt: ac tenebræ tandem densæ ac crassæ, id est, bruta quædam Dei ignorantia, & secura vitæ profanitas, ipsos totos invadunt & occupant. Et hos quidem actus sequitur aliquando etiam exemplaris[h] quædam, & publica, inque oculos omnium incurrens istorum hominum in hac vita punitio.

a. Is. 6:6, Matt. 13:14-15, John 12:40, Acts 28:26.
b. Rom. 9:18 & 11:8.
c. Rom. 1:24, 26ff.

2. The acts pertaining to this life are reprobation and desertion, likewise blinding and hardening and other temporal punishments of this kind, of which the first is the just casting away of wicked men, that is, when God will no longer desire to have them for his people[a] and therefore rightly withdraws from them the often-spurned grace of his Holy Spirit.[b] Indeed he sometimes refuses to confer upon them those outward means which he usually employs for the salvation of his people, namely, leaving them in their own darkness and sins, without true pastors, godly teachers or counselors and diligent searchers of truth.

b. John 12:35, Luke 13:24 & 17:22, Matt. 10:14ff, Acts 14:16, . 2:5ff.

3. Then follows blinding and hardening,[a] namely, when these sinners, now being deprived of the light of heavenly truth, by God's permission and just judgment are profoundly involved in gross ignorance and errors[b] and seduced in surprising and diverse manners. And when they are given up to their own impure lusts,[c] or permitted their filthy affections, or are exposed on every side to the temptations, delusions and snares of Satan,[d] or likewise, when their wicked counsels, pursuits and deeds are allowed to flow with some happy success, and they themselves sin with impunity,[e] and finally, when multiplied occasions of erring and sinning are cast before them, and their consciences in the meanwhile are not moved to some sad remorse or serious sorrow for their sins, etc.,[g] all such things indeed, and very many more of the same, profane men often turn to their own destruction. From this there grows more and more a strange blindness of mind, an enduring hardness of soul and filthy zeal for sinning, and finally a dense, thick darkness, that is, some brutish ignorance of God, and secure profanity of life totally seizes and possesses them. And sometimes indeed those acts are followed by some exemplary and public punishment of these men in this life, occurring before the eyes of all.[h]

e. Ps. 10:4ff, 71:4ff, Jer. 44:17-18, Deut. 32:14, 19.
f. Ez. 14:5, 9, Is. 63:16-17.
g. Eph. 4:19, Rom. 11:8.

d. 2 Cor. 4:4, 2 Thess. 2:11-12.

4. Actus pœnales ad futuram vitam pertinentes, continentur fere vocibus iræ ac vindictæ divinæ, item judicij[a] & condemnætionis,[b] qua Deus non modo immortalem gloriam[c] impiis & incredulis irrevocabiliter tunc abjudicabit, sed & cruciatus infernales atque æterna supplicia infliget. Quod quidem palam futurum est in extremo illo die, cum eos in æternum ignem, una cum diabolo & angelis ejus, præcipitabit,[d] ubi pendant pænam æterni exitii, expulsi à facie Dei, & à glorioso robore ipsius.

a. Mark 2:29, Rom. 2:5, 2 Thess. 1:5, 2 Pet. 2:9 & 3:7, Jude v. 7.
b. Rom. 5:16 & 8:1.

5. His autem omnibus ita peractis, continuo[a] novus ille orbis existet, in quo justitia habitat: & ubi Jesus Christus suis omnibus, regnum Deo[b] & Patri suo restituet, ut Deus porro sit omnia in omnibus.

a. 2 Pet. 3:13, Rev. 21:1ff, & 22:1ff.

h. Ex. 9:16, Acts 12:21 & 5:5, 1 Cor. 10:5ff, 2 Pet. 2:5-6, Jude vv. 4-5.

4. The penal acts pertaining to the future life are most usually contained in the words of divine wrath and vengeance, likewise of judgment and condemnations[a] by which God will not only irrevocably deprive the wicked and unbelievers[c] of immortal glory,[b] but will also inflict hellish torments and eternal punishments. That indeed will be openly done in the last day, when he will throw them, together with the devil and his angels, into everlasting fire where they will pay the penalty of eternal destruction, expelled from the face of God and his glorious power.[d]

c. Matt. 8:12, 22:13 & 25:41-46.
d. Matt. 25:41, Jude v. 7, 2 Thess. 1:9.

5. And these things being thus finished, then the new world will appear,[a] in which justice dwells, and where Jesus Christ will restore the kingdom to his God and Father, that God from then on may be all in all.[b]

b. Rev. chs. 2 & 3, 1 Cor. 15:24ff.

• CHAPTER 21 •

CAPUT XXI.
De misterio verbi divini,
deque ordinibus Ministrorum.

1. Et hæc quidem est voluntas divina, acitu nobis necessaria, quippe sanctissimis hujusmodi *præceptis* & *promissis* tam excellentibus constans, quæ ut miseris mortalibus innotesceret & semper ante oculos versaretur, voluit miserator ille generis humani, eandem non tantuma per privatam S. Scripturæ lectionem iis tacite insinuari: sed etiam per apertem ac publicam prædicationem passim, promulgari, ac quotidie

CHAPTER 21
On the ministry of the Word of God,
and orders of ministers.

1. And this indeed is the divine will which is necessary for us to discharge, consisting of such most holy commandments and so excellent promises that they must be made known to miserable mortals and be always set before their eyes. He who has great mercy for the human race wanted that it not so much be only tacitly pressed to them by private reading of the Sacred Scripture,[a] but also that it should be everywhere proclaimed

palam iisdem velut inseri & inculcari.

through open and public preaching, and daily and openly as it were implanted and inculcated into them.

a. Matt. 28:19-20, Acts 10:41ff, Rom. 10:14-15, 2 Cor. 5:19-20, 2 Tim. 4:2ff.

2. Id autem ut recte fieret, necessaria imprimis fuit solemnis & immediata quorundam hominum, ad id muneris obeundum, tum electio vel segregatio,[a] tum *missio* atque *ablegatio*; & quidem conjuncta cum infallibili instructione, & irrefragabili quadam auctoritate, seu spirituali potestate. Quocirca designavit[b] sibi Dominus Jesus primitus extra ordinem legatos quosdam, eximios & singulares ministros: eosque omnibus ad legationem istam obeudam necessaris donis[c] ac sancti Spiritus virtutibus instruxit:[d] assidueque ita rexit, gubernavit, roboravit & confirmavit, ut non tantum divinam hanc voluntatem palam semel puliceque annunciarent, & solide omni signorum ac miraculorum genere stabilirent ac confirmarent: sed &[e] cœtus piorum sibi ubique colligerent, in quibus illius ipsius voluntatis prædicatio, quoad ejus fieri posset, perpetuo vigeret, & sarta tecta conservaretur, ad continuum scilicet omnium vocaturum in vera & salutari fide Jesu Christi ædificationem.

2. And that it might be done rightly, first was necessary a solemn and immediate election or separation, then the sending and dispatching of certain men, to attend to this service, and indeed conjoined with infallible instruction and a certain irresistible authority or spiritual power.[a] For this [reason], in the beginning the Lord Jesus designated certain extraordinary ambassadors as his eminent and special ministers[b] and furnished them with all the gifts and virtues of the Holy Spirit necessary for the discharge of their mission.[c] And thus he so continually ruled, governed, strengthened and confirmed them,[d] that they not only many times openly and publicly declared this divine will and solidly established and confirmed the same by all kinds of signs and miracles, but also everywhere gathered to themselves congregations of godly men,[e] among whom they preached his will, that as far as possible, it might perpetually flourish and be preserved whole and protected, namely, for the continual edification of all who were called to true and saving faith in Jesus Christ.

a. Acts 1:8 & 10:41ff, 1 Cor. 12:28ff, Eph. 4:11.
b. Mark 16:15ff, Acts 2:1ff, 2 Cor. 12:13, Heb. 2:3-4.

c. Acts 13:1ff, & 16:6-7.
d. Eph. 4:12, Acts 14:21ff, 15:36 & 19:8.

3. Ac hi quidem primi ac præcipui præcones, fuerunt[a] *Apostoli*: qui sicut in docendis & colligendis cœtibus, ita in iisdem regendis & conservandis, ejusmodi sunt usi auctoritate,[b] qualem à Domino Jesu immediate acceperant: quæ[c] videlicet irrefragabilis & ἀνυπεύθυνα erat, & cui absolute fideles omnes obsequi ac parere tenebantur. Et hisce quidem adjuncti fuerunt, tum[d] *Prophetæ* & *Evangelistæ*, tum *Doctores* & *Pastores*, aliique tales: qui operam & ipsi suam aut cœtibus & Ecclesiis novis colligendis, aut per Apostolos jam collectis deinceps sovendis & amplius erudiendis sedulo navarent, atque impenderent.

3. And indeed these first and principle heralds were the apostles,[a] who used the authority[b] which they had immediately received from the Lord Jesus as much for teaching and gathering churches as in governing and protecting them, which was obviously irrefutable and ἀνυπεύθυνα,[c] and to which all believers were absolutely bound to obey and bear. And to these indeed were joined first prophets and evangelists,[d] then teachers and pastors, and others like them, who did their best and devoted themselves either to the gathering of new churches or assemblies, or later to the nourishing, feeding and further instructing of these already gathered through the apostles.

a. Matt. 10:1ff, 28:19-20, 1 Cor. 12:28.
b. 1 Cor. 5:3ff, 2 Cor. 10:1-2 & 13:10, 2 Thess 3:6, 14.

c. 1 Thess. 2:13, 2 Thess 2:19, 2 Tim. 3:14.
d. Acts 15:32 & 21:8, 1 Cor. 22:28, Eph. 4:11-12.

4. Cæterum ubi per hos fundamenta jam ac primordia ejusmodi jacta essent, ne aut absentibus, aut mortuis illis, cœtus isti iterum diffluerent ac dilaberentur, atque ita doctrina hæc divina & salutaris paulatim evanesceret; designarunt illi passina sibi successores illis in locis, in quibus cœtus jam collecti erant: puta,[a] *Episcopos*, *Presbyteros* & *Diaconos*: quorum opera & studio cœtus ista assidue conservarentur, & quantum fieri potest, etiam numero multiplicarentur: utque idem semper & ubique deinceps in cœtibus omnibus fieret, expresse iidem monuerunt: addita[b] etiam accurata descriptione, quales eos esse oporteat, qui porro cætibus in hunc præficiendi essent.

a. Acts 14:23, 20:28, Heb. 13:7, 17, Phil 1:1, 1 Tim. 4:16, 5:17.

5. Ac Episcopos quidem & Presbyteros[a] ideo designarunt, ut utrique Evangelium prædicando, veritatem salutarem docendo, errores contrarios refutando; item hortando, consolando, reprehendendo, corrigendo, regendo, denique[b] exemplo suo aliis prælucendo &c. Ecclesias jam plantatas conservarent, & continua successione, pro virili sua propagarent. Diaconos vero,[c] ut cum probati prius essent, eleemosynis colligendis ac distribuendis & pauperibus in cœtibus istis pie curandis, diligenter occuparentur. Unde nata est totius ministerii Ecclesiatici perpetua necessitas, & multiplex utilitas.

a. Acts 20:28, 2 Tim. 2:24-25 & 4:2, 5, Titus 1:9ff, & 2:5, 17.

6. Quia vero post Apostolorum, priorumque Evangelij præconum, sive Ecclesiæ fundatorum, tempora (cum jam plene satis proposita, & abunde judicio Dei confirmata, & literis denique clare cosignata esset Evangelij doctrina) cessabat immediata ministrorum missio, simulque infallabilis instructio, & indubitata Sancti Spiritus assistencia: idcirco irrefragabilis etiam potestas, sive infallabilis auctoritas, in docendo, & regendo, locum amplius non habuit. Quod & testatum facere voluerunt ipsi Apostoli, cum

4. But when such foundations and first beginnings had now been laid by them, lest by their absence or death these congregations were again scattered and dispersed and so this divine and saving doctrine should disappear little by little, they everywhere in those places where congregations were already gathered, appointed them their successors: bishops, elders and deacons,[a] by whose labors and zeal those congregations might continually be preserved, and as much as possible, multiplied in number. And they were expressly commanded that what was always done in all places afterwards should be done in all congregations, giving an accurate description of what kind of persons they ought to be who were later to be put in charge among them.[b]

b. 1 Tim. 3:1ff, Titus 1:5ff.

5. And they therefore indeed designated bishops and elders,[a] that by preaching the gospel, teaching saving truth, refuting opposing errors and likewise exhorting, comforting, reproving, correcting, ruling and finally by their example shining before the others, etc., they would preserve those churches already planted, and in a continual succession,[b] propagate more of the same by their strength. And [they designated] deacons,[c] that after they had first been tested, they might diligently be occupied with gathering and distributing alms, and in godly concern and care of the poor in those congregations. From this was born the perpetual necessity and multiple usefulness of the whole ministry of the church.

b. 1 Tim. 4:12, Tit. 2:7, 1 Pet. 5:3.
c. Acts 6:1ff, 1 Tim. 3:9ff.

6. However, after the time of the apostles, those first heralds of the gospel and founders of the church, when the doctrine of the gospel had already been sufficiently proposed and in the judgment of God abundantly confirmed, and finally, clearly committed to writing, the immediate sending of ministers ceased and with it the infallible instruction and the unquestionable assistance of the Holy Spirit. Consequently, the irresistible power or infallible authority in teaching and ruling no longer has any place. The apostles themselves

Episcopis & Presbyteris,[a] certam ac perpetuam doctrinæ regulam dederunt, & disciplinæ formam relinquerunt: juxta quam in posterum Ecclesias hi docerent, ac regerent: iisque expresse mandarunt, ac serio præscripserunt, ut[b] ὑποτύπωσιν seu formam sanorum sermonum, quos ab ipsis audiverant, sedulo retinerent: utque[c] fideles doctrinæ illius, quam discerant, memores ac tenaces essent: ac proinde iis, qui diversam ab ea, quam ipsi tradiderant, doctrinam afferrent,[d] anathema dixerunt,[e] Ecclesisque simul injunxerunt, ut præter eam, quam ab Apostolis acceperant, doctrinam, aliam nullam admitterent, etaimsi vel Angelus eam de cælo adferret.

a. 2 Tim. 3:10, 14, Acts 15:24, 1 Cor. 14:37-38, Tit. 1:5.
b. 2 Tim. 1:13-14.

7. Cæterum cum Episcoporum & Presbyterorum[a] omnium munus atque officium sit, juxta propositam ab Apostolis formama Ecclesias docere, ac[b] regere, manifestum satis esse videtur, aliis in alios[c] imperium ac potestatem, proprie dictam, nullo jure divino competere. Nequi id circo tamen omnino improbamus, multo minus superbe rejicimus, gradus illos docentium, ac regentium, qui in variis Christi Ecclesis, ordinis & decori, sive εὐταξίας conservandæ caussa, jam olim institui sunt, & passim hactenus obtinent. (Neque enim confusionis[d] auctor est Deus, sed ordinis) si modo ii tandem non degenerent in tyrannidem, & dignitatis potestatisque cujusdam mundanæ potius, quam spiritualis ministerii, & Christi Discipulos docentis modestiæ, speciem se ferant.

a. 2 Tim. 1:13.
b. 1 Pet. 5:2-3.

8. Cæterum si quis hujus ordinis prætextu ad superbiam & fastum abutatur; & speciatim, si quis per istos gradus eo usque ascendere non dubitet, ut sibi non tantum supremum jus de Religione statuendi, & controversias omnes fidei decidendi, arroganter assumat,[a] sed & dominatum in clerum Domini, inque conservos

wanted to testify about this, when they gave to the bishops and elders a sure and perpetual rule of doctrine and left a form of discipline, according to which they were later to teach and rule the churches.[a] They expressly commanded and seriously charged them that they should carefully retain the ὑποτύπωσιν or pattern of sound words which they had heard from them,[b] and that they might hold and remember the faithful doctrine which they had learned.[c] And from this they called "anathema" those who brought a doctrine different than that which they themselves had given,[d] and at the same time, enjoined the churches that they should not admit any other doctrine except that which they had admitted from the apostles, even if it were brought by an angel from heaven.[e]

c. Tit. 1:9.
d. Gal. 1:8-9.
e. Rom. 16:17.

7. Since, however, it is the duty of all bishops and elders to teach and rule the churches[b] according to that form proposed by the apostles,[a] it appears sufficiently manifest that they are not permitted by any divine right to any command and authority[c] properly called over one another. And yet concerning this we do not utterly disallow, much less proudly reject, those degrees of teachers and rulers who were appointed long ago in various churches of Christ, and obtained it throughout, for preserving the cause of order and decorum, or εὐταξίας, or for preferring good order. For indeed God is not the author of confusion but order.[d] In the end, they were not to degenerate into tyranny and make a showing of some worldly dignity and power, rather than of a spiritual ministry, and the modesty and moderation of disciples of Christ.

c. Matt. 20:25ff, & 23:8.
d. 1 Cor. 14:33, 40, 1 Tim. 3:15.

8. But if anyone abuses this order as a pretext for pride and arrogance, and in particular, if any by these steps does not hesitate to ascend so high so as arrogantly to assume to himself not only the supreme right of determining matters of religion and deciding all controversies of faith, but also to seize lordship over the Lord's possession and his

suos, imo reges, principesque usurpet: quin imo potestatem, sive directe, sive indirecte, coactivam (hoc est, vi externa armatam, aut seculari brachio innixam) in alios animadvertendi, imo gladio & morte eos puniendi, qui istam ipsi auctoritatem deferre per conscientiam nequeunt (aut dogmatis, decretis, statutisque ipsius subscribere gravantur) licet alioquin & probi & fideles Reipub. subditi sint: si quis talem, inquam, potestatem in Ecclesia Christi, per hanc ὠτάριον, aut aliam quamcunque similem, usurpet; vel saltem verbis sibi tribuat, aut ab alijs tribui sinat, næ in nobis quam longissime à veri Episcopi officio recedere videtur.

fellow-servants,[a] indeed over kings, and princes; indeed further, whether directly or indirectly, oppressive power (that is, the power of external arms, or supported by the secular arm) for judging others, indeed punishing with sword and death those who cannot out of conscience defer to him this authority (or who hesitates to subscribe to his dogmas, decrees and statutes), although in all other respects they are good and loyal subjects of the republic. If any, we say, usurp such power in the church of Christ, through pretense or anything similar, or at least verbally attribute it to himself, or permit it to be attributed by others, truly he appears to us to withdraw very far from the office of a true bishop.

a. Matt. 24:49, Luke 12:42ff, 3John v. 9, 2 Thess 2:4ff, 2 Pet. 2:1ff, 2 Cor. 11:20, Rev. 11:7 & 13ff., Gal. 4:29.

• CHAPTER 22 •

CAPUT XXII.
De Ecclesia Iesu Christi, ejusque notis.

1. Porro cœtus illi, qui aut publica horum ministrorum opera, aut alioqui per verbum Evangelij, quocunque modo prædicatum, lectum, auditumve, in unum quasi corpus congragantur (cujus omnia & singula membra, & mutuam quandam inter se, & cum unico ac vero capite suo Dn. N. J. Christo, spiritualem communionem obtinent) sicut revera sunt; ita etim jure vocantur Ecclesia Jesu Christi.[a] De qua utraque Ecclesia, nimirum, & ejus communione, in Symbolo Apostolico dicimus: Credo Sanctam Ecclesiam Catholicam, communionem Sanctorum.

a. Matt. 16:18 & 18:17, Acts 20:28ff.

2. Ecclesia enim hæc aliud nihil est, quam cœtus hominum per Evangelium vocatorum,[a] & in Jesum Christum credentium, aut saltem

CHAPTER 22
On the church of Jesus Christ, and its marks.

1. Furthermore, those congregations which are gathered as it were into one body either by the public labor of these ministers or otherwise by the word of the gospel preached, read or heard in whatever way (whose members, each and every one, obtain a certain mutual communion with one another and a spiritual communion with their one and only true head, our Lord Jesus Christ), as they really are, so also are they rightly called the church of Jesus Christ.[a] We speak concerning both, namely, the church and its communion, in the Apostles Creed: "I believe in the holy Catholic church, the communion of saints."

2. For this church is nothing else but an assembly of men called by the gospel,[a] and believing on Jesus Christ, or at least professing

nomen & doctrinam ejus, tanquam salutarem, ore profitentium: licet alii magism alii minus, aut sincere ac pure, aut firmiter ac constanter, in Christum credant, aut soris saltem ore ac ritibus Christum pofiteantur.

a. Rom. 10:10, 14ff., Eph. 5:23ff.

3. Dupliciter namque Ecclesia Christi, dum in terra militat, juxta S. Scripturam considerari solet. I. ut cœtus^a vere piorum & credentium, qui doctrinam J. Christi salutarem, quam ore profitentur, ex animo etiam amplectuntur, & toto corde tenet, juxtaque eam mores suos componunt. Qui cœtus^b soli Deo visibilis, ac certo cognitus: nobis autem inaspectabilis est: quum veram fidem ac pietatem, intus in corde latentem, nemo præter Deum, unicum scilicet cordium ac renum scrutatorem, intueri possit.

a. Eph. 5:23, 25, Gal. 6:10, 16, 1 Pet. 1:22-23.

4. Doctrinam autem, Jesu Christi salutarem tenere, non continuo est,^a omne id quod doctrina Christi quoquo modo continetur, adeo perfecte cognitum habere, ut in nullo prorsus articulo, in nullave s. historia, aut sensu S. Scripturæ, erres aut hæsites: sed id saltem omne^b probe tenere, sine quo fidei & obedientiæ mandata rite observari, & proinde venia peccatorum ac salus æterna obtineri ex Dei ipsius sententia, nequeunt. Quocirca omnes illa Ecclesias, quæ in necessaria veritatis ac professione consentiunt, pro Ecclesis Jesu Christi veris habendas esse credimus: etiamsi in multis aliis interim dissentiant, & à veritate alicubi non leviter aberrent.

a. Rom. 14:1ff, 15:1ff, Phil 3:15-16.

5. Secundo consideratur Ecclesia, ut est multitudo aspectabilis, fidem ac doctrinam Jesu Christi publice^a profitentium, licet forte non vere in ipsum credentium: quæ quoad externam oris confessionem, & alia id genus aperta fidei indicia, nobis etiam sat nota, & per se visibilis est: licet alias magis,^b alias minus evidenter, aut splendide nobis appareat.

a. Acts 2:41ff, 5:11, 8:1ff, & 14:32.

with their mouth his saving name and doctrine, although some more [and] others less, whether sincerely and purely, or firmly and constantly, believe on Christ or at least outwardly in words and rites profess Christ.

3. For the church, while it battles on earth, is customarily considered in a two-fold manner according to the Scriptures. First, as an assembly of the truly godly and believing,[a] who they embrace with the mind and hold it with their whole heart the saving doctrine of Jesus Christ, which they confess with their mouth and build their lives according to it. This assembly is visible and certainly known only to God,[b] but invisible to us, since true faith and piety, which lie hidden within the heart, none but God can behold, the only searcher of the hearts and inward parts.

b. Rom. 2:28-29, 8:17 & 10:9, 1 Cor. 4:5, Rev. 2:23.

4. But to hold the saving doctrine of Jesus Christ is not necessarily all that which is contained in the doctrine of Christ in whatever manner,[a] so as to have such perfect knowledge as to never err or hesitate in absolutely any article of faith, sacred history or meaning of Holy Scripture, but to hold properly all that without which the commandments of faith and obedience cannot be rightly kept,[b] so the forgiveness of sins and eternal salvation cannot be obtained from God. Therefore we believe that all those churches which consent to the belief and profession of necessary truth ought to be held as churches of Jesus Christ, even if, in the interim, they dissent in many other things and not lightly deviate from the truth.

b. 1 Cor. 7:19, Gal. 1:6 & 6:15.

5. Secondly, the church is considered as a visible multitude publicly professing the faith and doctrine of Jesus Christ,[a] even if they do not truly believe in him, as long as the outward oral confession and other indications of that kind of faith is of itself sufficiently known, and so is visible to us even if sometimes it appears less evident or splendid.[b]

b. Rom. 10:9-10 & 11:-34, 1 Cor. 4:4ff.

6. Utraque rursus vel ut Catholica[a] sive universalis, spectari potest, quæ per universum terrarum orbem diffusa, omnes simul, aut vere credentium, aut fidem saltem profitentium, cœtus complectitur: vel ut topica, seu particularis,[b] quæ certis in locis secundum partes seorsim colligitur; verbi gratia, Corinthiaca, Galatica, Ephesina &c. Quarum ista, quæcunque tandem sit, non tantum in doctrina errare, sed etiam à vera fide, ejusque professione, deficere potest: imo sæpe etiam (manente interim salvâ atque integra Ecclesia Catholica) à vera fide[c] reipsa deficit. Neque enim promissum ullum divinum extat, quo certæ alicui particulari Ecclesiæ, vel cœtui incorrupta doctrinæ veræ professio, inque ea perpetua successio, aut continuæ Spiritus S. assistentiæ, fideique orthodoxæ numquam interrupta & uniformis duratio (eaque semper conspicua futura) promittatur: imo vero & exempla &[d] præsagia defectionis multorum passim in S. literis obvia sunt.

a. 1 Cor. 1:2, Rom. chs. 10-13, 1 Cor. 12:12ff, Eph. 1:22-23 & 5:23-24.
b. 1 Cor. 1:2, Gal. 1:2, Rom. 1:7 & 16:1, 4-5.

6. Again, both may be considered either as catholic or universal,[a] which being diffused throughout the whole world, contains all congregations together which either truly believe or at least profess faith, or as local or individual church which is gathered in a certain location in smaller groups,[b] for instance, at Corinth, in Galatia, at Ephesus, etc. Whether universal or local, both may not only err in doctrine, but also fall away from the true faith and its profession. Indeed it often really does fall away from the same (the catholic church in the meantime remaining safe and whole).[c] Nor indeed does any divine promise exist by which a certain particular church or congregation is promised the uncorrupted profession of true doctrine and a continual succession in it, or continual assistance of the Holy Spirit and an uninterrupted and uniform duration of orthodox faith (and that to be always clearly seen). Indeed both examples and prophecies of the falling away of many are obvious everywhere throughout the Holy Scriptures.[d]

c. Rev. chs. 2 & 3.
d. 1 Thess. 2:3, 4:1ff, 2 Tim. 3:1, 2 Pet. 2:1ff, Acts 10:29-30.

De notis Ecclesia visibilis.

7. Notæ porro, quæ Ecclesiam, aut Christianum cœtum, qui jam per prædicationem verbi collectus est, clare nobis indicant, & visibilem (certæ quidem & minime fallaces) ad unicam generalem reduci possunt, nempe, ad professionem[a] sacræ ac salutaris doctrinæ, per Jesum Christum traditæ, eamque conjuctam cum externa saltem[b] mandatorum J. Christi observatione. Quum enim vera fides, quæ doctrinæ Jesu Christi salutari adhibetur, tanquam interior forma, & quasi anima, Ecclesiam Jesu Christi veram atque invisibilem constituat: necessum utique est, ut sola ilius veræ & salutaris fidei professio, qualem diximus, visibilem nobis eandem faciat.

a. Matt. 10:32-33, John 10:4, 5:27, 12:42-43, 13:34-35, 14:21ff.

8. Alias autem notas, per quas ii, qui plane adhuc nesciunt, quid sit vera Christi Ecclesia, vel

On the marks of a visible church.

7. Again, the marks which are certain and least fallible, which clearly indicate to us and make visible a church or Christian assembly which is already gathered by the preaching of the Word, may be reduced to one in general, that is, the profession of that sacred and saving doctrine delivered by Jesus Christ,[a] in conjunction with at least the external observing of the commandments of Jesus Christ.[b] For while true faith which partakes of the saving doctrine of Jesus Christ constitutes the more inward form and almost the soul of the true and invisible church of Jesus Christ, it is certainly true that the profession of that true and saving faith alone, of which we have spoken, makes the same visible to us.

b. Acts 2:41-42 & 4:32ff, Rom. 10:9, 1 Tim. 3:15.

8. But it is altogether vain and foolish to painstakingly seek or show to others the other marks

quæ salutaris illius doctrina, in Ecclesia veræ, ac consequenter in veritatis ipsius, cognitionem certo atque indubie perveniant, operose aut quærere, aut aliis indicare velle, vanum ac prorsus ineptum est; quia sic progredi, nec[a] necesse, nec utile, imo nec, ut rite fiat, possibile est. Tantum abest, ut ejusmodi notæ iis in rebus sitæ sint, quas mundus & ratio carnalis, magni æstimare solent: puta, in Antiquitate, Multitudine, Consentione, personarum Successione, externo cœtum Splendore, aut mundana Felicitate &c. de quibus jamdudum inaniter multi gloriantur.

a. See the places above, already quoted.

through which they who are plainly ignorant of what may be the true church of Christ, or of that doctrine of salvation in the true church may certainly and undoubtedly arrive at the truth itself. For to proceed so is neither necessary or useful, nor possible that it could be rightly done.[a] But far be it that the marks of a true church would be localized in such things which the world and carnal reason is accustomed to value so greatly, namely, antiquity, majority, consent, succession of persons, external splendor of congregations, or worldly happiness, etc., in which many recently boast in vain.

9. Officium porro eorum, qui ad Ecclesiam hanc visibilem pertinent, non tantum in eo positum est, ut pro se quisque doctrinam Jesu Christi salutarem[a] ore ac vita profiteatur: sed ut juncti[b] etiam inter se fideles, plures, paucioresve, ea faciant, quæ ordinarie non nisi in cœtu peragi possunt, ac solent, quæque cœtum ipsum magis illustrem ac conspicuum reddunt.

a. Mark 8:38, Rom. 10:9.

9. Furthermore, the duty of those who belong to this visible church does not just consist in every individual professing with their mouth and life in this saving doctrine of Christ for themselves,[a] but also in believers being united and joined together among themselves,[b] whether they be many or few, in their doing those things which ordinarily cannot be completed except by a group, which renders such groups more illustrious and visible.

b. 1 Cor. 11:20ff. & 14:4, Acts 2:41-42, Matt. 18:16, 1 Cor. 16:1ff.

10. Qualia officia, præter verbi prædicati auditionem, ac fidei professionem jam dictam, duo præcipua sunt:[a] usurpatio Sacramentorum, quæ vocatur, &[b] disciplinæ Christianæ exercitium, de quibus statim amplius.

a. Acts 2:41ff, 8:12ff, & 20:7.

10. The other duties, aside from the hearing of the Word preached and the profession of faith already mentioned, are primarily two: the use of the sacraments, as they are called,[a] and the exercise of Christian discipline,[b] about which more immediately [follows].

b. Matt. 18:17, 1 Cor. 5:4, 1 Tim. 5:1-2, 20.

• CHAPTER 23 •

CAPUT XXIII.
De Sacramenti, alijsque sacris ritibus.

1. *Sacramenta* cum dicimus, externas

CHAPTER 23
On the sacraments and other sacred rites.

1. When we speak of the sacraments, we

Ecclesiæ ceremonias, seu ritus illos sacros ac solemnes intelligimus, quibus veluti fœderalibus[a] signis ac sigillis visibilibus, Deus gratiosa beneficia sua, in fœdere præsertim Evangelico promissa, non modo nobis repræsentat & adumbrat, sed & certo modo exhibet atque obsignat: nosque vicissim palam publiceque declaramus ac testamur, nos[b] promissiones omnes vera, firma, atque obsequia fide amplecti, & beneficia ipsius & grata semper memoria celebrare velle.

a. Rom. 4:11ff, 1 Cor. 10:1-3, 16ff., 1 Cor. 12:13.

2. Hujusmodi autem ritus, si proprie & accurate sit loquendum, in N. T. duo tantum sunt: *Baptismus* scilicet & *Sacra Cœna*. Ex quibus ille[a] signo Circumcisionis, quod sub Veteri T. sacræ initiationis, sive institutionis cujusdam in populum Dei,[b] signum erat; hæc vero[c] *agni Paschalis* esui, qui ritus erat solemnis Eucharistiæ, seu publicæ gratiarum actionis, ad Deum, pro typica populi Isrâelitici redemptione, hoc est, liberatione ex Ægypto, palam laudandum ac celebrandum, non malec per analogiam quandam respondent.

a. Gen. 17:10ff, 1 Som. 17:36.
b. Ex. 12:26ff, Lev. 23:5ff.

De Baptismo.

3. *Baptismus* est primus N. Testamenti publicus & sacer ritus: in quo fœderati omnes (nullo aut æteris, aut sexus discrimine) per solemnem aquæ ablutionem Ecclesiæ inseruntur, & cultui divino initiantur: sive idcirco *in nomen Patris, & Filij & Spiritus S.* aquæ immerguntur,[a] vel aqua abluuntur, ut hoc veluti symbolico signo, ac sacra tessera, confirmentur de gratiosa Dei erga ipsos voluntate, quod sicut aqua sordes corporis abluuntur, ita ipsi per sanguinem & Spiritum Christi (modo sua ipsorum culpa gratiosum hoc fœdus irritum non fecerint) intus purgandi, sive à reatu omnium peccatorum plenissime liberandi, & tandem gloriosa filiorum Dei immortalitate, atque æterna fælicitate donandi sint: ac simul etiam ex altera parte ipsi obligentur,[b] eoque palam declarent, se omnem salutem suam à solo Deo

understand the outward ceremonies of the church, or those sacred and solemn rites, by which as by covenantal signs and visible seals[a] God not only represents and sketches out his gracious benefits to us, especially those promised in the covenant of the gospel, but also in a certain way exhibits and seals them to us. And in response we openly and publicly declare and testify that we embrace all the promises of God with a true, firm and obedient faith,[b] and that we will always celebrate his grace and benefits.

b. Rom. 6:-34 & 2:25-26, 1 Cor. 10:16ff., & 11:25ff.

2. If we speak properly and accurately, there are only two rites of this manner in the New Testament: baptism and the sacred supper. Of them, the first corresponds as a good analogy to the seal of circumcision,[a] which was a seal under the Old Testament of sacred initiation or a certain ingressing into the people of God.[b] The other corresponds to the eating of the Passover lamb,[c] which was a rite of solemn blessing or public thanksgiving to God, as a symbol for the redemption of the Israelite people, openly praising and celebrating their liberation from Egypt.

c. 1 Cor. 10.

Baptism

3. Baptism is the first public and sacred rite of the New Testament, by which all who belonged to the covenant were engrafted into the church by the solemn washing with water without distinction of age or gender, and initiated into the worship of God. For this, they were immerged or washed in water in the name of the Father and the Son and the Holy Spirit, that by a symbolic sign and sacred token, they were confirmed concerning the gracious will of God toward them, that just as the filth of their bodies is washed away by water, so they themselves were purged within by the blood and Spirit of Christ (if they do not make this gracious covenant void through their own fault), and most fully delivered from the guilt of all their sins, and finally were granted the glorious immortality and eternal happiness of the sons of God. And at the same time, they for their part were obligated openly to declare

& Domino Jesu Christo, unico Mediatore, Sacerdote ac Regno suo constanter exspectare, ipsi ex animo considere, eique abjectis peccatorum omnium sordibus atque inquinamentis, virtute Spiritus S. per omnem vitam obedire velle.

a. Matt. 3:21 & 28:19, Mark 16:16, John 3:15, John 4:1, Acts 2:41ff., 8:12, 36-38, & 10:47ff.

De S. Cœna Domini.

4. *S. Cœna* est alter N. Testamenti sacer ritus, à Jesu Christo ea, qua proditus fuit, nocte institutus, ad celebrandum eucharisticam & solemnem mortis suæ[a] commemorationem, in quo fideles, postquam seipsos explorarunt, inque vera fide approbarunt, sacrum panem, in cœtu publice fractum, edunt; & simul vinum, publice fusum, bibunt: idque ad cruentam Domini mortem, pro nobis obitam (qua sicut corpora nostra cibo & potu, seu pane & vino sustentantur, ita corda nostra in spem vitæ æternæ aluntur ac nutriuntur) cum solemni gratiarum actione annunciandum: suamque vicissum cum crufixo Christi corpore, & effuso sanguine (sive cum ipso Jesu Christo, pro nobis crucifixo & mortuo) eoque beneficijs omnibus, per mortem Jesu Christi partis atque acquisitis, vivificam & spiritualem communionem, & mutuam simul inter se charitatem, coram Deo & Ecclesia publice testificandum.

a. Matt. 26:26-28, Mark 14:22-24, Luke 22:19-20, 1 Cor. 10:16-17, & 11:23-25.

5. Porro ex iis, quæ de universo hoc S. ritu, deque rebus per ipsum significatis, in Scriptura[a] passim leguntur, quæque ipsi fidei articuli (de vero Christi humano corpore, veraque in[b] cœlos ascensione & exaltatione &c.) nobis suggerunt, & denique ipsa recta ratio dictat; facile apparet, nullam hic fieri. 1. Substantialem signorum in res signatas[c] transmutationem, puta, panis & vini in corpus & sanguinem Domini: 2. Nec localem aliquam utrorumque conjunctionem, seu corporalem inclusionem, aut physicam aliquam alligationem. 3. Tantum abest, ut hoc pretextu altera signorum pars (puta, calicis, seu poculi sacri usus) fidelibus eripienda sit: Utque

that they constantly look to God alone and the Lord Jesus Christ, their only mediator, priest and king, for all their salvation, and to reflect on him from the soul, and casting off all the filthiness and iniquities of sins to desire to obey through the power of the Holy Spirit for their whole life.

b. Rom. 6:3-4, 1 Cor. 12:13 & ch 13, Gal. 3:27, 1 Pet. 3:21.

The Lord's Supper

4. The Holy Supper is the other sacred rite of the New Testament, instituted by Jesus Christ the night in which he was betrayed, for a eucharistic celebration and solemn commemoration of his death by which believers,[a] after they have examined themselves and truly proved themselves to be in true faith, eat the sacred bread publicly broken in the congregation, and at the same time drink the wine publicly poured, and that to declare with solemn thanksgiving the Lord's bloody death, a death for us, undergone for us (just as our bodies are sustained by food and drink, or bread and wine, so our hearts are fed and nourished in the hope of eternal life). In return, they testify publicly before God and the church of their enlivening and spiritual communion with the body of Christ crucified, and his shed blood (or with Jesus Christ himself, who was crucified and died for us) and all the benefits acquired through his death and at the same time their mutual charity for one another.

5. Certainly the following can be easily seen from those things which are read throughout Scripture concerning this whole sacred rite and the things signified by them,[a] and which the articles of faith (concerning the truly human body of Christ and his true ascension into heaven and exaltation,[b] etc.) themselves suggest to us, and finally what right reason itself dictates. 1. There is no change of substance made of the signs into the things signified,[c] namely, of the bread and wine into the body and blood of the Lord. 2. Neither is there any local conjunction or bodily inclusion, or some physical bond. 3. Far be it that under this pretext one of the signs (namely, the use of the chalice or

4. verum & vivificum illud, sive expiatorium, Jesu Christi sacrificium[d] jam olim pro peccatis nostris, ab ipso Christo, unico Pontifice nostro, semel oblatum, reipsa hic repetim, ac quotidie de novo peragi credendum sit: ut denique 5. Symbola ipsa, quasi corporis & sanguinis J. Christi latibula, religiose nobis adoranda sint: hocque ipso finem, aut publice in templis proponenda, aut ciboriis includenda, aut in processionibus circumgestanda &c.

a. Luke 22:19-20, 1 Cor. 11:24.
b. Acts 1:9-11 & 3:21, Heb. 8:4.

sacred cup) be taken away from believers, and 4. that the true and life-giving or expiatory sacrifice of Jesus Christ, now long since offered once for our sins by Christ himself,[d] our only high priest, is to be believed to be really repeated or daily performed again, and finally, 5. that the symbols themselves are to be adored and worshipped by us, and for this same purpose, either publicly displayed in temples, or enclosed in coffers, or carried about in processions, etc.

c. Matt. 26:27, 1 Cor. 10:16 & 11:24ff.
d. Heb. 7:27-28, 9:25-28, & 10:10-14, 18.

De alijs S. ritibus, sed adiaphoris.

6. Præter sunt & alii S. ritus, generatim sic dicti: qui tametsi ex diserto aliquo Christi præcepto in perpetuum, ac necessario, à fidelibus servandi non sint; tamen boni ordinis, aut externæ disciplinæ caussa, jam olim fere ab Apostolis, eorumque discipulis observati sunt: & citra impietatem saltem, ac superstitionem, observari etiam nunc libere possunt, & quidem satis utiliter: verbi gratia, *Impositio manuum*,[a] eaque multiplex, puta tum in *ordinatione ministrorum*; tum in[b] *examinatione* ac *confirmatione neophytorum*, seu *Catechumenorum*; denique in[c] *publica receptione*, seu *reconciliatione pœnitentium, graviter ante lapsorum*: item *solemnis conjugum copulatio*, seu *benedictio conjugij in cœtu Ecclesia* &c. modo hinc absit vana superstitio, sive opinio divini cultus, item præcise necessitatis &c. contraque ordinis tantum & decori, publicæque ædificationis ratio habeatur: & denique vera in talibus libertas,[d] & Christiana charitas (eoque vera etiam inter dissentientes ἐπιείκεια & tolerantia mutua) semper illibata conservetur: neque pax Ecclesia, propter externos ejusmodi, & per se adiaphoros ritus, temere turbetur.

a. Acts 6:6 & 13:3, 1 Tim. 1:14, 2 Tim. 1:6.
b. Acts 8:17ff, & 195-6, Heb. 6:2.

Other sacred but unnecessary rites

6. Besides these there are also other sacred rites, generally so called, which even if they are not necessarily and perpetually kept by believers from some expressed commandment of Christ, yet for the cause of good order or external discipline, have now long since been generally observed by the apostles and their disciples, and may be even observed freely now without the least ungodliness and superstition, and indeed profitably. For example, laying on of hands for various reasons, such as in ordaining ministers,[a] in examining and confirming new converts or learners[b], in the public reception or reconciliation of penitents[c] who had fallen grievously before, likewise in the solemn joining of marriage and the blessing of the couple in the congregation of the church, etc. Such a case is far removed from either vain superstition, or an absolutely necessary opinion regarding divine worship, etc. On the contrary, they are justifiable for order, decency and public edification, and finally that true liberty[d] and Christian charity may always be preserved in such things (and also a true ἐπιείκεια and mutual toleration between those who disagree), and the peace of the church not be rashly disturbed for the sake of such outward and unnecessary rites.

c. 1 Tim. 5:22.
d. Rom. 14, *per totam*.

7. Huc etiam referri possunt *Ecclesiaticæ* seu *liturgicæ* observationes illæ (per se quidem adiaphoræ, sed quibus tamen externi ac publici

7. At this point we may make reference to those ecclesiastical or liturgical observations which are not required in themselves, but without

fidelium cœtus ægre carere possunt) circa publicum in Ecclesiis, legendi, orandi,[a] psallendi, prophetandi, eleemosynas colligendi, item genua[b] inter orandum flectendi &c. ordinem ac modum: item circa publica[c] jejunia, & solemnes supplicationum seu precationum dies, aliaque id genus externa, ac per se mere ritualia, attamen nevertheless pia exercitia; non quidem in specie divinitus præscripta (nedum gratiæ divinæ, aut vitæ æternæ meritoria) sed tamen ad externam Ecclesiæ εὐταξίαν[d] seu decoram πολιτείαν utiliter spectantia: imo etiam piam devotionem in animis nostris aliquatenus aut excitantia, aut foventia, eoque non facile per se contemnenda, nec, ubi publice recepta sunt, temere ac cum scandalo piorum abroganda.

a. 1 Cor. 11:2ff. And ch. 14 *per totam*, 16:1.
b. Acts 20:36 & 21:5, Eph. 3:4, Matt. 27:39, Mark 14:34-35, Luke 22:41.

8. In his enim omnibus (ut in tota S. liturgia, totoque externo Ecclesiæ redimine) id unice curandum, ut *decenter*[a] *omnia*, & *ordine*, in *domo Domini fiant*, utque[b] *ædificationi* omnium, maxime[c] infirmorum[c] (sed tamen veræ pietatis studiosorum) semper inserviant: non[d] autem laqueum cuiquam injiciant, aut[e] libertatem Christianam lædant, aut denique scandalum ullum infirmis præbeant.[f] Ad quem finem melius & facilius adsequendum, accurata externi, jamque recepti, ordinis,[g] honestatis, ac decori, item diversorum locorum, temporum, aliarumque circumstantiarum ratio ubique habenda est: & speciatim *Christiani Magistratus* auctoritas, ubicunque haberi potest, ob publicam Ecclesiæ tranquilitatem, in talibus semper attendenda.

a. 1 Cor. 14:33, 40.
b. 1 Cor. 14:26.
c. Rom. 14:13, 15, 19, 21 & 15:12.
d. 1 Cor. 6:12 & 10:23-24, 29.

which the external and public congregations of believers can hardly be without, such as public order and methods of churches, reading, praying; singing, prophesying, gathering alms, and kneeling in prayer, etc. Likewise [there are] public fasts and solemn days of supplication or prayers, and other external things of that kind, in themselves mere ritual, but still godly exercises, not indeed divinely prescribed in kind (much less deserving the grace of God or eternal life) but yet profitably serving for the outward discipline of the church, or of decent conduct, indeed also for a certain stirring or warming pious devotion in our minds, and therefore not lightly to be condemned for themselves, nor, where they are publicly received, rashly abrogated to the scandal of the godly.

c. Acts 12:12, 13:2 & 14:23.
d. 1 Cor. 14:33, 40 & 11:16.

8. For in all these things, as in all of sacred worship and the whole external governing of the church, this only is to be sought, that all things in the house of the Lord be done decently and in order, and always serves for the edification of all, especially the weak which are none the less zealous for godliness, but not cast a snare upon any one, or infringe Christian liberty, or finally offer any scandal to the weak. For the better and easier achieving of this end, there must be an exact regard for externals, and acceptance, order, honor and decorum, likewise of diverse places, times, and other circumstances. In particular, the authority of the Christian magistrate, wherever it exists, must always be obeyed in such things for the public tranquility of the church.

e. Gal. 5:1ff., Col. 2:8, 16, 18, 20.
f. Rom. 4:13, 1 Cor. 8:13.
g. Rom. 12:17, Phil. 4:8.

• Chapter 24 •

CAPUT XXIV.
De disciplina Ecclesiastica

1. Quia vero cœtus nullus, quntumvis recte institutus & bonis legibus informatus, diu subsistere potest, nisi certa ratione ac *disciplina* gubernetur, per quam etiam continuo in officio contineantur ii, qui ad illum pertinent: hinc est, quod in Ecclesia Dei visibili (quæ domus,[a] familia,[b] civitas[c] & regnum Dei[d] est) hujusmodi disciplinam, qualis à Domino[e] & Rege nostro præscripta est, vigere atque exerceri, tum utilissimum, tum æquissimum esse statuamus.

a. 1 Tim. 2:15., Eph. 2:19-21.
b. Luke 12:40ff.
c. Heb. 12:22, Rev. 21:2-3.

2. Ea autem consistit in fraterna & mutua *admiratione*, *reprehensione* & *correctione* eorum,[a] qui peccatum aliquod nobis notum, maxime vero in aliquod enorme crimen prolapsi sunt: ut scilicet mature resipiscant, & ad bonam frugem reddenat: aut si aliquoties moniti, pertinaciter tamen pergant resipiscere nolint, in ipsorum *vitatione* ac *secessione*[b] à fraterno eorundem commercio: quippe qui jam indignos seipsos reddiderunt amabili fratrum nomine, sive eorum, qui sanctissimum Christi nomen invocant, & pietatis ac sanctissimæ alumnos se profitentur: idque totum hoc fine, in Religio Christi & Ecclesia ipsius per ipsorum consortium male audiat, & detrimentum aliquod patiatur: sed omnium potius Ecclesiæ membrorum salus sedulo procuretur.

a. Matt. 18:15ff., 1 Cor. 5 *per totam*.

3. Versatur autem hæc disciplina, tum circa *Pastores* ac *præfectos* Ecclesiarum, tum circa ipsas *oves* vel *auditores*. Circa Pastores[a] &

CHAPTER 24
On church discipline.

1. Because no society, however well established and shaped by good laws, can long subsist unless it is governed by a certain reason and discipline, through which those who belong to it may be continually kept to their duty, hence it is that in the visible church of God (which is the household, family, city and kingdom of God), we think it first most profitable and then most just that such a discipline as was prescribed by our Lord and King should flourish and be exercised.

d. Luke 1:32-33.
e. Matt. 28:20.

2. For this consists in fraternal and mutual regard, in reproof and correction of those[a] who have fallen into any sin known to us, and especially into any enormous crime, that they may repent quickly and return to being honest men. Or, if having been admonished several times they still obstinately go on and refuse to repent, [it consists] in avoiding them and withdrawing ourselves from fraternal relations[b] with them as those who have now rendered themselves unworthy of the pleasant name of "brothers," or of those who invoke the most holy name of Christ and profess themselves as most holy learners of godliness. And all this is to this end, that the religion of Christ and his church may not be maligned and receive some detriment by their partnership, but rather that the health of all the members of the church may be carefully sought.

b. 1 Thess. 5:14, 2 Thess. 3:6, 14, 15, 1 Tim. 5:19-20.

3. And this discipline includes both pastors and leaders of churches as well as the sheep themselves or hearers. Concerning pastors[a] and leaders, they

must profitably conduct their office in the church, whether in ministering, teaching and ruling the church, or themselves, or their families, without generating scandal. For example, in teaching,[b] they must not demand those things which are forbidden by the laws of Jesus Christ, or forbid what they command, or allow what is prohibited, or require things which are free and indifferent, or strive too sharply obstinately for things unnecessary or of no great use and disturb the church with factions and to tear it in pieces. In their teaching, they must maintain that method which is fitting for serious teachers of godliness, and which does not foment contentions, quarrels and strifes rather than promoting spiritual edification, and more for the cooling of pious zeal than inflaming. In governing themselves,[c] they must be blameless, husbands of one wife, vigilant, temperate, grave, well-ordered, hospitable, moderate, just and impartial, and free from drunkenness, anger, the love of money, fighting, hypocrisy and avarice. In governing their own family,[d] they must keep their children in subjection, with all honesty. And finally, in ministering,[e] they must faithfully, cheerfully and prudently manage those things that are committed to them.

c. 1 Tim. 3:2ff., 5:17ff., Tit. 1:6.
d. 1 Tim. 3:4-5, Tit. 1:6.
e. Acts 6:3ff., Rom. 12:7-8, 1 Tim. 3:8, 12.

4. Concerning the sheep[a] or hearers, they must not carelessly neglect or knowingly and willfully disregard those things which are divine commands, or commit acts which are not agreeable to the commands of Jesus Christ. In matters otherwise indifferent,[b] they must not disturb the public order and peace of the church and consequently do things which are prejudicial both to their own salvation and the edification of their neighbor.

b. 1 Cor. 11:1ff., ch. 14 *per totam*, Rom ch. 14 *per totam*.

5. Otherwise, this discipline must be exercised with all charity,[a] prudence and discretion, according to diverse qualities and various reasons, whether of persons and sins, to the greatest profit

ipsorum peccantium, tum aliorum omnium utilitatem, idque per gradus certos in verbo Dei indicatos. Et primo quidem *personarum* justa ratio habenda. Seniores[b] enim increpandi non sunt, sed tanquam patres momendi: Juniores, tanquam fratres: Seniores mulieres, tanquam matres &c. Imprimis vero ratio habenda est earum personarum, quæ in auctoritate & munere publico constituæ sunt. Contra[c] Presbyteros enim non facile admittendæ sunt accusatiores: at ubi peccaverint (id est, manifeste peccasse comperti fuerint) coram omnibus arguendi sunt, ut reliqui timeant. Similis vero ratio est[d] Magistratuum, & eorum omnium, qui in sublimitate aliqua positi sunt.

a. Gal. 6:1ff, Matt. 18:15ff.
b. 1 Tim. 5:1ff.

6. *Peccatorum* vero diversorum accurata etiam ratio vel imprimis habenda est. Si enim peccatum sit[a] *clandestinum*, seu publice nondum notum, sola admonitione privata opus est: eaque aliquoties iterata, etiam adhibitis consciis, aut testibus, si opus sit. Si vero[b] *publicum* crimen sit: id est, peccatum non grave tantum, sed & cum publico scandalo Ecclesiæ ipsius perpetratum: aut[c] si alioquin admonitiones privatæ omnes contumaciter rejicia; coram omnibus, vel in cœtu Presbyterorum,[d] admonitio instituenda est, ut auctorum pudeat, utaque alii ejus exemplo à peccando deterreantur. Quod si etiam accedat ad peccati enormem gravitatem, notoria peccantis *pertinacia*, & admonitionum omnium contemptus, ita ut nulla sequatur vitæ emendatio:[e] tum vitandum est familiare, seu fraternum peccatoris consortium: (si forte hac ratione pudor ei incuti, & ipse ad salutarem pœnitentiam adduci possit) addita, si necessitas extrema postulaverit, expressa & seria Ecclesiæ declaratione, eum, quamdiu impœnitens manserint, alienum à regno cœlorum esse: quippe qui in manifesto crimine, seu carnis opere, sciens prudens perseveret. At vitatis tamen ipsis, sive à communione fraterna exclusis, post probabiliter testatam pœnitentiam, Ecclesiæ pax, seu dicta communio, serio[f] præsertim eam petentibus, prompte semper restituenda est.

both of the sinners themselves, or of all others, and that, by certain steps indicated in the Word of God. And first indeed there must be had a just regard of persons. Older men[b] are not to be rebuked, but entreated as fathers, younger men as brothers, older women as mothers, etc. But one must have a special regard for those people who are constituted in authority, and public office. Accusations are not to be easily admitted charges against elders,[c] but if they have sinned (that is, they are plainly discovered to have sinned) they are to be rebuked before all, that the rest may fear. One must also have similar regard for magistrates,[d] and all who are set in high places.

c. 2 Tim. 5:19-20.
d. Rom. 13:7, 1 Pet. 1:17.

6. In truth, an accurate understanding of the diversity of sins is of principle importance. For if the sin is secret[a] or yet not publicly known, only a private admonition is needed, and that sometimes repeated, summoning accomplices or witnesses if useful. But if the crime is truly public,[b] that is, not just a grave sin, but also perpetrated to the public scandal of the church itself, or if otherwise all private admonitions be obstinately rejected,[c] then an admonition is to be made before all, or in the assembly of presbyters,[d] that the perpetrator may be ashamed and that by his example others may be deterred from sinning. But if he adds notorious obstinacy of sinning and contempt of all admonitions to the enormous weight of sin, so that no amendment of life follows,[e] then all familiar or brotherly consorting with the offender is to be avoided (if perhaps for this reason shame may be instilled in him and he himself may be brought back to saving repentance), adding, if extreme necessity require it, an expressed and serious declaration of the church that as long as they remain impenitent they are not worthy for the kingdom of heaven, as one that knowingly and foreseeingly perseveres in a manifest crime or work of the flesh. But the peace and communion with the church must always be promptly restored to those who have been shunned or excluded from brotherly communion, after probable testimony of repen-

prompte semper restituenda est.

a. Matt. 18:15ff.
b. 1 Thess. 5:14, 2 Thess. 3:6, 15.
c. Matt. 18:16.

7. At veritatione tamen ista, quam diximus, quoad domesticam vitæ consuetudinem, eximendi sunt illi, qui vel contractu divino, & indissolubili, ut^a conjuges, vel naturæ^b lege, ut liberi, vel officij necessitate, ut^c servi & ancillæ, vel sibi ipsis invicem, vel alteri saltem alteris, obligati sunt & obstricti.

a. Matt. 19:5, 1 Cor. 7:10ff., Eph. 5:22ff.
b. Eph. 6:1-2.

8. Disciplina porro hæc non est ejusmodi actio, quæ cum^a carnali potestate, seu mundana auctoritate, aut vi ulla coactiva, ab Ecclesia exercetur: sed tantummodo^b voluntaria ipsius Ecclesiæ secessio, aut segregatio ab eo, cum quo, tanquam cum discipulo J. Christi, amplius vivere ipsis non licet. Ita ut non tam proprie Antistites Ecclesiæ illum à se, quam seipsos, una cum suis, ab illo (idque jussu ipsius Christi, Domini sui) sejungant, ac separent: neque cum eo aliter, quam cum^c ethico & publicano, sive cum quolibet peccatore publico, & profano, conversari possint ac velint: quandiu quidem ipse impœnitens manserit.

a. 2 Cor. 10:3-5, 1 Cor. 5:10-11.
b. Rom. chs. 16-18, 2 Thess. 3:6, 14, Tit. 3:10-11, 3 John

9. Quare, qui disciplinam hanc non tantum cum potestare carnali, & vi coactiva exercent: sed etiam ad corporales punitiones, & supplicia capitalia extendunt (præsertim sub prætextu hæreseos, vulgo sic dictæ) potestatem miniam, imo prorsus alienam,^{a} & illegitiman, sibi arrogant, quinimo conscientiarum, ac prophetiæ libertatem^b reipsa opprimunt: & salutare hoc remedium, à Servatore nostro ad peccatores emendandum, sapienter institutum, in morti ferum deleterium transmutant: quodque saluti illorum destinatum erat, ad evertendum ac destruendum eosdem, convertunt. Quocirca etiam, qui hareticidio, aut simili^c tyrannidi, aut persecutione ob conscientiam, ullo modo patro-

tance,^{f} especially if they seriously desire it.

d. 1 Cor. 5:3-4, 1 Tim. 5:20.
e. Matt. 18:17, 1 Cor. 5:11, 2 Thess. 3:6, 14.
f. 2 Cor. 2:7-11 & 7:8-12.

7. But from this shunning about which we have spoken, they who are either obligated and bound by some divine and indissoluble contract, such as couples,^{a} or by law of nature,^{b} such as children, or the necessity of duty, such as servants or maids,^{c} are exempted as far as domestic customs of life, whether reciprocally, or merely one to the other.

c. Eph. 6:4-5, Tit. 2:9-10. Phil. v. 10ff, 1 Pet. 2:18-19.

8. Further, this discipline is not that manner of action which is exercised by the church with carnal power,^{a} or worldly authority, or some coercive power, but it is only the church's own voluntary withdrawal^b or separation from him with whom they may no longer live as with a disciple of Jesus Christ. Thus the leaders of the church must exclude and separate the said person from themselves, or sever and separate themselves from him, together with their people (and that by the command of Jesus Christ himself, their Lord), and cannot nor will not converse with him [any more] than as with a gentile and a publican,^{c} or with any public and profane sinner, so long indeed as he remains unrepentant.

vv. 10-11.
c. Matt. 18:17.

9. Those who exercise this discipline not only with a carnal power and coercive force, but who also extend it to corporal and capital punishments (especially under the pretext of heresy, so vulgarly called), claim for themselves a power of threatening indeed utterly alien and illegitimate,^{a} and in fact truly oppress liberty of consciences and preaching,^{b} and change that healing remedy wisely instituted by our Savior for correcting sinners into a most deadly poison. And that which was destined for their salvation, they twist to their overthrow and destruction. But concerning those who in some way sponsor the killing of heretics or similar tyranny or persecution for the sake of conscience,^{c} we judge that they are utterly foreign to the most

cinantur, eos tum à mitissimo Christi spiritu prorsus alienos esse, tum ineptis ac præposteris adversum hæreses pugnare, adeoque gravissimo peccato se coram Deo obstringere, arbitramur.

a. Matt. 13:28-30, Gal. 4:29, Luke 9:55.
b. 1 Thess. 5:20-21, 1 Cor. 14 *per totam.*

gentle Spirit of Christ, and also fight against heresies with inept and preposterous weapons and consequently bind themselves to a most grave sin before God.

c. 2 Cor. 10:3ff, 13:10, Eph. 6:11ff.

• CHAPTER 25 •

CAPUT XXV.
De Synodis, seu Concilijs, eoramque modo & usu.

1. Et sic quidem singulæ Ecclesiæ, seorsim acceptæ, à suia Ministris, hoc est, Episcopis & Presbyteris regendæ sunt. Quod si quid interim magis arduum in doctrina, aut moribus, aut ritibus Ecclesiæ propriis, disceptandum inciderit, quod vel omnes, vel pluries saltem Ecclesias concernat: tum Synodi, seu conventus Ecclesiastici utiliter institui possunt, ac quandoque debent (idque exemplo ipsorum[a] Apostolorum) iique vel majores, vel minores, prout rei necessitas postulare videntur. Possunt, inquam, utiliter institui; siquidem legitibus in ijs ordo ac modus servetur: imprimis autem, si hæc sequentia capita diligenter observentur.

a. Acts 15:1ff.

2. 1. Si in iis ad nullam humanam[a] norman, aut regulam fictitiam, quæcunque tandem ea sit, sed ad solum Dei verbum, dogmatum omnium tum veritas, tum utilitas, ac necessitas expendatur & examinetur. 2. Si libertas[b] unicuique plenaria concedatur, sine scrupulo, aut periculi metu sententiam suam dicendi; in aliorum autem opiniones inquirendi; & rem totam, de qua controvertitur, rite examinandi. 3. Si in iis non admittantur, nisi viri apti & idonei, hoc est, rerum divinarum periti,[c] & qui in

CHAPTER 25
On synods or councils, and their manner and use.

1. Individual churches are to be ruled by their own ministers, that is, by bishops and elders. But if in the interim anything more difficult in doctrine, or customs, or rites proper to the church, which concerns either all or at least many of the churches should happen to be debated, then synods or ecclesiastical gatherings may be, and sometimes ought to be, usefully appointed (and that by the example of the apostles themselves[a]), whether large or small, as the necessity of the matter appears to demand. They may, we say, usefully be appointed and held, if indeed a legitimate order and manner be preserved in them, first and foremost if what follows is diligently observed.

2. 1. If in them first the truth, and then the usefulness and necessity of all dogmas are weighed and examined, not by any human square[a] or counterfeit rule of whatever sort, but only by the Word of God. 2. Full liberty must be granted to every one to speak his opinion,[b] without scruple or fear of danger and to enquire into the opinions of others and rightly examine the whole matter which is being questioned. 3. No one is to be admitted into them except men who are able and suitable, that is, who are experts in matters of divinity and powerful in the

Scripturis potentes sunt, sensusque habent ad discretionem veri & falsi exercitatos, imprimis autem pii, prudentes, graves, moderati, veritatis juxta & pacis studiosi: item vere liberi, & durante litis examine, nulli vel personæ, vel Ecclesiæ, vel Confessioni &c. sed soli Deo & Christo, ejusque S. verbo, simpliciter obstricti: ab omni denique pravo affectu, ira, odio, & partium studio prorsus alieni. 4. Si in iis id præcise aut præcipue non agatur, ut controversiæ fidei, quocunque demum modo, tollantur, aut in alterutram partem decidantur: idque ad externam tantum Reipublicæ quietem seu politicam tranquillitatem, vel procurandum, vel conservandum: sed imprimis opera detur[d] ut hæreses, scismata, aliaque publica id genus vitia, & scandala, ante omnia ac Ecclesis arceantur, aut jam invecta tollantur: atque ita pietati & veritati, item libertati, & charitati Christianæ, semper in iis consulatur: Ac proinde 5. si in iis plana, salutaris atque necessaria veritas arcte quidem retineatur: at dissentientibus tamen, & veritatem adhuc nescientibus, periculum idcirco nullum creetur,[e] nec vis ulla conscientijs inferatur: sed cum summa lenitate, animique mansuetudine, veritas salutaris unice iis persuadeatur: inreliquis autem moderata dissentiendi libertus certis legibus salva maneat, & pacis ac concordiæ mutuæ remedia commode conquirantur. 6. Denique, si quod in iis statuum est, libero[f] semper examini, & ulteriori revisioni, subjectum relinquatur; imo, diligenter ad Dei verbum decreta earum omnia expendantur, serio jubeatur ac mandetur: nec invidia cuiquam hoc nomine, aut periculum ullum unquam creetur.

Scriptures[c] and have their senses exercised to discern between true and false, but especially godly, prudent, grave, moderate men who are loyal to the truth and zealous for peace. Likewise, [they must be] truly free, and during the time of the elimination of the controversy, simply bound to no one, whether a person, church or confession, etc., but only to God, Christ and his sacred Word, and finally, utterly foreign to all corrupt affections, wrath, hatred, and love of divisions. 4. In them, it must not be absolutely or principally urged that controversies of faith be removed by any means whatever, or decided for one party or the other, only for the seeking and preserving the external quiet and political tranquility of the republic. Instead, in them it must principally paid attention that heresies, schisms and other such public faults and scandals,[d] before all else, be kept out of the churches, or removed if already brought in, and thus godliness and truth, likewise liberty and Christian charity always be consulted. And therefore, 5. plain, saving and necessary truth must be certainly, strictly retained by them, and yet so that no danger is created for those who dissent or are still ignorant of the truth,[e] nor any violence inflicted upon their consciences, but that they be persuaded of the truth of salvation only with highest gentleness and meekness of mind. But in the things remaining, a sober liberty of dissenting must remain safe on certain conditions and the remedies of mutual peace and oneness suitably sought out. 6. And finally, that which is established by them must always be left open to a free examination and later revision,[f] indeed, it must be seriously ordered and commanded that their decrees be diligently examined by the Word of God, not any hatred or danger ever be created to anyone on that account.

a. Gal. 1:9, Acts 17:11ff.
b. 1 Thess. 5:21, 1 John 4:1, Acts 17:2-3, 1 Cor. 14 *per totam*.
c. 1 Tim. 4:12ff., & 6:3-4, 11ff., 2 Tim. 2:2, 14, 24-25, 3:8, 16, & 4:3-5, Heb. 4:14, Ja. 3:13ff.

d. 2 Tim. 2:22, Matt. 7:15-16, Rom. 16:17, 2 Cor. 11:33, Gal. 5:11-12.
e. 2 Cor. 4:1-2 & 10:4, Ja. 4:11-13, 2 Tim. 2:22, 2 Pet. 5:3, col. 3:12-13, Eph. 4:1ff.
f. 1 John 4:1ff., 1 Thess. 5:19-21.

3. Debet autem his Synodis, post Dei Christique authoritatem summam, etiam intervenire authoritas Christiani Magistratus, tanquam Ecclesiæ nutritij[a] si quis modo talis sit

3. But after the supreme authority of God and Christ, the authority of the Christian magistrate ought also to intervene in these synods as one who looks after the church,[a] if there be such a person in

the church whose duty, following the example of godly kings and princes of the Old Testament,[b] is architecturally to moderate the outward order and rule of the church, and preserve the public worship of God whole and complete therein. And for this, as often as is beneficial, by the powers of his office, he himself ought to and rightly can convoke synods, and preside over them, propose together with ecclesiastic persons the things which must be treated, peacefully hear all opinions, even of dissenters, carefully search out the truth of God's Word for himself and collect the free votes of others, that everything in them be conducted according to God, and through his power to provide for such.

a. Is. 49:23ff. & 60:1ff.
b. John 24:1ff., 2 Ki. 13:19ff., 2 Chron. 17:5ff, & 31:2ff.

4. Nevertheless, it is neither his right nor duty to command the execution of the decrees of synods by any secular power, and to coerce and repress those who hesitate to subscribe to them for conscience's sake, either with threats or fines,[a] still less with exiles, imprisonments, chains and finally death or other such kinds of atrocious punishments. Moreover, neither ought he nor rightly can he trouble with edicts, proscriptions, attacks by soldiers and other violent means of acting,[c] those who desire for the sake of religion and conscience to meet outside in public,[b] while modestly and always preserving due obedience to their superiors, which always remain subject to the right of the magistrates, but he is held to care for and pay attention to preserve whole and protected[d] their liberty of publicly worshipping God, and that religious divine truth be protected by spiritual arms alone,[e] and to be persuaded only by reason, lest otherwise he appears to bring violence to the consciences of his subjects, and crush Christian liberty,[f] and finally, to will to usurp the rule which belongs to God and our Lord Jesus Christ.

a. Rom. 13:1ff.
b. Acts 1:13ff, 13:1ff., & 20:7ff.
c. Acts 4:1ff., 5:17ff & 6:9ff, and so throughout the entire book.
d. Acts 5:34ff., 18:12ff., & 26:31ff.
e. 2 Cor. 10:4-5, Eph. 6:12ff.
f. 1 Thess. 5:19ff, 1 Cor. 14 *per totam*, 2 Cor. 1:24, 3:17 & 4:2ff.

· CONCLUSION ·

Conclusio

Atque hæc demum est nostra de omnibus, saltem præcipius, Religionis Christianæ articulis sententia, ex qua facile intelligere, & clarissime perspicere potes quisquis es, Christianæ, immunes & alienos nos esse ab omnibus iis, quæ per calumniam nobis hactenus ab adversariis nostris impacta sunt, hæresibus, schismatis aliisque noxiis atque impiis opinionibus. Neque refodere nos, aut novo, quod dicitur, paxillo suspendere erronea ulla & ab antiqua ac primæva Christianitate damnata placita: non item convellere, nec labefactare quæ universali Ecclesiæ Christianæ consensu stabilita sunt: non definire nec decidere præfracte ac superbe, quæ in ancipiti controversia jam olim posita sunt, quæque nec ad divinæ gloriæ, nec ad nostræ aut proximi salutis promotionem magnopere faciunt: non denique scrutari operose aut subtiliter, quæ nobis revelata non sunt: ne scilicet pedem inferamus in ea, quæ sapientissimus Deus arcana esse voluit. Sed id operam dare unice, ut veritatem quæ secundum pietatem est, quamque solide scire nostra omnium interest, sartam tectam conservemus, & quæ ad mutuam inter omnes Christianos pacem, atque concordiam, tum fovendam, tum restituendam, faciunt, ubique sectemur, & quantum in nobis est, promoveamus; memores illius, quod Apostolus monet ad Titum 3. 8. *Fidus est hic sermo, & hæc volo te asseverare, διαβεβαιοῦσθαι, ut qui crediderunt Deo, curent bonis Operibus præstare caeteris*: *Hæc sunt illa præclara & hominibus utilia:* & ejus, ad quod alibi hortatur; *Pacem sectamini cum omnibus, & sanctimoniam, sine qua nemo videbit Dominum.*[a] In hisce duobus præcipua Christianæ

Conclusion

And this at last is our opinion of all, or at least the principle, articles of the Christian religion, by which, Christian reader, whoever you are, you may easily understand and most clearly examine that we are free and unworthy of all the heresies, schisms and other noxious and ungodly opinions which have previously been thrown against us through their slander. And neither do we dig up or, as they say, hang on a new peg any errors which were decidedly condemned by the ancient and early Christian leaders, nor likewise convulse and shake those things which were established by the universal consent of the church, nor define or abruptly and proudly make decisions regarding things which were settled long ago by doubtful controversy nor greatly promote the glory of God nor our salvation or neighbor's, and finally, laboriously and subtly scrutinize those things which were not revealed to us, lest indeed we stick our feet into that which the most wise God wants to be kept secret. But we give attention only to that truth which is according to godliness, and preserve whole and protected that which solidly concerns us all to know, and that we everywhere pursue and, as much as we can, promote those things which make both for the cherishing and restoration of mutual peace and unity between all Christians, remembering that which the Apostle admonished in Titus 3:8, "This is a faithful saying, and these things I want you to declare, that those who have believed in God be careful to render good works to others. For these are noble and useful to men." And that which he elsewhere exhorts, "Pursue peace with all men, and the holiness, without which no one will see the Lord."[a] The glory of the Christian religion is especially placed in these two. Therefore we

Religionis gloria posita est. In his itaque toti huiusque sumus. De non necessariis autem, nec apprime utilibus ad salutem, serram contentionis reciprocare nolumus: & mysteria quidem sublimia atque abstrusa, simplici & ab omni scrupulosa subtilitate aliena, fide recipimus, nec nisi sobrie ac parce, &, ut veterum aliquis non male dixisse legitur, sine fortipe ferrum candens non tractamus. Speculationes autem infructuosas & inanes argutias procul habemus, quippe quæ rixas potius ac quæstiones pariunt, *quam ædificationem Dei, quæ est per fidem.*[b] De adiaphoris, item ritibus ac ceremonijs in Ecclesia, nemini facile molestiam facessimus, dummodo scandalum infirmorum sedulo vitetur, & superstitio sollicite caveatur. Denique omnia nostra studia eo dirigimus, ut, quæ ad solidam pietatem æternamque salutem nostram aut necessaria, aut valde utilia sunt, firmiter retineamus: in cæteris vero quosvis à nobis dissentientes libenter toleremus, & cum omnibus Ecclesis Jesu Christi, licet opinione nostra errantibus, pacem & concordiam ex animo colamus & foveamus.

a. Heb. 12:14.

Quæ cum ita sint, obnixe te per Dominum oramus atque obsecramus, Christiane Lector, ne contrarijs suspicionibus locum apud te ullum concedas, neque iniquas hostium nostrorum accusationes, calumnias & obtractationes admittas, aut facile aurem iis præbeas, quorum maxime interest, ut male nos audiamus, ne immerentes & innoxios scilicet sine causa damnasse, ac proscripsisse videantur: sed ut quæquitatis accurata ratione habita, ex hac nostra confessione ac fidei publica declaratione de nobis judicium facias. Sicubi forte errare nos credas, instrue nos spiritu lenitatis ac mansuetudinis, qui servos Jesu Christi quam maxime decet. Parati sumus omni loco & tempore meliora ostendentibus cedere, & divinæ veritati, quæ nobis omni alia re pretiosior est, locum dare. Sicubi nihilominus dissentiamus in rebus scitu non necessariis, feramus invicem in Domino, & charitatis simul & prudentiæ Christianæ memores, studeamus servare unitatem

have been wholly concerned with these things. But concerning things unnecessary nor especially useful for salvation, we do not want to draw back and forth the saw of contention, and the mysteries that are truly lofty and hidden, we receive with a simple faith, free from all scrupulous subtleties, and as one of the ancients is reported to have said well, we do not handle the glowing iron without tongs, unless soberly and sparingly. However, we hold at a distance unproductive speculations and inane word games, because they engender quarrels and questions, rather than "the edification of God which is by faith."[b] Concerning non-essentials and likewise rites and ceremonies, we make trouble for no one lightly, so that scandalizing the weak may be carefully shunned and superstition anxiously carefully avoided. And finally, we direct all our studies to this, that we may firmly retain those things which are either necessary or very useful to real godliness and our eternal salvation. And in other things we freely tolerate all those who disagree with us, and from the soul we honor and cherish peace and unity with all the churches of Jesus Christ, even if in our opinion they are in error.

b. 1 Tim. 1:4.

These things being this way, we resolutely ask and implore you by the Lord, Christian reader, that you not give any place in yourself for any suspicions to the contrary, nor receive the unjust accusations and slanders of our enemies, or easily give an ear to those whose greatest interest it is that we should be heard evilly, lest they should be seen to have condemned and banished us without cause, [we who are] undeserving and innocent. But [we pray] that, having a careful regard for justice, you would judge us according to this our public confession or declaration of faith. If at any place you happen to believe that we have erred, instruct us in a spirit of gentleness and meekness which most fitting for the servants of Jesus Christ. We are prepared at any place and time to yield to those who shall show us better, and give place to divine truth, which is more precious to us than anything else. If at any place we disagree in things not necessary to be known, let us bear with one another in the Lord; and remembering both Christian charity and

spiritus per vinculum pacis.[a] Tantum in eo, ad quod duce Christo pervenimus, eadem incedamus regula & itidem simus affecti: "si quid autem aliter sentiamus, hoc quoque nobis reteget Deus."[b]

a. Eph. 4:3.

Faxit, ut in vera fide, pietate, charitate, prudentia, lenitate, mansuetudine, aliisque sanctis dotibus atque Christianis virtutibus, indies magis magisque ad ipsius gloriam proficiamus, atque alij aliorum infirmitates, errores, & lapsus patienter ferre ac placide corrigere studeamus, quo in charitate radicati & fundati, veleamus adsequi, cum omnibus sanctis, quæ sit illa latitudo & longitudo & profunditas & sublimitas, omnique cognitione superior charitas Jesu Christi, ut ita implemur ad omnem usque plenitudinem Dei. Ei vero, qui infinita cum redundantia potest omnia facere supra ea, quæ petimus aut mente concipimus, pro vi illa agente in nobis, Ei, inquam, sit gloria in Ecclesia per Jesum Christum in omnes ætates seculi seculorum. Amem.[a]

a. Eph. 3:17-21.

prudence, let us be zealous "to keep the unity of the Spirit in the bond of peace."[a] But in that to which we have arrived by the guidance Christ [our] leader, let us walk by the same rule, and be like-minded. "And if in anything we think otherwise, God will reveal even this to us."[b]

b. Phil. 3:15-16.

May he grant that we, to his glory, daily progress more and more in true faith, godliness, charity, prudence, gentleness, meekness and in the other holy gifts and Christian virtues, and strive patiently to bear and peaceably amend one another's infirmities, errors, and fallings, that being rooted and grounded in love, we may be able to understand, together with all saints, what is that width and length, and depth and height and the love of Jesus Christ which is superior to all understanding, that we may thus be filled up with all the fullness of God. To him, who with infinite abundance is able to do beyond all that we ask or think, according to the power working within us, to him be glory in the church through Jesus Christ, in all ages, forever and ever. Amen.[a]

Lightning Source UK Ltd.
Milton Keynes UK
UKHW030129280122
397835UK00002B/40